EPIC

John McEnroe,
Björn Borg,
AND
THE GREATEST TENNIS
SEASON EVER

MATTHEW CRONIN

WILEY

John Wiley & Sons, Inc.

Published by John Wiley & Sons, Inc., Hoboken, New Jersey
Published simultaneously in Canada

For general information about our other products and services, please contact our Customer Care Department within the United States at (800) 762-2974, outside the United States at (317) 572-3993 or fax (317) 572-4002.

Wiley also publishes its books in a variety of electronic formats. Some content that appears in print may not be available in electronic books. For more information about Wiley products, visit our web site at www.wiley.com.

Library of Congress Cataloging-in-Publication Data:
Cronin, Matthew.
  Epic : John McEnroe, Björn Borg, and the greatest tennis season ever / Matthew Cronin.
    p. cm.
  Includes bibliographical references and index.
  ISBN 978-0-470-19062-3 (cloth); ISBN 978-1-118-01595-7;
  ISBN 978-1-118-01596-4; ISBN 978-1-118-01597-1
1. McEnroe, John, 1959– 2. Borg, Björn, 1956– 3. Tennis players—United States—Biography. 4. Tennis players—Sweden—Biography. 5. Wimbledon Championships (1980) 6. U.S. Open (Tennis tournament) (1980) I. Title.
  GV994.A1C76 2011

  796.3420922—dc22

  [B]

                                2010048272

Printed in the United States of America
10 9 8 7 6 5 4 3 2

To my father, Dr. William T. Cronin, 1933–1999, who taught me the value of serve and volleying and chip and charging, both on court and in life. Without his and my mother Joan's love of the sport, I would never have gotten as hooked on tennis as I did in 1980.

CONTENTS

ACKNOWLEDGMENTS

Writing this book has been a long and interesting process, as it's not only the first time that I've written one, but also the first time that I've had to write a long tome about a sport that I've been covering for the past eighteen years and not actually been in the press rooms at tournaments around the globe with my pen poised. What was most pleasurable was going back to 1980, a summer that I recall very well—the season I graduated from high school and visited Europe for the first time. I was as deeply enchanted with tennis then as I am now, but then I was merely a wild junior player who would come off the courts dripping thick New England sweat ready to discuss the era's greatest rivalry, Borg versus McEnroe.

I clearly recall that my Connecticut hometown, filled with tennis players as it was immersed in the tennis boom, literally stopped so that everyone could sit in front of their TVs and cheer during the Borg-McEnroe Wimbledon final. I also recall returning from Europe in late August, making my annual trek as a fan to the U.S. Open, and getting a look at the superintense McEnroe and the cool-handed Borg and literally praying that they would reach another Grand Slam final that summer. They did and put on a spectacle that is nearly equal in quality and drama to that of their more historically noted Wimbledon clash.

Some thirty years later as I write this, I'm thinking about how many people of my generation have come up to me to ask whether I miss tennis's old days, when great rivalries were compelling and you could really relate to the personalities. While I understand this train of thought, I'm so involved with the modern game and with its often thrilling personalities and various styles that I'm usually a bit taken aback by that perspective. But what I will say—and I've covered plenty of amazing summers of tennis since 1992—is that no two men have ever offered such a stark and invigorating contrast as McEnroe and Borg, which is why, to so many folks who lived through that brilliant summer, those two stand alone. When it comes to conjuring up memories of what made tennis so inviting to people who grew up in the 1960s, 1970s, and 1980s, it's the classic clashes of the New Yorker and the Swede that first come to mind.

I spoke to so many people for and about this book that it would be too long a list to mention them all. I'd like to thank everyone who spoke to me on the record or on background, and, of course, everyone who helped me with the actual process. Many friends in the tennis world have offered support in one way or another, and first off, I would like to thank all my colleagues in the International Tennis Writers Association, who, more than the players, have kept me loving the game with their wit and wisdom.

Some special thanks must go out to writers Richard Deitsch, Scott Price, Joel Drucker, Andrew Friedman, Sandy Harwitt, Ron Cioffi, Jon Wertheim, Chris Clarey, Pete Bodo, Steve Tignor, Bud Collins, Alix Ramsey, Eleanor Preston, Cindy Schmerler, Richard Osborn, Bill Simons, Bonnie Ford, Richard Evans, Brad Falkner, Steve Flink, Howard Fendrich, Doug Robson, Chris Bowers, and Lisa Dillman. I also want to thank my great buddies Tim Corridon and John Nielsen, who listened to me gripe again and again in my down hours.

This book would be nowhere without the patience and always jolly support of my agent Bob Shuman, who could teach more than a few tennis players about the importance of staying positive, as well as Peter Rubie of FinePrint Literary Management.

Stephen Power, my editor at John Wiley & Sons, Inc., exhibited a huge amount of patience with the project and had the concept nailed down from the get-go.

Two men helped close this project out and spent a huge amount of time on it: the accomplished author Paul Robert Walker gave this book a hard, appropriate, and excellent edit; and my friend Tom Tebbutt, the longtime tennis correspondent for the *Globe and Mail*, picked out many unforced tennis writing errors.

Not everyone can say that they come from a fabulous nuclear family of tennis lovers, but I can, and my mom, Joan Rezzonico Cronin; my brothers, Mark and Paul; and sisters, Tami and Megan, have always lent me their ears.

I've been quite fortunate to have been married to Patti Orozco since 1991 and to consider her side of the family to be my own. Patti and our kids, Cassandra, Connor, and Chiara, had to watch me toil writing this book while working full time on other things, and they were simply heroic in putting up with my cursing in the wee hours of the morning or on alleged holidays. It was worth it to me and I hope to everyone else.

FOREWORD

by Tracy Austin

When players are floating in their tennis bubbles, as John McEnroe and Björn Borg were doing back in 1980, they don't realize how popular they are. However, there's no question that the two men were larger than life.

Their rivalry was such a great clash of personalities and styles that it captured the world's attention, perhaps more than any other rivalry in tennis history. I knew both guys from the time I was a teenager, and although we laced up our tennis shoes in different locker rooms, I had a good sense of how intense they were, how serious they were about their craft, and how much they wanted to beat the other guy down on the world's biggest stages.

Björn was quieter than John, but he oozed self-confidence. John was more colorful than Björn, and his sensitive side could come out both on court and off. With his long blond hair and fathomless eyes, Björn had the look of an old-style Nordic warrior, while McEnroe's frizzy dark hair and contorted facial expressions might have cast him as a child musical prodigy.

John had the best hands I've ever seen, and due to his remarkable touch he could get away with a lack of technique. Björn amazed me with his ability to track down one ball after another, his consummate calm, and his relish for playing the big points.

I knew John better than Björn, whom I admired more from afar and who had godlike status in the locker room. Björn seemed to approach the game much the same way that I did, wearing down his foes from the baseline and waiting for the right opportunity to strike. On the other hand, John was more like one of my great rivals, Martina Navratilova, an emotional serve-and-volleyer with incredible feel who was always looking for ways to attack.

Fans took notice of John and me at the same time, at 1977 Wimbledon. He came out of high school, qualified for the tournament, and reached the semifinals, while I played the main draw as a fourteen-year-old. We both lost to America's best and most popular players at the time, Jimmy Connors and Chris Evert, but analysts predicted that we would soon become two of their greatest rivals. That prediction would come true a couple of years later.

After John and I won our first U.S. Opens in 1979, both of our lives changed. Even though my parents tried to keep my life as normal as possible and expected me to behave like every other responsible and well-brought-up teenager, I was clearly in the spotlight. I could no longer walk through my high school corridors without someone looking at me like I was a little different. I'm sure that much the same happened to John. A New York native, he won the U.S. Open in his hometown, and New Yorkers love to celebrate their own.

There was no end to the press and sponsor requests as our public profiles took substantial leaps: John's as he became the great Borg's primary challenger, and mine as I threatened the extremely popular Chrissie Evert.

Great champions are so single-minded in their pursuit of on-court success that they rarely realize they've entered the public mind to such an extent, but Björn and John had to know at least to some degree how closely the world was following their rivalry in 1980. It seemed like everyone picked sides when the two faced off in the 1980 Wimbledon and the U.S. Open finals. Some liked the cool and seemingly indomitable Swede, and others sided with the temperamental and artistic New Yorker. Some liked the cool tactician, others liked the fiery shotmaker. Plus, their styles were remarkably different: one was a vintage serve-and-volleyer and the other a tireless baseliner.

Great rivalries come not only from a clash of styles but from the fans' emotional attachment to the competitors. Without question, fans either loved John or hated him, and much could be said about their reaction to Björn, whose cold dominance turned a lot of people off. People so closely watched their matches because they were so emotionally invested in the outcome.

Both finals were absolute classics that can be watched again and again, and appropriately, Borg and McEnroe split them, giving their devoted fans something sweet to remember during the cold winter days that followed.

While the sport has advanced to new heights since that storied season, it's hard to remember a time when tennis meant as much as it did during the summer of 1980.

Tracy Austin is a two-time U.S. Open champion.

INTRODUCTION

July 5, 1980

It's cold and still a bit wet as the wind whips through Wimbledon Park and down the narrow streets of Wimbledon Village, forcing ticket holders lunching on Church Road to throw on their sweaters.

Down the hill, Björn Borg and John McEnroe, each man with his own entourage, approach the All England Lawn Tennis Club, soaking in the deep greens and purples that surround the wood and polished brick on the buildings. Soggy ivy is allowed to climb some walls, but it's never allowed to grow beyond its decorative bounds. There's no tolerance at the club for headstrong plants that don't know their place.

The players enter the grounds through tall iron gates staffed by ushers and head up the smooth walkways to the locker room, which feels like a plush, old-school men's club. McEnroe wears tight white sweatpants, a red, white, and blue Davis Cup jacket, and half-calf white socks. Borg has his bright red Fila warm-up jacket draped over his shoulders while he signs autographs for the attendants.

Despite the all-white clothing rule, "Johnny Mac" will be allowed to don his devilish red headband and Borg will strap on his red, tan, and blue Fila colors. Ironically, Mac wore the Borg headband when he fell to Jimmy Connors as a pudgy-faced kid at 1977 Wimbledon. But not this day.

Out on Centre Court, teenage American darling Tracy Austin and her brother John win the mixed doubles title after feeling anxious that they might not finish in time to allow the main event to go on when scheduled at precisely 2 p.m.

As the men's finalists walk onto the court, McEnroe looks jumpy, fidgeting with his headband, while Borg follows him out stoically, chin up, feet straight and marching forward, one definitive step at a time. The Swede looks up briefly at the Royal Box, then begins to warm up. His long hair bounces off his neck and he is purposely unshaven. McEnroe's dark curls fly as he flings his racket bag under his chair, while Borg deliberately uncovers each frame. The crowd begins to clap and whistle.

In the stands, Borg's anxious fiancée, Mariana Simionescu, looks sharp in a pink outfit, while a few chairs down, John McEnroe Sr., who hates to be called "Senior" and would rather his son be addressed as "Junior," wears a silly floppy hat to cover his balding head. Borg's coach, the stoic Lennart Bergelin, bows toward John Sr.

The anticipation in the crowd is palpable, as it is for every Wimbledon final, but this one feels different. "McBrat" is about to face the "Ice Man," a slightly crazed serve-and-volleyer confronting the vintage baseliner. It's brunet vs. blond, a ballistic up-and-comer versus a calm and collected veteran. It's Borg, the teen idol with his long flowing hair and subdued smile, against Johnny Mac, the teen rebel with his unkempt locks and ferocious frown. Around the world, millions of folks watch on television or listen on the radio, following what will become the most storied rivalry in tennis history.

On this cool, rainy July day, Borg vs. McEnroe—a competition that has been growing for almost two years—will explode into a unique rivalry with heavyweight implications in the style of Ali vs. Frazier, Chamberlain vs. Russell, and Nicklaus vs. Palmer.

It matters a great deal in 1980, in large part because of the dramatic tennis played between fierce competitors and polar opposites, but also because the world needs a diversion from increasing chaos. It is McEnroe, defending American pride wounded by the seemingly unending hostage crisis in Iran and an Olympic boycott against the Soviet Union, against Borg, an island of stability in a Europe fraying at the edges as the Soviet Empire begins to crumble.

This rivalry is largely responsible for the U.S. tennis boom of the late 1970s and early 1980s, when everyone from clumsy kids to suburban moms and baseball-loving dads picks up rackets and floods private clubs and public parks. Children dress the part—McEnroe fans in their fiery red headbands imitating his crazy corkscrew service motion, and Borg fans in their classy white Fila outfits trying to smooth two-handed backhands down the line.

Americans see in a McEnroe a heroic young gunfighter who can still save the town from land-grabbing outlaws, while Europeans see in Borg a representation of the glory days of lofty monarchies when perfectly sculpted athletes would put on shows for the pleasure of princes and princesses.

Peter Fleming, McEnroe's close friend and doubles partner, recalled, "Sitting in the stands, the guys who were the punk rockers were for Junior. He was the Sex Pistols of tennis. He was Mr. Antiestablishment."

A creature of his era, McEnroe is only twenty-one and deeply into rock and roll, fast cars, and the blond, ponytailed girls who cruise around his Long Island neighborhood. As mentioned in his autobiography, one of the highlights of his life this year was when he and his friend and fellow New York tennis star Vitas Gerulaitis went to a Rolling Stones concert at the Meadowlands and smoked pot with Mick Jagger before the lead singer went onstage, holding up the show—just as Mac held up plenty of tennis shows with his tantrums.

Borg likes to party too, but he is so calm and dominant on the court, so regal and graceful, that he's been nicknamed the "Angelic Assassin"; he's a machinelike player with incredible physical gifts and a steely focus. He looks and acts so much the part of the perfect athlete that *Time* magazine put him on its cover with the headline THE INCREDIBLE TENNIS MACHINE. Some call him "the Stone Man," others a "Cold-Blooded Viking." One of his foes, Ilie Nastase, the colorful Romanian, described him as a Martian.

On this day in 1980 it really does seem as though Borg is from another planet. He has won the last four Wimbledon titles and is now trying to gain his fifth in a row, to tie Englishman Laurie Doherty, who won five straight titles from 1902 to 1906 and set a new benchmark in the modern era. All that stands in his way is a wild, talented New Yorker three years his junior and already infamous for self-imploding with his hot Irish temper.

The two men take quick sips of water from a cooler near a drink dispenser with a Coca-Cola logo that also contains bottles of Robinsons Barley Water, not exactly the juice of today's champions but very much part of English popular culture. Then they walk toward the baselines. Waiting for the first booming ball off the upstart's racket, Borg crouches low behind the line. McEnroe rocks back and forth, winds up with his corkscrew motion, and pounds the first ball into the net. On his second serve he comes in and knocks off a routine backhand volley winner. Borg then rips a forehand winner return.

The match is on.

PART ONE

WIMBLEDON

1

Taming a Passionate Spirit

Björn Borg's father, Rune, loved table tennis, but it didn't put bread on the table in his town of Södertälje, Sweden, so he kept his day job selling clothes while his wife, Margarethe, stayed at home. But Rune still competed like mad, and in 1965 he won first prize at the city table tennis championships: a tennis racket. He gave it to his only child, nine-year-old Björn, who immediately headed off to discover what it would feel like to hit larger balls into a larger court and at the same time actually run after them, unlike in the more stationary table tennis.

Björn's first wife, Mariana Simionescu described his hometown, Södertälje, as "a row of little cubes." She says there is a sameness there, a consistency, that informs the character of the man she married.

There was a small tennis club in Södertälje, but as a beginner Björn had a hard time getting matches. So he did what every kid of his era did: he found something to hit against that would hit back. That turned out to be the family's garage door, and it would be a perfect opponent. When boy hits ball against door, ball always comes back—unless boy misses and sends ball over it or off to the side.

"I was obviously crazy about tennis from the beginning," he said.

So were many of his countrymen. In 1881, the crown prince who was to become King Gustaf V built Sweden's first proper court at Tullgarn, his private country castle. The first covered court was built in Stockholm in 1896. During the nineteenth century, eight tennis clubs were founded, and by the mid-1950s that number had reached four hundred. When Borg began to play, approximately eight hundred clubs existed with some sixty thousand players.

King Gustaf, who occupies a critical place not just in Swedish tennis lore but in European tennis as well, was said to have played two three-set matches in one day at the age of eighty-four.

Borg likely knew little of Curt Östberg, the first significant male player from his country, who beat French Hall of Famer Jean Borotra to win the British indoors in 1934, but Östberg's status as a top-flight player confirmed that Sweden was there to be reckoned with as a tennis power. Once Borg grew older, he was surely made aware of Sven Davidson and Ulf Schmidt, who became the first Swedish pair to win a major when they won the 1958 Wimbledon doubles.

After banging and thumping balls at the thick garage door for up to four hours a day, Borg learned all the tricks of tennis wall ball: which height, spin, and amount of velocity to use to get the desired return. Slugging against backboards bores some people, but not players like Borg, who enjoyed the monotony of its consistency. You couldn't hit through the wall, you couldn't coax an error out of it, but what you could do was imitate it: hit the ball back again and again until the human became as steady as the wall.

Borg would set up tests for himself, imagining that he was playing for Sweden against the United States or Australia, the two preeminent Davis Cup nations. "I used to say if I miss one the Aussies or U.S. will win the Cup," he said. "Or if I don't miss for ten shots, Sweden wins."

Borg won his first junior tournament at age eleven at the Sorm-land County Championships. One day a top Swedish coach, Percy Rosberg, saw Borg play when he was scouting a couple of older kids and invited Björn to train with him at the Salk Club in Stockholm, even though he didn't like Borg's table-tennis-style flick of a fore-hand. For the next five years, Björn made the ninety-minute train trip from Södertälje to Stockholm every day after school.

At first, the club's better players regularly destroyed him. Two years later, he took them all down. "His footwork was fantastic," Rosberg says. "Even then he would hit one more ball back against the opponent."

Borg's parents never pushed him, and he lived a fairly normal boyhood, also playing soccer and ice hockey. In the summer he and his parents would take a small boat out and sometimes sail past Stockholm to the island of Möja. On the journeys he would gaze at the water, perhaps designing combinations that would make it impossible for fellow players to send him off the court. He likely dreamed of being a king, not of his nation's political courts like Gustaf, but of the world's tennis courts, where majestic ability mat-tered more than royal blood.

He didn't take tennis lessons for his first three years, which is one of the reasons why he started to play with two hands on both sides—that and the fact that his racket was too heavy for him and he simply wasn't strong enough to produce enough pace. He didn't develop classic strokes, but he honed his own, which were consistent and full of topspin. As he grew stronger, he began to hit a one-handed forehand but kept his left hand on the racket while whip-ping backhands.

"Some people at the club said I'd never amount to anything with my two-handed shot," Borg said. "Maybe the reason why I got so far was because I wouldn't listen."

Later he would say his success was made possible because of his "crazy" western forehand grip and "wristy" two-handed backhand, both of which forced him to hit with exaggerated overspin. "Violent topspin is my trademark, and if I hadn't had the courage to improvise when I was young, and shatter the conventional beliefs about grips and depth, I might still be struggling through the qualifying rounds at Wimbledon rather than shooting for a string of successive titles."

When the cold Swedish springs turned to summer, Borg would get up at dawn and head to the courts. His mother wouldn't pick him up until ten at night, when the sun was still high in the Scandinavian sky. He played as much as he could, and when he wasn't hitting he watched others compete.

"Even at night I felt like getting up to play," said Borg, who added that the winters weighed on him heavily because he could only play two hours a day indoors and because school sucked up a lot of his time.

"He'd spend eight hours a day on these courts," said Leif Johansson, a future Davis Cup teammate who was three years older than Borg and who trained at the same club. "He was out here always."

Another Swedish player, Tenny Svensson, pointed to Borg's independent streak and singular focus. "He wants to do things his way. That's probably why he became the best: he made up his mind he was going to do it, and he went for it."

It was then that the stories of the petulant young Björn popped up. He would later be called "Ice Borg," but as a young teenager while playing at the clubs, he admittedly had a terrible reputation as a racket thrower and a player who would loudly curse his own mistakes, his foes' good shots, and questionable line calls.

In early Borg lore, after Rune saw his son throw his racket, he wouldn't allow him to play for six months, which is why Björn eventually developed an icy exterior. Whatever the truth of that story, there is no doubt that young Borg fought to control his temper. "I wanted to win so badly that it drove me mad when I lost," he said. "One day they suspended me for two months and I was forbidden to go to the club. They said anyone who behaves like you has no business to be on a tennis court."

Borg said he learned a lot in those two months and realized that he would perform better if he stayed calm. Lesson learned. Later, in his pro career, his most famous confrontation fittingly came when he gave the umpire the silent treatment after a bad call and was nearly defaulted at the 1981 Masters at Madison Square Garden.

At twelve, Borg won his age division in the Swedish school championships. At thirteen, he traveled south to Meln for the nationals and won the fourteen-and-unders. He was selected for the Swedish traveling team and dropped hockey. In 1971, at the age of sixteen, Borg won the prestigious Orange Bowl junior championships in Miami, and in 1972 he won the Wimbledon boys' championships and the Orange Bowl again.

As he grew older, the shy Borg saw his friends spreading their teenage wings, but he kept his growth spurts for the tennis court. He lifted weights, he ran, he did little more than eat, breathe, and sleep sports. He practiced seven hours a day at the age of nine, and by age twelve, nine hours a day wasn't uncommon. Those beloved little boat trips he took with his parents were now fewer and farther between. He realized early on that if he wanted to win, he'd have to be fresh for matches and for practice. He said that he never had much time to see friends, but the close ones understood. "Sometimes I had the impression they thought I was mad," he recalled. "The most important thing if you want to become a champion is to decide that your sport comes before everything else. Even after all if you don't manage it, you know you have tried."

By the time his future coach, Lennart Bergelin, saw him in 1970, he was stunningly good—a tremendous athlete with lightning foot speed whose strokes were nearly impenetrable. "Anyone who saw him play when he was thirteen, had seen his groundstrokes and knew how much he loved practicing, would have realized he'd be very good," Bergelin said. "I've never seen such magnificent groundstrokes, or anyone who moved so fast; he gets away from the ball and always has time to play his shots."

Bergelin, a shrewd and good-natured coach, had a few notable victories of his own as a player, leading Sweden to an upset of Australia in the Davis Cup in 1950 when he beat Frank Sedgman and John Bromwich on wet lawns at the Westchester Country Club in New York. He also won the Swedish indoors three times.

Even with Bergelin at his side, Borg continued to develop his unique style. He was stubborn but was also smart enough to see that what he was doing was working on court. He was grinding all styles of players down with his heavy topspin and quick feet. If he was beating everyone his age then, why couldn't he do the same in the pros? In that way, he was like John McEnroe, perfecting his own craft while dismissing the criticisms of the tennis in-crowd.

"The first thing I did in tennis was wrong according to all the teaching pros," Borg said. "I used the western forehand grip with a closed racket face which everyone said was too 'wristy' and unreliable. I was told that no modern champion uses the western grip, and there was a lot of advice in the beginning to change to a more accepted approach. Well, it's become my best shot. I'm glad I didn't listen. The point is that tennis is a highly personalized game. You should do what seems to work for you, rather than be regimented into a lockstep stroke that may be safe and easy to teach but does not allow your possibly unique talent to emerge."

Whether Borg was any good in school is debatable. Some Swedish journalists say he didn't have the aptitude for it, but Borg maintained that he was a decent student who left school at fifteen to see whether he could become a successful pro, and if he hadn't made it, he would have gone back. "In life," he said, "if you see there's a good chance to make it, you have to take the chance."

That year, he fell behind in his work due to what he says was a tremendous emphasis on tennis; in one class the teacher called him lazy and stupid. At first the headmaster denied his request to travel to multiple tournaments and miss school, but, pressured by the Swedish Tennis Federation, he eventually let Borg go, just in time for the Davis Cup. Borg simply could not stop playing or practicing. "I felt like if I leave [tennis] for five minutes it will all break down," he told Bergelin.

Saddled with a mediocre Davis Cup team in 1972, Bergelin knew that he needed another gutsy player and turned to the fifteen-year-old Borg to play against New Zealand in the Swedish seaside resort of Båstad, which has hosted tournaments since the

turn of the twentieth century. Things didn't go swimmingly in practice as, while he was losing a challenge match to Ove Bengtson,
Borg questioned a few of Bergelin's calls, going so far as to call him
a cheater. Bergelin was so angry that he pushed Borg over a bench
and threw a racket at him. But despite being disturbed by the precocious behavior of his young colt, Bergelin named Borg to the team
anyway. He knew he had a real player on his hands.

"Borg's greatest victory," Bergelin said, "was not the way he came
to master his forehand and backhand, but the change he under-
went, with terrible determination, to tame his passionate spirit."

Later, as Borg's career blossomed and he became more of a partyer, some saw Bergelin as an enabler. While he ruled Borg with a
steady hand early, he rarely interfered in his off-court forays, feeling that it was beyond his call of duty and, of course, a risk to his
position. The American player Billy Martin, who practiced with
both of them and knew them well, said that Bergelin acted more
like a coach and a friend, not a father figure, toward Borg. But
Bergelin put himself out front and center whenever there was a
playing crisis, and he later railed against Borg's agency, International Management Group (IMG), encouraging his pupil to save
himself from wear and tear by not playing a lot of big-money exhibitions.

Borg's first Davis Cup match was against the seasoned Onny
Parun, and he quickly fell behind two sets to none. In the third set,
Bergelin gave him a lighter racket. Borg was freed up to swing away,
and, steady as his garage door, he spun ball after ball back on the
slow red clay. Although he was exhausted by the fourth set, he upset
Parun 4–6, 3–6, 6–3, 6–4, 6–4. "Parun was in good shape," Borg
said, "but didn't like to rally forever." Just shy of his sixteenth birthday, Borg was the youngest player ever to win a Davis Cup match.

He then beat Jeff Simpson in straight sets on the final day, and it
wouldn't be until eight years later in the U.S. Open final against
McEnroe that he looked completely unsure of himself.

"No one thought I would win those matches," Borg said, "but I
played well and won. When I was fifteen and sixteen I beat some

very strong players. I never thought I'd be able to beat people of that standard so young. That's when I began to think I would be a good tennis player, but I didn't think I'd make a career out of it. I said to myself that if I worked hard and practiced a lot, perhaps I could become somebody in tennis, but that depended on me."

After those wins, Borg signed his first commercial contract with a racket manufacturer, and his parents breathed a sigh of relief, because the decision to leave school seemed sounder.

Later that same year, Borg played on the hallowed turf at SW19, the tony London postal address of the most important tennis tournament in the world, reverently called "the Championships" by the British. There he won the Wimbledon boys' singles title, when he defeated Britain's Buster Mottram in the final. He again showed incredible resilience, coming back to win the trophy after being down 5–2 in the deciding set.

Borg reveled in his success, but at times regretted his loss of a normal teenage life, which perhaps was the reason why he retired so prematurely and eventually went off the boil. He said that there were occasions when he thought he was practicing too much and wasn't having the same type of fun as his friends, who were having a blast going out and dancing. "There were times when I hated tennis. I would tell myself, 'I'm stopping now and I'm going to be like my friends. I want to go out and have fun.'" But that sentiment never lasted long, because he loved tennis too much. So he kept grinding, ignoring the sea, the sun, the beach, and all the things he would speak fondly of later.

Bergelin worked hard to get Borg to focus, as his temper was not yet completely in check. One time when he was playing his rival and Södertälje neighbor Leif Johansson on national TV, he went to the other side of the court to question a call and circled it—a huge no-no in tennis. The great, extroverted Swiss player Martina Hingis, while playing against the beloved German Steffi Graf at the 1999 French Open, would cross the court early in the second set and do the same, inciting the crowd to rain down boos and whistles at her for the rest of a match that turned out to be one of the greatest implosions (and defeats) in modern history.

Borg lost that match to Johansson, and he regretted his actions after the local press questioned his sportsmanship. "He changed completely after that," Johansson says. "I never saw him lose control again."

Borg then began to pick up a trait that would carry him through win after win: focusing just as much in practice as in matches. That trait is learned and not innate, especially with young players whose minds naturally wander. But Borg kept pushing himself in practice to concentrate harder and for longer periods, and by the time he was sixteen he was pretty good at it.

While much of Europe in the 1970s was churning, Sweden, which did not participate in World War II, stayed to itself, avoiding alliances and remaining as neutral as possible during the cold war. Its Social Democratic governments had spent much of the 1950s and 1960s reconstructing its economy and attempting to form a more productive welfare state, called *Folkhemmet* (the People's Home), fueled by a postwar economic boom. But the economy began to struggle during the 1970s, and, as in much of the Western world in the late 1960s and early 1970s, radical leftism swept the country, with riots breaking out in Båstad and students occupying the student union building at Stockholm University.

With the Social Democrats still in power, however, there were no extended violent confrontations, and with the election of the noted Swedish prime minister Olof Palme in 1969, the nation had become a much more vocal actor on the world stage. While Borg was less than a year away from being named to the Swedish Davis Cup team, the activist Palme was condemning the American bombing of Hanoi in Vietnam, famously comparing it to Nazi war crimes such as the destruction of Lidice and Oradour-sur-Glane. The United States responded by calling home its ambassador.

In 1973, Borg marched out onto the ATP (Association of Tennis Professionals) Tour, and while he had a relatively slow start, it was clear that he was a true up-and-comer. His first four matches on clay in Europe were against two excellent Italian players, Adriano Panatta, a colorful and attacking player who would win the 1976

French Open, and Corrado Barazzutti, who was able to mix up his attacks enough to trouble Borg. Most Italian players tended to make their living from the back of the court, but not the tall and statuesque Panatta, who had traveled to Australia when he was fifteen, undergone a growth spurt, and been taken by the serve-and-volley game.

Panatta broke out in 1973 and busted up Borg, whom, ironically, he would later coach during Borg's quickly aborted comeback attempt in 1992, when the worn-down Swede unsuccessfully tried to win ATP Tour matches with an antiquated wooden racket. In 1973 his thick wooden frame worked just fine, except against Panatta in their first two matches. "His game didn't bother me too much," Panatta said of Borg.

Borg would have his way with Barazzutti just a few weeks later at Monte Carlo, but in their first match in Barcelona, Barazzutti, who would later reach No. 7 in the world, went into his rope-a-dope routine, where the Italian's negative body language would make his opponent believe he was out of a match, and then Barrazzutti would catch fire. Borg failed to pummel his foe into the ropes with enough stinging body blows.

But then Borg went to Monte Carlo, one of the crown jewels of the European claycourt swing, and made himself known, wasting Barazzutti in the fourth round and eventually reaching the final, where he would go down to the clown prince of tennis, Ilie Nastase, in straight sets.

He was off to the races, and at his first French Open he stunned the steady and gritty American Cliff Richey, the savvy Frenchman Pierre Barthes, and the attacking American Dick Stockton before taking a four-set loss to Panatta, who would win the prestigious title in 1976.

Richey recalled, "My sister Nancy [who won the French Open in 1968] asked me who I was playing, and I said, 'Some guy named Borg. Never heard of him. He's only sixteen.' . . . He had huge groundstrokes. No variety then. Just boom, boom. Even without variety, he was good enough to crunch most players."

Borg then traveled to Wimbledon, which was embroiled in controversy. The player field was devastated by withdrawals as the newly founded men's ATP Tour pulled out eighty-one of its top players from the tournament because the International Tennis Federation had suspended one of the ATP members, Niki Pilic, for refusing to play in the Davis Cup. Wimbledon upheld the boycott. A few notables didn't honor it, including Britain's Roger Taylor (out of loyalty to his nation's top tournament), who ended up beating Borg 7–5 in the fifth set of the quarterfinals.

"I'd won, but Borg was mobbed," Taylor said. "Screaming girls stepped on court to mob him. It's the first and last time I've seen something like that."

Borg recalled the headline in the *Daily Mirror*: A STAR IS BJÖRN.

Borg would make his first visit to New York later that summer and stunned former Wimbledon champion and soon-to-be American icon Arthur Ashe in the third round of the U.S. Open (which was still being played on grass), before falling to none other than the Wimbledon-suspended Pilic. He admired Ashe's quiet and classy demeanor.

"It was the first time I had beaten a superstar on turf. I hadn't been expected to win; my serve was weak and I had a nonexistent volley . . . but the experience was critical in building my confidence that one day I would play well at the mecca of grass tournaments, Wimbledon."

The Swede would win his first professional title in San Francisco over a declining Roy Emerson, the great Aussie who won twelve Grand Slam titles. Borg ended the year ranked in the coveted top 20 at No. 18.

Toward the latter part of 1973, Borg bought his parents a grocery store to run in Södertälje. But they wouldn't be long behind the cash registers. The following year, Borg left Sweden and took refuge in the tax paradise of Monaco. While his nation struggled to define itself on the world stage, Borg waved goodbye with his father and mother at his side and went south. So did some of his countrymen's feelings toward him, and he was heavily criticized for abandoning his homeland.

While he was stung by the criticism, Borg never shied away from expressing how much he disliked seeing most of his income go elsewhere, saying one of the reasons that he left was "to avoid the 90 percent tax bite Sweden was taking from my prize money."

He was resentful, as he thought that by flying his patriotic flag playing for the Swedish Davis Cup team he was showing loyalty to his homeland. He also defended the move by saying how much more convenient it was to live in more central Monte Carlo, given his travels, and that he loved the warm weather. There, in the southern European tax haven, he bought and opened up a tennis shop that his dad could run.

Said Borg, "I took absolute hell from people for leaving Sweden. I was called unpatriotic, selfish, and money-hungry by the Swedish press, which didn't ease my distrust of tennis writers."

2

A Losing Set Is Not So Much after All

Borg hasn't shaven in weeks. His hair falls past his shoulders, and his blond beard looks full of Nordic snow. Mac might be a bit nervous, but his muscular legs are churning forward and he signals to Borg that he will be up to the net as quick as the hungry foxes that prowl Wimbledon Village after midnight. He adeptly varies his serves and holds to 1–0.

McEnroe may have a slight upper frame, but his thighs, encased in tight white shorts, appear massive, two blocks of Stonehenge rock. Like Borg, he stands five feet eleven inches tall.

After nearly two weeks of play, Centre Court is badly beaten up, resembling the pockmarked face of an aging Central Park hot dog vendor who has just battled twelve hours of heat and crowds during a Billy Joel concert. Divots cover the center areas and stretch out a good seven feet toward the sidelines inside the service boxes. There will be few pure bounces on this historic day, when a pumped-up McEnroe goes straight at the cool Borg.

Borg is wielding his black Donnay racket with his trademark long grip for two-handed backhands. Mac spins his signature Dunlop racket in his hands, a mostly white stick with brown trademarks and trim.

Mac is light on his feet and covers the net quickly, with little fear of impending lobs, swooping within inches of the cords. His lefty slice serve is troubling the Swede, and Borg can't jump on his backhand quickly enough to push the New Yorker back.

McEnroe's crazy dark curls fall off his head and look like corkscrews drilling into his shoulders. Still feeling his oats at 0–1, 30–30, Borg approaches the net and hits a very deep backhand approach shot that McEnroe somehow manages to muscle past him off the backhand side for a winner with a lethal long swing. At break point, Borg charges the net again, but this time pushes an atrocious shot approach short, and McEnroe flips a topspin lob past him that the Swede has no chance of chasing down. The American has grabbed the crucial first break to 2–0, and Borg gently taps the ball he has dug out of his pocket toward the umpire's chair. He's already aware that if he doesn't up his level quickly he could be in big trouble. McEnroe isn't going to offer the types of opportunities that Sandy Mayer and Brian Gottfried handed him in previous rounds. It's very early, but McEnroe is right where he wants to be. With a break in hand, he's at full sail, able to focus on delivering significant, varied first serves. He holds at love to 3–0, because even when Borg is able to get his racket on the ball, he's unable to predict where McEnroe is going and therefore is merely reacting, rather than being able to plan where his returns will land. Mac is finding his way to the net way too often, and the steely Swede is without confidence. A small group of 1970s-style hippies stand up and clap loudly for the American.

The Swede knows he has to take care of his serve to get a toehold in the match. He decides to put more mustard on his first serve and on his approach shots. He drills a forehand crosscourt that punishes Mac's backhand, and then after a torching first serve hammers a forehand swing volley into the open court to grab his first game to 3–1.

Borg pulls his hair back, blows on his left hand, which is slightly bandaged across his knuckles to prevent blistering, and rocks back and forth, awaiting Mac's serve. He's finally able to nail a return of serve with a whipping backhand that's too low and hard for McEnroe to handle, and it's 15–15. But McEnroe continues to sprint gamely toward the net. A split second after he's made contact with the ball on his serve, he's already nearly three feet inside the court. One long step, followed by another bunny hop into his split step, and he's standing on the service line absorbing where Borg is going with his return. Two more quick strides and he's swooping all over the cords. The Swede manages to dip one return that troubles McEnroe, getting to 30–30, but then, harried, he buries a negotiable backhand pass into the net. Borg feels crowded as he tries to wedge a slice backhand past McEnroe down the line, and the American watches it drop wide and goes ahead 4–1.

Borg has no rhythm and is broken again, this time to 5–1, with a series of uncharacteristic unforced errors, along with a brilliant jumping backhand approach shot and backhand down-the-line winner from the New Yorker. After poking a backhand volley into the net early in the game, the Swede uncharacteristically displays a small flash of disgust, slapping a ball from his hand harder into the turf than he normally would and catching it again before he goes up to serve. When the game concludes, an unidentified American in the audience yells out, "Oh yeahhh!" as McEnroe's backhand winner skids off the line.

The match is twenty-two minutes old and Borg has only won four points on Mac's serve. In this game, he'll do no more than try to reestablish his strokes, but he's very much aware that the set is all but over. Mac is carving his lefty serve to the ad court with fresh new blades and is so confident that he's even able to put in a more difficult serve for a left-hander: a flat heater out wide to the deuce court that gives him his first ace and a 30–15 lead. A let cord return coaxes an error out of McEnroe, but then Borg tries to step way over to his left to take a McEnroe serve on his forehand side and puts it into the net. Set point number one for McEnroe sees him fly a backhand volley just long, and he nearly argues the call, but instead runs his fingers firmly down his cheeks and goes back to serve again. This is no time for a temper tantrum. At deuce, Borg decides to try and take a floating volley out of the air and go behind McEnroe, but he again finds the net. McEnroe wins the first set 6–1 when he takes a let cord return from Borg and dips a backhand half volley cross-court for an impossible winner.

Simionescu is chain-smoking and says her heart is heavy.

Bergelin thinks, "You can't bet on red in roulette ten times in a row. A losing set is not so much after all."

3

"A Little Boy or a Midget in Disguise?"

Like many athletes who weren't blessed with a large frame and Olympian genes, John McEnroe describes his rise to the top of the tennis world as improbable. But it really wasn't. From the time he first picked up a racket, he had a few intangibles that would work in his favor—an unquenchable thirst to win, a frenetic competitiveness, and amazing hand-eye coordination.

John Patrick McEnroe Jr. was born on February 16, 1959, at the American military base in Wiesbaden, Germany, where his father, John Patrick McEnroe Sr., often known as J.P. McEnroe, was stationed with the air force and his mother, Kay, worked as a surgical nurse. After J.P.'s discharge in 1960, the family moved to Flushing, New York, and later settled in Douglaston, a middle-class section of Queens. There were two younger McEnroe brothers, Mark (born 1962) and Patrick (born 1966), the latter of whom became a fine tennis player himself. J.P. earned his law degree in night school, and was talkative, demanding, and full of life, with a loud joke or opinion always on hand. Kay, a no-nonsense mother who describes herself as someone who likes "everything done yester-day," had a harder view of life and never trusted outsiders.

"Unfortunately, I'm like her in that way," said her oldest son.

McEnroe described his Douglaston neighborhood as something out of *Leave It to Beaver*, where he and his friends would spend long summer nights playing stickball out on Rushmore Street—a fine way to improve the eye-hand coordination so necessary for tennis. But much as he loved to play sports, McEnroe wasn't physically blessed, and in his youth he was short and pudgy and had a target on his chest for the neighborhood bullies. He was called a runt by older kids but continued to engage in every sport available to him. He never minded getting his nose bloodied or causing a few scrapes and bruises himself. Early on, he developed a Napoleon complex.

Kay quickly instilled a no-quit attitude in him. Once, after he fell off his bike and hurt his arm, she told him to grit his teeth and go play tennis. Three weeks later they discovered that McEnroe had actually broken his arm. "We were rookies at the parent job," his father said, "but we got better at it."

Nothing would stop the McEnroes from climbing up the social ladder, and they moved three different times while in Douglaston. "They fully bought into the American dream," John Jr. said. "But it was a restless dream, and a big part of it was where you lived."

His father likes to tell the tale of how one day in Central Park he was pitching balls to his little son, who proceeded to crack one hard line drive after another. A woman walked up to McEnroe Sr. and asked, "Excuse me, is that a little boy or a midget in disguise?" The story smacks of urban legend, but somebody somewhere saw that Johnny Mac had a unique understanding of games played with balls. Eventually they would become his puppets.

Blessed with an amazing touch, McEnroe picked up tennis quickly and once said that he could actually feel the balls through the racket strings—no small feat for even the most superior of ath-letes. He was competitive in everything, saying that he had a "rage not just to compete, but to compete and win." He never got used to losing and absolutely hated defeat. As a kid, he would scream at himself when he missed a negotiable shot and cry when he lost. No linesmen were around to yell at back then, so he took every error out on his own psyche.

Strangely, McEnroe also began to resent the spectators who came out to watch him play, saying that he couldn't stand that they were having a jolly old time eating, drinking, and discussing life in the stands while he was on court laying it on the line.

McEnroe was a smart kid who did well in elementary and middle school and enjoyed chess. His mother recalled a time when he came home from the seventh grade and said, "'John Dupont got a 98 in the lab and I only got a 96.' I told him to sit down and study and he won the academic medal. He was a competitor."

J.P. was an ambitious father who loved his son's sport so much that he not only attended just about every one of John's matches, but would also watch him practice hour after hour. This can be an incredibly boring experience given the monotony of tennis drilling routines, where a player can be asked to hit fifty balls down the line with the same stroke. John Jr. would say that at times he tried to push his dad away, thinking that instead of watching him drill he should be taking his wife to lunch. But J.P. McEnroe never went away. Even in 2006, when McEnroe returned to the ATP Tour to play doubles at a tournament in San Jose, J.P. was there soaking it all in at courtside. He thoroughly enjoyed himself as John won his seventy-eighth title with Swede Jonas Björkman over a group of underwhelming twentysomethings.

Even though Douglaston had decent public schools, like many Irish Catholics at the time, the McEnroes decided to send their kids to a Catholic school, St. Anastasia's. But when John was in first grade, a nun told Kay that he was too smart for his class and to send him elsewhere. So off little Johnny went to Buckley Country Day School, a twenty-five-minute ride away in the exclusive Roslyn town. He excelled there, always wanting to score the highest grades, a commitment that was obvious to his teachers.

After a move to the more prestigious Douglaston Manor, the McEnroes joined a small nearby tennis and swimming club, the

Douglaston Club, in 1967. J.P. liked tennis and put rackets in his boys' hands. It was a way of climbing the middle-class ladder, because tennis was still an exclusive sport and still a year away from breaking out of its amateur status.

Johnny Mac began to take lessons and his talent was unmistakable. Two weeks after his first lesson at the age of eight, he entered the club twelve-and-under tournament and reached the semifinals. Three weeks later he beat all three of the other twelve-year-olds who had attained the semis. The club pro, Dan Dwyer, said at a banquet, "I'm predicting we are going to see John at Forest Hills someday." (The U.S. Open didn't move to its current site in Flushing Meadows until 1978.)

McEnroe says that as a kid he was fast, could see the ball like a grapefruit, and could anticipate where his opponent's balls were going. That ability made him the player he would later become, as he always seemed to be in the right spot at the right time. That ability is also a crucial part of a net rusher's success, since a large part of being a successful volleyer is understanding where your opponent is going to aim his passing shots.

Due to his small stature, McEnroe was not a serve-and-volleyer at a young age. He was a scrapper who dug out balls time and time again and began to adeptly mix up speeds and spins. Mac watched the game and learned all its potential shots. He tried different lengths of backswings, slid his hands up and down the racket to test its weight, stood in varied positions, tried topspin, backspin, and sidespins. He hit high, he hit low, he hit between heights and aimed down the middle. Like Borg, he pounded balls against the backboard when he couldn't get a match. The racket became an extension of his arm.

McEnroe joined his United States Tennis Association (USTA) section, the Eastern Lawn Tennis Association (now the USTA Eastern) in 1968, the same year that the International Tennis Federation and the Grand Slams decided to allow pros to compete in the major tournaments and formally collect prize money, the dawn of the Open Era.

It was a cataclysmic change for the once amateur sport and was the death of "shamateurism" (the practice of remaining amateur but collecting under-the-table payments). Under the old system, the true champions were not always crowned, since during much of the 1940s, 1950s, and 1960s many of the top players—such as McEnroe's hero Rod Laver—joined barnstorming pro tours in order to make a living. Once they did, they were no longer allowed to compete at the still amateur Grand Slam tournaments, which is why the tennis history books prior to 1968 are full of unworthy champions. Without the players who played for money, the fields did not reflect the true talent of the time.

Still just a kid and mostly unaware of the free-love, free-dress cultural movements of the time, Mac put on his pair of tight white shorts, his collared short-sleeved shirt, his high white socks, and his canvas tennis shoes and took his tennis up to another level, as the USTA tournaments featured the best players. Against better competition, he improved his arsenal. His mom and dad drove him around the Northeast and sometimes even hopped on a plane to go farther. He progressed quickly but didn't shoot up the charts immediately.

John recalls one of his first big junior tournaments at Forest Hills when he was ten or eleven and way too sure of himself and went down to a player he thought he could beat. "I played Larry Linnett, who was the top player at the time," he said. "I called my parents and said, 'Don't worry, it's under control. I'm gonna beat this guy. He can't play at all; he's got no forehand.' I saw that he sort of chipped his forehand. Then I went out and won [only] two games. I was like, 'Wait a minute, something's wrong here.' I was an Eastern ranked player but it was a humbling experience. It's tough as a kid to lose; you're losing most of the time, at least once in a tournament."

When he was twelve, McEnroe was ranked No. 7 nationally in the twelve-and-unders, but he didn't win his first national tournament until he was sixteen, when he took the title at the National Clay Courts. He was essentially out there alone, since he lacked a traveling coach and his dad wasn't an accomplished enough tennis tutor to help him out much.

"When the kids were in the juniors, the rule back then was you couldn't coach unless the kids split sets and then in between sets," recalled his father. "Other kids would be there at nationals with teaching pro coaches. I didn't know anything. I was a lawyer. When they split, I'd say to John, 'Play the way you played the set you won; don't play the way in the set you lost.'"

Most important, McEnroe never thought that he was losing to better players, saying that the reason for his defeats was that the other boys might be bigger, stronger, or from other different regions of the country where they played a style he couldn't yet contend with. The East Coast vs. West Coast rivalry was big then, and while most of the easterners grew up on clay, the Californians were learning a faster, hard-charging game on hard courts.

"He was very shy when he was young," his father recalled. "He held back emotionally. The first time that he met Stan Smith, John raced behind his mother's skirt and peeked out. It wasn't that many years later when he beat Smith in Philly."

Even at that age, little Johnny always thought he could see the lines better than anyone, and if his opponent questioned one of his calls, his face would get tomato red. After defeats, those who knew him well would wait for the inevitable as his eyes would start to well up and a flood would descend upon his tennis shoes. His legendary temper tantrums at linespersons, umpires, fans, media, photographers, and other players had yet to emerge.

"The only time I was called when he was in grammar school," said Kay, "is when he got mad in basketball and the school was upset that he was trying to be the coach. John just won't accept anything that, in his judgment, is wrong. It's as simple as that."

Kay apparently didn't accept John's misbehavior, either. Her third and youngest son, Patrick, said that she was especially tough on John (perhaps because he was the firstborn), and opined that "it had a lot to do with his eventual toughness and grit as a competitor."

Quite remarkably, growing up just down the street from the McEnroes was Mary Carillo, who would later become in many folks' opinion the most brilliant women's sports broadcaster of her era. A true jock early on, she too was a member of the Douglaston Club who spent much of her childhood playing games until it got dark. "The rule was that we had to be inside when the streetlights came on," she recalled.

Carillo was a better swimmer than tennis player, but a bad case of swimmer's ear took her out of the pool, so she eventually picked up a racket and began to play at the age of ten. Two years older than John, Carillo was a bright, talkative daughter of an advertising man.

At first no one would play her, until she ran into Johnny Mac, who was willing to spar until the sun set. Like Mac, Carillo was a lefty. Like Mac and Borg, she idolized Laver. They played day in and day out at a fairly even level until Mac hit about ten years old and wiped her out 6–0, 6–0. Flustered, Carillo turned to him and said, "You know something, someday you're going to be the best tennis player in the world."

"Shut up," John replied.

"He was operating in a place no one else was," Carillo says. "Even then, he had this amazing touch game."

By the time McEnroe reached age eleven, his skills began to out-grow the Douglaston Club, and his parents discovered the Port Washington Tennis Academy (PWTA) on Long Island, where former Mexican Davis Cupper and Wimbledon doubles champ Tony Palafox was heading up the program in 1970. A number of factors came together to make PWTA the training ground for many of the nation's great juniors, an unusual distinction considering that tennis is a warm-weather sport, the primary reason so many of the nation's good players come out of California and Florida.

The kids from Queens were multisport athletes and the area was by no means a tennis mecca. That was until, as Carillo says, "Vitas happened."

Then and there the Gerulaitis phenomenon hit the fan. A flam-boyant and charismatic kid who was liked by all and worshipped by some, Gerulaitis brought a certain magnetism to the Port Washington Tennis Academy. Sure, once the kids were already into tennis they would flock to PWTA to learn their trade at the hands of cool-handed Palafox and legendary Harry Hopman, who had been both a great player and a coach of twenty-two mostly success-ful Australian Davis Cup teams. But children tend to gravitate to their more popular peers rather than to adults with sound reputa-tions. Five years older than McEnroe, Vitas had long, curly blond hair, was a stylish dresser, could crack jokes and woo girls and men, and my, could he move about the court!

The PWTA was the brainchild of Harlem-born Hy Zausner, a former dairyman who received his first lesson from Nick Bollettieri in 1964 when the then rookie teaching pro was stationed at a club in Puerto Rico. A relentless self-promoter, Bollettieri would later become one of the world's most famous tennis coaches, eventually opening one of Florida's first boarding academies, the NBTA.

"When I left Puerto Rico, the bill for my lessons was more than the hotel bill," Zausner later said. "Bollettieri was a good promoter."

Within a year, Zausner became a very good player, and with Bollettieri's urging helped found the nonprofit PWTA in 1965 to give kids a wholesome alternative to the so-called bad lifestyles. Bollettieri coached there for a year and left for Florida, but Zausner kept at it and grew the site into a seventeen-court facility that accommodated a hundred students at a time and hosted some 150 tournaments a year. Zausner declared that tennis had become almost a necessity to families on Long Island.

"When I was growing up the best players were from California and Florida," Carillo says. "New York didn't have it, and then Port Washington happened and then Vitas happened. Vitas was every-body's hero and John idolized him. One of the reasons why John and Borg had something special was because of Vitas, who was best friends with the two of them. He was friends with everybody: with Connors, who John hated, with [Guillermo] Vilas, who was kind of a nut, with Borg, who wasn't really friends with anybody. Vitas was a rock star. Before he got rich and famous he was famous to us at

Port. He was such a good junior, so stylish and fast, and had long hair and looked more like a rocker than an athlete. He lived that lifestyle as well. Even when he was a just a guy from Howard Beach, Queens, he walked into PWTA and changed everything."

The PWTA became the precursor to the huge Florida academies and was the East Coast's answer to the smaller yet renowned West Coast clubs like the Los Angeles Tennis Club, which produced Grand Slam winners Ellsworth Vines, Bobby Riggs, Jack Kramer, and Billie Jean King, and the Berkeley Tennis Club, which produced the likes of legends Don Budge, Helen Wills, Helen Jacobs, and Bill Johnson.

Never before had so many terrific players flocked to a northeastern locale, and it hasn't happened since. Vitas and his sister, Ruta, came over from Howard Beach, Queens. From Douglaston came the McEnroe boys and Carillo. Peter Rennert came in from Great Neck, Peter Fleming and Fritz Buehning from New Jersey. Billy Martin, who now coaches the UCLA's men's tennis team, would come in from California. Two-time U.S. Open champ Tracy Austin also visited during the summer.

A sign hung in the PWTA lobby, boldly stating, "Tennis isn't a matter of life and death, it's more important than that."

"It was a hotbed and people would come in and play from all over the world," said Patrick McEnroe. "It was like today's Florida academies but wasn't like a factory. It's hard to say whether it was a fluke or not, but when you have that much good competition you are bound to produce some good players. But there's no doubt that PWTA and Glen Cove [where the McEnroes later trained, again under Palafox] had some effect, because since I retired, we've only had one decent player from the New York metropolitan area, Justin Gimelstob [from New Jersey]."

Palafox wasn't immediately impressed with McEnroe and threw him in with the less talented group, so McEnroe's dad stepped in and asked 1963 Wimbledon titleist Chuck McKinley—who had competed against Palafox in the amateur ranks and Davis Cup—to ask his buddy Palafox to take a look at little Johnny again. Palafox gave McEnroe another chance and began to see a little of himself in John—incredible anticipation and the ability to work the court. Palafox also saw in Mac a bit of former Aussie lefty standout Neale Fraser, a guy who has the innate ability to do different things with his service delivery.

Palafox taught Mac to take the ball on the rise and with short swings. He taught him how to anticipate the right time to attack, how to properly move forward, how to finish off points. He taught him how to slow the racket upon impact in order to keep the ball on the strings for a split second longer, thereby gaining more control. He taught him to see the court differently, to make his opponents move into uncomfortable positions. Palafox was all about teaching his players how to use the right angles of the court. Few players in history ended up using the hard dimensions of the rectangular box with more aplomb than McEnroe.

Stylistically, Palafox was much the same sort of player as McEnroe—a feel player, but without the evil, twisting serve. Palafox had a solid yet unspectacular career in singles, but did win numerous doubles titles with his flamboyant teammate Rafael Osuna, widely regarded as the best player in Mexican history, who tragically died in a plane crash in 1969. Like Johnny Mac, Osuna was full of vim and vigor, so Palafox was well suited to take on the young New Yorker. Plus, he was a man at ease who knew how to communicate calmly and directly, perfect for the volcanic McEnroe.

"Tony was extremely mellow, which is why he was so successful with John," said Patrick, who was also trained by Palafox. "He was so calm it was like he was sleepwalking. . . . He'd have these two-hour drills where we'd be working really hard, and he'd come over and say, 'Just try to focus hard for twenty minutes.' . . . Even when John became great and was driving people crazy with his antics, he'd always come back to Tony because he was such a calming influence."

Mac was not only fortunate in getting a high-quality coach near home in Palafox, he was additionally blessed: in 1970, the same year McEnroe arrived at PWTA, the great Australian coach Harry Hopman joined the Port Washington staff. A notorious taskmaster,

Hopman was famous for having his teams perform numerous hours of rigorous off-court training so as to instill a never-say-die attitude on court. Called a no-nonsense asshole by some and a brilliant disciplinarian by others, he coached Aussie Davis Cup teams between 1939 and 1967, only once failing to reach the final round. He had under his tutelage such legendary notables as Lew Hoad, Ken Rosewall, Rod Laver, John Newcombe, and Roy Emerson, all of whom would be inducted into the International Tennis Hall of Fame. Emphasizing super-fitness, Hopman drove and inspired his teams and helped build up their underpopulated country's pride in beating the rest of the world.

Everyone who played for Hopman called him "Mister," even though in his playing days the dapper five-foot-seven, 133-pound scrapper was merely known as "Harry" to his peers and had a marginal singles career, his best Grand Slam result being a trip to the 1938 U.S. Championship quarterfinals, where he was thrashed 6–3, 6–1, 6–3 by the great Don Budge, the first man to win the calendar-year Grand Slam.

A better doubles player, who won the Australian doubles title with Jack Crawford in 1929 and 1930 and four mixed-doubles titles with his first wife, the former Nell Hall, Hopman found his true calling as a coach. He led his teams to fifteen Davis Cup victories in twenty-one Challenge rounds. (Until 1972, the Challenge round was the final round, in which the winner of the elimination rounds, called ties, challenged the previous year's champion, who only had to play the final round.) Australian writer Harry Gordon called him an exceptionally hard taskmaster and the shrewdest tennis brain in the world. He was admired and feared and used authoritative yet practical measures to guide his teams. American Davis Cupper Tony Trabert once said after a defeat at the hands of teenage Hoad and Rosewall, "We were beaten by two babies and a fox."

Australian Davis Cup captain Colin Long, who led his nation before Hopman, said his successor's objective was to "have his boys be faster, sharper, and peppier than the opposition. He drives them hard. Then, when they think they are as fit as they can be, he drives them harder." Hopman made sure that his players lifted weights but also had exercises specially tailored to them so they didn't get too top-heavy. He understood specialty training before there was even a term for it.

Hopman knew how to spot talent, but he had eased up a bit by the time he arrived in Long Island. The often caustic man had a sweet spot for McEnroe, who said that Hopman would occasionally allow him to skip the off-court workouts because he knew that he was a match addict who worked himself into shape on court.

When former pro Chuck Kriese, who would become a renowned instructional author and the men's tennis coach at Clemson, asked him if there were any really promising young players at his academy, Hopman said, "Well, I have two who may amount to something, but one is more promising. His name's McEnroe and he's twelve years old."

Kriese, who went on to train with Hopman, said of his approach, "Very seldom did I hear Hopman talk about certain shot techniques, and when he did, it was always in a way that gave leniency to the player's individual form and style allowing the player to immediately adapt. . . . He could coax the inner part of a player to produce the results that he wanted, but always in a unique way, suiting each player's personality."

That style worked well with McEnroe, who was an unorthodox player and personality. He wasn't the type of player who could be force-fed instruction. He had to believe in his teachers, and Hopman already came with impeccable credentials in McEnroe's eyes, as he was junior coach to his and Carillo's hero, Rocket Rod Laver.

Bob Brett, who coached under Hopman at Port Washington and later became a highly successful coach himself, remembered, "When McEnroe was ten or eleven, everyone was expected to do exercises at the end of their lessons, and apparently John used to leave and go to the toilet when the exercises were about to start. Some of the kids asked, 'Where's McEnroe?' and Mr. Hopman said, 'Don't worry about McEnroe, he's his own man.'"

McEnroe wasn't quite a man at the age of twelve, but he was certainly ultracompetitive. Plus, he had begun to get a taste of the pros, specifically Borg, whom he had first seen play when he was working as a ball boy at the U.S. Open at Forest Hills in 1971. He was entranced. "The Fila outfit, the tight shirts and short shorts . . . I loved that stuff!" he said. Shortly afterward, a Borg poster joined Laver and Farrah Fawcett on his bedroom wall.

Peter Fleming, who would become one of McEnroe's best friends and main doubles partners on tour, first encountered Johnny Mac at the PWTA in 1972. Fleming—much taller and four years older—was ready to put the brash boy in his place. He ran into McEnroe in a coffee shop, and one of Fleming's buddies looked over at McEnroe and told Fleming what an excellent player the kid was.

"I thought, 'C'mon, how good can he be?'"

He made a bet with one of the coaches that he could give "that scrawny kid a 4–0, 30–0 of a start and kill him. I'll kick his ass! I was the typical cocky sixteen-year-old. We went out right after lunch; I gave him 4–0 and 30–0, and he beat me five sets in a row. He won the 30–0 game every time. I hit two balls in the fence, and he'd win, and then I knew he was pretty good. He was a precocious kid. He just bunted the ball back and ran and ran and ran. Even at that age, once John McEnroe got his teeth into you he never let go. He was a unique talent."

Despite the age difference, a friendship was struck. The PWTA didn't allow cards or TV, so Fleming and McEnroe would go at it in marathon chess games that would last two and a half hours, many of which ended in draws. A considerate and thoughtful person, Fleming could tell that McEnroe was more intelligent than his years let on.

He and McEnroe became regular practice partners and joined up with Gerulaitis and another one of their talented friends, Horace Reed, for sessions at the academy. Hopman would encourage take-no-prisoners competition, even if it included himself.

"We'd do goofy games at the net and we'd make up the rules—you get a point if you hit somebody," Fleming recalled. "Mr.

Hopman would feed us and we'd try to hit each other with full-swing volleys, and we'd even go for Mr. Hopman once in a while. I remember once I even hit Mr. Hopman and this little grin came over his face. He liked that we tried to test him. It was a big-time, vibrant atmosphere."

Hopman was a man of few words, but they were always significant to the juniors. He wasn't always immediately visible, but he kept a close eye on all of his better players.

"In two years, Mr. Hopman probably said five things to me, and four of them were, 'Go for the lines,'" Fleming recalled. "Once I played another kid from New Jersey at some Christmas tournament and he beat me 6–4, 6–1. I was meant to be this stud from New Jersey, and he was a year younger and I choked like a dog. Two months later I was scheduled to play against him again at the Port Washington Invitational. As I was walking on court, Mr. Hopman sprung out of the curtain he was always surreptitiously hiding behind to see what was going on and asked, 'Peter, can I have a word with you, please?' I said, 'Yeah, yeah, yeah, what?' He said, 'Peter, go for the lines.' I said, 'Wow, Mr. Hopman thinks I'm good enough and can be successful enough to go for lines.' I said, 'I'm going for it,' and I beat that kid 6–0, 6–0. Just that one little thing; he didn't speak much, but it was like that EF Hutton commercial: when he talked, you listened."

During that time, the top juniors at PWTA would also go over to ball boy at the U.S. Open. Mac was actually a ball boy for Borg in one match against Croatia's Niki Pilic.

"Forest Hills was a special place for me," McEnroe said. "I played tournaments under the 59th Street Bridge, like the Easter Bowl, where you couldn't hear yourself think. I played in sweats and it was so hot they stuck to my pants and I couldn't get them off. But most of my memories are of trying to become ranked high enough so I could go to national events, of the fear, of how nervous I was the first time I played at Forest Hills."

In 1974, the boys of PWTA and their coach, Palafox, brought their skills to Forest Hills in, of all tournaments, the U.S. Open, when coach Tony and McEnroe, who received a wild card, went up against Fleming and Gerulaitis and fell in straight sets.

Everyone had a Johnny Mac story from PWTA. Bill Scanlon, who would later become a journeyman player and thorn in McEnroe's side, wrote a book called *Bad News for McEnroe*. He remembers being a sixteen-year-old player at PWTA playing Mac, winning the first set, going ahead in the second set, and then, remarkably, watching Mac walk off court and default. In no uncertain terms, Scanlon said that McEnroe quit, a devastating accusation and one that Mac disputes.

Still, something in Scanlon irritated McEnroe, and in his autobiography Mac writes that the reason for his dislike of Scanlon was that when they were on the Junior Davis Cup team together, Scanlon ignored him. Scanlon says that he was never a member of the Junior Davis Cup team and that it was a case of mistaken identity, but the bitterness lasted well into their pro careers.

There was no mistaking who the main two characters at PWTA were: Gerulaitis and Hopman. Palafox was the gentle technician, Zausner ruled from his owner's roost, and Mac, Fleming, Carillo, Rennert, and Vitas's sister Ruta were the standout juniors, but it was very much Hopman's program and Vitas's circus tent. "Hopman adored Vitas," Carillo said. "He had favorites like Emerson and Hoad, and I would put Vitas right after those guys. Back in the day before he started wasting himself with drugs, Vitas was a very hard worker."

Johnny Mac was still doing things his way, which included frequent bathroom breaks when it came time for off-court work. He loved to compete, but the monotony of standard exercises and hitting ball after ball crosscourt or down the line bored him.

"John didn't like drilling," Carillo remembered. "It was mind-numbing to him. He always resented players like [Ivan] Lendl who were metronomic and automaton-like."

Another junior player at PWTA said that one day, Hopman asked him and McEnroe to do a two-on-one with Gerulaitis (where two players work over the other player to death in relentless drills). The junior was particularly excited about the chance to hit with the popular Vitas, but Mac just looked at Hopman and said, "No, I don't do two-on-ones."

Although Hopman gave McEnroe plenty of slack and would later become an overly loyal defender of his on-court explosions, there were times when his pupil tried his patience. One day when he was supposed to be drilling, Mac instead decided to try to get the most out of his magic wand.

"He was shifting the ball around, hitting no-look volleys and fade volleys up at net and the other kids were trying to copy it and of course no one else could," Carillo recalled with a laugh. "Hopman caught John doing it and said he was disrespecting his court and compromising the practice session. . . . 'You want to hit and play like a girl, you go play on the girls' court!' Thirty minutes later, Hopman checked the girls' court and there were all the girls, hitting no-look volleys. John had poisoned the entire pool."

The Australian Alex Aitchison, who was working as a coach under Hopman at the time, recalled one of his first memories of watching McEnroe at Port Washington from his office window. McEnroe had missed an easy forehand volley and was so angry that he ran toward the back fence, clawed at it, smashed his racket, and then went to his bag, got another playing stick, and continued on as if nothing had happened.

Aitchison encouraged Hopman to discipline him, but to no avail. "What a turnaround I was seeing from the man whose reputation had branded him as possibly the toughest disciplinarian the game of tennis had ever seen," Aitchison said.

But Hopman never turned his back on the temperamental McEnroe, the opinionated Carillo, or Gerulaitis, who later developed into a hard-core partyer. Hopman liked players who set their own standards very high. "I liked John's temperament because he was always striving for the perfect shot," Hopman said.

He demanded loyalty, and when he got it, he stood loyal to his students.

"He knew how good John was but at times there was not much to defend, even when Vitas was going down with stories of his drug use and he swore it couldn't be true," Carillo said. "He was very loyal and honestly believed that one of his kids couldn't do something wrong. He couldn't imagine Vitas doing something like that, and he knew John was stepping over the line—maybe he was blind loyal to John."

Fleming remembers a story told to him by former British Davis Cupper John Barrett, who brought a team over to compete against Port Washington. Hopman took Barrett on a tour, pointed out Mac, and said, "He's going to be number one in the world."

By the time he was sixteen, McEnroe was attending the exclusive Trinity School in Manhattan, where he did well in math and in other subjects. Mac took a long subway and bus ride into the city by himself that averaged around an hour each way. He got a close look at humanity on those subway rides, from the poor to the rich, from the crazy to the sane. He recalls being mugged once, but it was nothing serious, and like any smart athlete without a death wish, he managed to run away from his attacker.

He still had his poster of Björn Borg in his bedroom, and while their childhoods were dissimilar, he was attracted to the Swede's class, the sleek way he moved, how he held his chin up high, how he was almost never fazed. McEnroe wanted to be seen as a regal character too, one who was holding up trophies, one who was praised by knowledgeable commentators, one who made the girls swoon. In short, he wanted to be cool, and for tennis to be cool too. If he could just be a little more like Borg, maybe he too would have the world at his feet.

McEnroe had quit playing football in the eighth grade after getting the wind knocked out of him, but he still played basketball and soccer in high school. He quit basketball after two years because he couldn't make an impression on the coach, but he stuck with soccer, and in his senior year, the same year he qualified for the French Open and Wimbledon, he led his team in scoring.

The headmaster at Trinity, Dr. Robin Lester, a huge tennis fan who had been attending Wimbledon long before McEnroe became a player, actually allowed John to make playing the French Open and

Wimbledon his senior project. At first Lester wasn't overly impressed: "If you lined up all 300 boys in his approximate age group . . . and asked us to place them in the order of who was most likely to succeed as an international athlete, John would have come in 299."

Mac's classmates knew him as funny and witty, and his teachers knew him as an opinionated student. "He was noted for quick, perceptive observations," Lester said, "and those remarks can be construed as wise or sullen and surly. I found him a challenging student because he was not a yes-man. He was nobody's man but John McEnroe's."

He held similar strong opinions about on-court proceedings. When he was fifteen, he was given a wild card into the U.S. Open mixed doubles with Port Washington teaching pro Lindsay Nevin, a decent player from England who had competed at Wimbledon. At dinner one night, McEnroe Sr. asked Jr. if he was going to go out to Port Washington and hit some with Nevin or even speak to her prior to the Open. John said no, and his father asked why, because his son had never played mixed doubles before. His father asked, "What do you know about mixed doubles?" Junior replied, "I only know one thing: your partner stinks."

When he was sixteen, Johnny Mac's rebellious side began to flourish, and at that time he received a six-month suspension from the PWTA for two pranks. The first occurred at the Concord Hotel in upstate New York when Mac and Rennert decided to light a towel on fire, put it in a pail, open up one of the rooms where the girls were staying, throw it in, and yell "Fire!" Then they doused them with water.

The other prank occurred when they delayed a Port Washington bus after a tournament. Mac and Rennert had decided to go into the gym to play pickup basketball, and apparently another junior who was supposed to tell them when it was time to leave decided to join their game instead. Mac claims that Zausner then came into the gym screaming, "I'm sick of your attitude!" and suspended him and Rennert for the rest of the summer. Unlike others, Zausner wasn't blindly loyal to Mac.

"McEnroe was a guy unto himself," Aitchison said. "He knew it all and you couldn't tell him anything. When we told him of the suspension he simply said, 'Fine, I don't need you.' I said, 'John, that's up to you, but you're suspended for six months whether you need us or not.'"

Later that same year McEnroe won the French Open mixed doubles title, qualified for Wimbledon, and went on to the semifinals in the main draw. The rest, as they say, is history. "I guess he didn't need us after all," Aitchison said.

McEnroe thought that Zausner had overreacted and refused to apologize. McEnroe Sr. would later say that Mac was upset that he was informed of the suspension by letter rather than being directly called by Zausner himself, whom he said he knew well.

What was clear to at least one of the teaching pros was that some of McEnroe's authority figures were becoming enablers. "Maybe, just maybe, if tighter control and better parental guidance had been applied, these young men might have acted like normal human beings and this situation never would have arisen," Aitchison said.

But the incident did cause a fissure in the relationship between Rennert and McEnroe as the Rennert family apologized and Peter had his suspension lifted. Mac didn't realize this and thought he was being played off against Rennert by the PWTA, so when he ended up playing him a short while later in the Easter Bowl quarterfinals, he throttled him, thinking, "I can't lose to this guy."

McEnroe also claims that on the first point of the match he hit a serve that bounced off the court and hit Zausner in the head.

Mac wouldn't return to the PWTA as a member, and fortunately, Palafox had moved to the nearby Glen Cove Racket Club, where he was reunited with John. Hopman would then found his own academy in Saddlebrook, Florida, but would keep in consistent contact with his student, even when Johnny Mac had earned the worldwide infamous nickname "McBrat."

Hopman knew he had a genius on his hands, manners be damned: "He's not so brash, he's not so docile, it's just that he's a New Yorker."

4

Better Call a Cab

At the start of the second set of the glorious 1980 Wimbledon final, John McEnroe bounces off his chair and is feeling very good about his chances. Björn Borg taps the strings of two rackets before taking the court again, trying to discover which tension will bring out the best in him. Borg has been in this position before, losing the first set of the 1977 Wimbledon final to Jimmy Connors and then the first set of the 1979 final to Roscoe Tanner. But he has never faced an artist with as many paintbrushes as McEnroe.

In the second point of the second set, Borg's racket flies out of his hand on a first serve and bounces crazily across the turf. A poltergeist has invaded the steely confines of Wimbledon's tried-and-true Centre Court. A frustrated Borg cannot seem to go on the offensive. Down 0–30, he digs in and stops the bleeding, firing a handful of stinging serves to hold to 1–0. The BBC's Mark Cox mentions that Borg has been forced out of his backcourt comfort zone because he doesn't want McEnroe to seize complete control of the net.

Instead of trying to step in on the twisting McEnroe serves into his backhand, Borg leans back and comes over a few with spin and authority. But Mac is smart and continues to mix up his deliveries, going hard at Borg's body with topspin serves and swinging out wide with his flat heaters. He looks like a giant cuckoo clock, gently swaying back and forth until it's time to ring the gong, and then clashing against it mightily.

The balls of 1980 did not bounce as high as those of today and did not penetrate the courts as much. To give the white pellets an eye-bursting ride, the competitors have to swing super hard and meet the ball in the center of their small wooden racket heads. There is no space-age graphite or superspin-producing stings like those that dominate the twenty-first century, when players can half frame a ball swinging as hard as they can from ten feet off the court and still find a corner. With the weaker wooden rackets and more vulnerable and unpredictable gut strings of 1980, hitting in the small sweet spot and telling your arm to control the ball was mandatory. The technology didn't do it for you.

Mac is absolutely dominating on his serve, but his return games are a bit funky. Borg is attempting to crowd the net on his service games in order not to concede the front-court offensive, and Mac has to push himself more with his returns, leaning into the ball as far as he can without toppling over. His slice backhand is carving up the blades. Borg isn't always coming in behind hard two-handed backhands, he's slicing with one hand and looking for depth to encourage Mac to try and overplay hard-core passing shots.

Borg realizes that he has to start nailing his passing shots if he's going to have any chance at a comeback. He pushes McEnroe in the second game, but still can't handle the American's whipping first serves, and it's 1–1. Borg plays an efficient game at the net to hold to 2–1 and signals to Mac that there's no chance he's going to try to win the final entirely from the baseline. He can spend part of this afternoon at the cords too. A McEnroe serve out wide produces a cracking sound from Borg's frame in the opening point of the fourth game. He pumps his fist after delivering another bullet down the T.

A solid volley and another excellent serve and Mac has held at love to 2–2. It's now 3 p.m. Borg must be patient until the serving torrent subsides, but after the American clips the line with a running forehand, he faces a break point. But Borg bombs one down the T, Mac can't lift a backhand over the net, and he yells out, "No!" McEnroe is using the lob intelligently and Borg is less than surehanded at the net. Borg's third ace and continued trouble from Mac's backhand side give the Swede the lead at 3–2.

On the changeover, McEnroe reties his shoes while Borg furiously wipes off his grip with a towel. The BBC's John Barrett opines that Borg is unhappy at having to play so frequently in the forecourt, but McEnroe is joyful there, slicing a backhand volley winner crosscourt with his hot racket face so wide open that he could grill some sausages on it. With his unkempt Civil War–style sideburns seemingly growing at light speed, McEnroe holds to 3–3 with a bone-crushing forehand volley.

Borg is still not volleying consistently, and after staring one into the net, he's down 15–30. But then the American seizes up a bit, missing a wide-open backhand pass with Borg completely off the court. McEnroe throws his hands up in the air, stares up at the sky, and then scrapes his feet on the turf. A huge opportunity has been wasted. He then misses a routine backhand approach and Borg booms his fourth ace to hold to 4–3.

Mac is a different man while serving, and Borg is a good seven feet behind the baseline to return. He blowtorches a serve and nearly loses his shoe after holding to 4–4, but he picks it up off the grass and relaces it. The sun has broken through and it's warmer now, and the once chilled crowd basks in the unusual rays of brilliant sunshine.

Mac charges and knocks off a sure-handed backhand volley to gain a break point, but Borg pounds a serve down the T to earn a deuce. Mac then yanks a backhand crosscourt pass and Borg hits another unreturnable serve. Borg is serving better now down the center and has taken dead aim at McEnroe's sporadic backhand return. Mac screams at himself after netting another one. But the ultraquick Mac is determined and scalds his most impressive backhand return of the match down the line as chalk clearly flies. He holds his third break point, but Borg stands up tall, smoking an unreturnable serve out wide, chucking in a forehand drop volley, and then watching the American overplay a forehand. McEnroe cannot completely shake him and the Swede holds to 5–4.

"Björn can make the ball drop so fast it will untie your shoelaces," said the legendary coach Vic Braden. "If you want to get back far enough to take it on the bounce, you've gotta call a cab."

Mac admittedly gets nervous, and Mariana Simionescu is thinking, "Who says the human heart is made to function for 150 years?"

But Borg's chin has hardened and his shots have more force. McEnroe looks clearly concerned and takes more time between serves, which is an effective strategy, and he holds contemptuously to 5–5. With Borg ahead 30–0, a clearly pressing McEnroe hits a wild backhand wide. Borg holds at love, and during the changeover he readjusts his thick wristbands while Simionescu rests her left cheek in her hand.

McEnroe begins the twelfth game with a fine serve out wide, but then muffs a drop volley right in front of the charging Borg. He tries another drop volley and the Swede is right there to clean up with a forehand crosscourt. Then Borg belts that McEnroe slice serve that has been working so well all day long right down the line, and he has two set points. One disappears as McEnroe jams one into his body, but he breaks Mac to win the set 7–5 behind a dipping backhand down low that Mac nets on an approach shot.

Cigar-puffing men leap out of their seats. The match is even at one set apiece. The frustrated New Yorker squats low as he feels the contest slipping away.

"Something in me deflated," McEnroe said. "I felt I should have been up two sets to love and the fact that I wasn't opened the gates to mental and physical fatigue."

5

The Sport's First Rock Star

In February 1974, Borg left Sweden to perform heroic tasks, rarely looking back at a country that was deeply affected by its own problems and those of Europe as a whole. Like Hercules, he had plenty of bulls and wild mares to tame. Despite his large reputation at home, he was considered no more than a wet-behind-the-ears up-and-comer, until he leapt into the ring and began to battle.

He traveled to London to play in an indoor ATP Tournament there, where he stunned Arthur Ashe and outsteadied his future Wimbledon and U.S. Open nemesis Roscoe Tanner, a kooky lefty serve-and-volleyer from Lookout Mountain, Tennessee. In the final, he dispatched a competent but physically limited British player, Mark Cox.

He then went back to Barcelona and passed Adriano Panatta again and again. But in the final, Ashe mixed and matched his shots beautifully and confused the still-raw Borg in three sets. However, Borg got revenge on Ashe two weeks later in the final of Sao Paulo.

Borg traveled stateside, lost to his junior nemesis Bengtson in the second round in Tucson, and then went west to Palm Springs and was undone by Tanner on hard courts. Not a week went by when he wasn't playing, and in Tokyo he got a real treat when he faced off against his boyhood hero, Rod Laver, who held the mantle of greatest player ever, having won the calendar-year Grand Slam in 1962 and 1969 (the four majors: the Australian Open, the French Open, Wimbledon, and the U.S. Open). Borg loved the quiet and deliberate way that Laver went about his business and how he always seemed to sense the right opportunity to strike.

Laver wasn't tall, but he was famous for his massive lefty forehand and how much spin he could put on the ball. He could serve and volley and pound balls off the ground. He could hammer his serve, use a light touch on his volleys, and come way over on his one-handed backhand and produce murderous topspin. Like Borg, he had beautifully timed shoulder turns and drove through the ball. He was fast and could produce winners on the dead run. He sliced when necessary and could flatten balls out. He could throw haymakers and counterpunch.

By the time that Borg faced his hero, however, Laver was thirty-five years old, riddled with back and knee injuries, and was clearly declining, having lost half a step of his foot speed. But he still knew how to master the angles of the court.

In their first match on hard courts, Laver knocked Borg out 6–3, 7–5. The two faced off again a couple of weeks later on clay in Houston, and remarkably, the old man had enough left in the tank to stop the young stallion again, 7–6, 6–2. In that tournament, Borg also bested an American backboard, Harold Solomon, as well as one of his eventual dogged rivals, the strong-legged Argentine poet Guillermo Vilas. But Laver was the bar that Borg had hoped to leap over, and he was unable to do so. Experience conquered youth in the same way that Hercules' enemy King Eurystheus schooled the strong yet overanxious demigod.

"He was a great counterpuncher, had a lot of speed, a lot of footwork," Laver said. "That was a lot of fun. I enjoyed competition. Got the adrenaline going. You get out there and do the best you can. Against Borg, I came to the net . . . had to volley aggressively and keep him off balance. And you had to cut out errors. That's the thing that everybody has to do: gotta cut out your errors but still hit with power and spin. You can't just play safe."

Borg would take that lesson to heart, and just a few weeks shy of his eighteenth birthday he claimed his first major career crown with an extraordinary run at the Italian Open, the most important clay-court event of the season after the more prestigious French Open. There he bested a slew of excellent dirtballers: Manuel Orantes, who would later grind Jimmy Connors down in the U.S. Open final; Vilas, in a meat grinder of a five-setter; and the zany Nastase, whom he crushed in straight sets.

Considered an incredible talent, Nastase tortured his fans with his up-and-down play, and officials and linespersons with his ballistic temper and sharp tongue. "Nastase would be a man of genius if he had command of himself but as things are he seems doomed to be merely talented," wrote the *Observer*'s Clive James.

Nastase called Borg "the Martian," or "the Alien," because he could never get behind his iron mask on court. In the locker room, the Romanian said, the Swede was robotic with his rituals, carefully folding his towels and diligently packing his racket bag while other athletes had strewn their clothes all over the floor.

While Nastase won his fair share of important tournaments, he's widely considered an underachiever, because when he was focused and on his game, no player of his era—until McEnroe came along—was able to magically produce as many gorgeous shots as the Romanian did.

"Nastase could come unraveled with surprising ease, needlessly quarreling with linesmen and umpires, berating himself in a variety of languages, tormenting his opponents with his tempestuous behavior," wrote the esteemed tennis historian Steve Flink. "He was a boy disguised in a man's body, snapping unreasonably even when barely provoked, turning from laughter to anger inexplicably. His fellow players seldom knew what to expect next from Nastase, and his mood swings were so extreme that he was usually hard pressed to understand them himself."

In essence, Nastase was McEnroe before McEnroe was McEnroe.

But in that Italian Open final against Borg, the incredibly talented Nastase could do very little as Borg mocked the tricks he had in his bag. "Borg plays like a pawnbroker," Nastase said. "He never gives points away."

Borg had come of age and felt ready to do battle on Europe's biggest claycourt stage, Roland Garros in Paris. Outside the tree-lined grounds, tension filled the air, as about a week before the tournament, on May 18, India had detonated a nuclear bomb in an underground explosion. The bomb was small—approximately fifteen megatons—but India thus became the sixth member of the so-called nuclear club, and the world seemed a less safe place.

But fans could take respite inside Roland Garros, and there Borg took everything that a variety of foes threw at him and chucked it back. In the round of sixteen, he needed five sets to put down the all-court repertoire of American Erik Van Dillen. In the quarterfinals, he came back from two sets down to defeat the seemingly tireless Mexican Raúl Ramírez. In the semis, he butchered Solomon, and then in the final he locked horns with Orantes, but this time he couldn't get off the mark quickly enough and needed his sturdy legs and balloon-sized lungs to carry him to victory.

He lost the first two sets 6–2, 7–6, but then turned up the heat and brutalized the Spaniard 6–0, 6–1, 6–1 to capture the first Grand Slam trophy of his career. At seventeen years and eleven months, he was the youngest ever male French Open champion, a record that would stand for eight years until his countryman Mats Wilander eclipsed him in 1982.

"My greatest point is my persistence," Borg said. "I never give up in a match. However down I am, I fight until the last ball. My list of matches shows that I have turned a great many so-called irretrievable defeats into victories."

Almost immediately, Borg's iconic stature was raised up a notch, because now he wasn't just a golden-locked teen idol; he had proved that he could play with the big boys on the world's most important stages.

The victory also had a major effect on his homeland, as Swedish boys began to pick up rackets and attempted to imitate their hero. "He really got tennis going in Sweden," said fellow Swede Anders Jarryd, who would later become a top 10 player. "There started to be indoor facilities to play in, which was good because you can only play outdoors there for about five months. Tennis got really big and we got the talented athletes who wanted to play tennis rather than other sports. It was a new generation. To see how he did at the Grand Slams, you wanted to play more and try to do the same shots that he had."

By then, Borg was completely dependent on Bergelin, who had become not only his coach but also his adviser. Borg respected Bergelin's place in the game (he won Monte Carlo in 1947 and reached the Wimbledon quarterfinals three times) and nearly everything he had to say about the sport. Bergelin would arrange practices, have his thirty to forty wooden rackets strung supertight (around 80 pounds, which would at times splinter the wood), call for transport, and screen all calls to Borg's hotel rooms. "I have every confidence in him," Borg said. "He knows exactly what I'm feeling when I win or I lose, when I'm tired or nervous or when I'm angry. And he has guided me gently, without ever pushing me. He's the perfect adviser."

After his French Open win, Borg was called the teenage Swedish whiz kid of the tennis future, and with the victory of the nineteen-year-old American girl-next-door Chris Evert in the women's singles in Paris, the sport and its fresh faces began to capture world attention. "He was the sport's first rock star," said Mary Carillo. "He was graceful, elegant, interesting, without even trying."

"He put professional sports on the business map," added Wilander, who eventually became Sweden's Davis Cup captain. "He made it marketable."

In Scandinavia, Borg immediately hit the top of the charts. Giggling girls began to follow him everywhere, hoping to catch a fallen strand of his blond mane. He could no longer go out alone without being disturbed, and due to both his victory in Paris and his obvious physical appeal, his face was splashed all over London's tabloid newspapers when he arrived in London for the Wimbledon Championships.

"When I have time off I prefer to go to Monte Carlo more than Sweden," Borg said. "In Sweden, it's impossible to be alone and have a rest for a couple weeks because everyone will bother me. It's just like when Nastase goes to Romania or Vilas to Argentina. But there are so many famous people in Monte Carlo, no one cares. . . . But I'm still a Swede and I miss Sweden and the Swedish people."

He was in no shape, physically or mentally, to make the clay-to-grass transition, and in the third round he was blasted by Egypt's Ismail El Shafei 6–2, 6–3, 6–1. The left-handed El Shafei was the only notable player from his tennis-starved and largely poor nation, but because he came from a wealthy family that could afford to pay for his travel, he was able to properly develop his game abroad. El Shafei delivered a hard lesson to the young Swede, who couldn't get his feet moving and failed to deliver the necessary dose of offense. He lost, and upon leaving London vowed never to take such a thumping defeat again.

While Borg packed his bags, the sport got a further bump when the American sweetheart Evert and her intense fiancé, Jimmy Connors, known as the "Sweetheart Double," won the titles in what was termed tennis's "Summer of Love." Connors destroyed the aging Ken Rosewall 6–1, 6–1, 6–4, while Evert got a stroke of luck when she only had to best the underwhelming Australian Kerry Melville in the semifinals. Her great rivals at the time, the talented yet mercurial Grand Slam champion Evonne Goolagong of Australia and Billie Jean King, America's most famous women's libber, had been upset.

A Borg-like player with a two-fisted backhand and precise, relentless groundstrokes, Evert then snuffed out Russian Olga Morozova, a colorful yet inconsistent player, 6–0, 6–4 in the final. "Was somebody on my side up there in those dark clouds?" Evert asked. "How else could Kerry Melville have beaten Evonne on grass and Olga snap Billie Jean's fifteen-match Wimbledon streak? It was like the silver plate was being offered to me on a silver platter, if I wanted to fight for it."

The tabloids had a blast, as the bookmakers had quoted odds of 33 to 1 on a "love double" for the engaged couple of Connors and Evert, who never did end up getting married but made those who placed adroit wagers on them quite content.

While Evert and Connors danced the evening away at the Wimbledon Ball, Borg had not entered his nightclub phase yet. Instead, in his free time he read comic books—preferring Disney characters Goofy, Donald Duck, and Pluto—watched TV, and listened to the Beatles and Elvis Presley. "Tennis is all I know and want to know. It's my life," he said.

Borg was never considered a complicated fellow by the press or his peers. He was reserved and quiet, and early on convinced onlookers that he preferred a sedate life when he was practicing. The older he got, the more he took to nightlife, but when he was younger he was good at hiding his tastes for women and alcohol.

Some believed that Borg played the press like a master violinist stroking his Stradivarius; others said he had a dull wit. But he did realize early on that he had some public obligations, so there were times he would dutifully sit and allow reporters to fire questions at him. Most of his responses were cliché-riddled, and he didn't deliver consistent tongue-lashings like Connors did.

"Borg was spartan, and emotionally restrained," said Patrick McEnroe. "He was all about action and physical superiority."

To Borg's friends, he was as loyal as a golden retriever. To some other competitors, he was as hard to read as his quick-fisted two-handed backhand down the line. "He's a very personable guy," said Gerulaitis. "He'll do anything for you. He's considerate, but he likes to do what he wants to do and plan the day the way he wants it."

Gerulaitis would later become Borg's best friend on tour and his regular practice partner. In 1980, he would host what was described as a wild bachelor party for Borg. But early on, he couldn't read Borg's personality. "We did the same thing every day—just work, work, work, break for lunch, and then go back and play," Gerulaitis said. "He's a great worker, a very hard worker, but other than that I don't know him. He's polite, he'll talk to anybody, but he doesn't socialize that much. He's not what I would call an outgoing guy."

One writer would compare him to the Swedish car the Volvo, declaring him "very dull." But Vilas, somewhat of a Renaissance man who played doubles with Borg on occasion and faced him countless times, disagreed that there was little more to the Swede than a hairdo and machinelike groundstrokes.

"He may not communicate things so well, but he is thinking all of the time," Vilas said. "Tennis was not invented yesterday; it's been around a long time. You can do some things without 100 percent concentration, but you cannot do great. Maybe he's so good that he doesn't have to think about the other guy and thinks only about himself. That's also a good approach. Let's put it this way: you cannot be stupid if you are best in the world at something. You have to be very intelligent, very bright. You have that kind of concentration, that kind of feeling, to be in that good shape physically. Borg has a very strong mind. On the court, he's playing with one mind. Off the court, he's very good about getting away from his fame."

Much later, reflecting on the cool, somewhat vacuous exterior that he perfected, Borg said, "It was an act and an act I came to perfect. But an act just the same."

Throughout the 1960s and 1970s Sweden was seen as taking a lead role in what is now referred to as the "Sexual Revolution." Gender equality was promoted, and during the late 1960s promiscuity was not discouraged and the country had an unusually high number of single men and women.

The 1967 Swedish film *I Am Curious (Yellow)* reflected a liberal view of sexuality, included scenes of lovemaking, and introduced the concept of the "Swedish sin." The film includes numerous scenes of radical politics, kitchen nudity, and staged sexual intercourse. In 1969, the film was banned in Massachusetts for being pornographic, and eventually the case went to the U.S. Supreme Court, where it won the day under free speech laws. As a result, many U.S. obscenity and pornography laws were lifted, allowing soft-core porn to enter the mainstream.

Borg was surely well aware of the film and its impact, but never copped to a reputation of being a womanizer, even though he couldn't go anywhere without women throwing themselves at him. Yet he did have a playboy image, and much later he appeared in advertisements where he urged his countrymen to stop Sweden's falling birth rate. Their tagline: "Fuck for the Future."

"It bothers me that they write that I'm a playboy, because I'm not a playboy and I never wanted to be a playboy," he said. "Maybe I'm the same guy I was when I was in school at fifteen. The only thing that has changed is that I'm playing better tennis, and that has led to a lot of things. But I always wanted to be the same guy."

Perhaps the reason Borg was so protective of his reputation was that he was also at times involved in allegedly monogamous relationships, including his 1980 marriage to the Romanian player Mariana Simionescu, whom he would later divorce. But some who knew him well would later comment that he had a voracious sexual appetite, including the author Richard Evans, who in his book *Open Tennis* described Borg's "capacity for excess during the midnight hours."

Whatever the truth, sex was a sideline to his physical acts on the court, and Borg knew he had to improve and hit the U.S. summer hardcourt circuit with a vengeance. He was still learning to hit through the ball on hard courts and to contend with all the serve-and-volleyers, as well as the lefty baseliners who gave him trouble. He lost in the final of Indianapolis to Connors and the quarterfinals of Canada to Vilas, and then he won Boston over the inventive Tom Okker.

The America that Borg found himself in at the time was shamed by the Watergate scandal that led to President Richard Nixon's resignation in August. Borg didn't fare much better than Nixon that month at the U.S. Open, when the attacking Indian Vijay Amritraj took him down 6–2 in the fifth set in the second round. Amritraj (who later starred in the James Bond movie *Octopussy*) never turned out to be a brilliant player, but given that the reason he began playing was to improve his health because he was a sickly child, he made quite a career for himself, becoming the No. 1 Asian player and also scoring wins over Connors, McEnroe, Ivan Lendl, John Newcombe, and Stan Smith. Although India was and still is a relatively poor nation that didn't have a lot of tennis courts, some of India's clubs, left over from British rule, featured grass courts, and Amritraj learned to cut his way through the blades.

Borg wouldn't win a title the rest of the year, but he competed fairly well except on grass, where he still had trouble adapting his defensive game to the quick surface. Yet with every match he improved slightly, and by the time 1975 rolled around he was a more refined product.

Borg began his 1975 season on the winter indoor circuit in the United States and Europe, and he and Arthur Ashe became the winter's hottest rivalry, facing off four times on indoor carpet, with Borg taking two tight decisions.

Borg's travel schedule was then off the charts. He went from Monte Carlo to Johannesburg and back to Stockholm, where as the biggest ticket in town he lost, stunningly, to countryman Tenny Svensson, 6–4, 6–4. The courts there were still too quick for his liking, and he stood too far behind the baseline to return cannon shots.

Then Borg got another crack at Laver, and this time young legs won out. In the semifinals of the World Championship Tennis (WCT) finals in Dallas, he took a 7–6, 3–6, 5–7, 7–5, 6–2 decision, but then fell to the more clever Ashe again. The congenial Ashe, matching his effect on much of the world through his diplomacy, writing, and political activism, would eventually have a strong influence on Borg and McEnroe, who years later were offered $1 million to play an exhibition in Sun City, South Africa, in an obvious attempt by the promoter to help legitimize South Africa's apartheid state. On the recommendation of Ashe, they turned it down and in some small way helped hasten the downfall of the scorned apartheid state.

In May, Borg went back to the Italian Open and failed to defend his title in a loss to Ramírez. It looked like the teen angel might be falling back to earth when he went to defend his French Open title.

But once there, Borg got a sweet whiff of the late spring Parisian air, and he locked in from the baseline and devastated the field. He crushed the American Solomon and the former Wimbledon and U.S. Open champion Stan Smith, had a four-set tussle against Panatta in the semis, and then wasted Vilas 6–2, 6–3, 6–4 in the final. There was no doubt then who was the king of clay. "He was physically the strongest and on a good day he was unbeatable," Vilas said. "I really believe he was unbeatable on clay."

Borg was consistently questioned about how he could wear down a man whose thighs looked a good three inches thicker than his and whose oversized left forearm resembled that of an arm wrestler. But while the Argentine had a heavy forehand, he had trouble hitting through the court, and the Swede's backboard was a few inches thicker than the Argentine's. Vilas was used to wearing foes down, and Borg was simply too tireless to impose a steady and monotonous game upon.

"I sense that if we rallied back and forth forty-seven times I would outlast him," Borg said. "Roland Garros was the toughest to win, both physically and mentally. It's on clay, and for two weeks you have to run, sweat, slide, and fight for hours and hours. But I always arrived really well trained, and I was very strong both physically and mentally."

Whether he could make the transition to grass was surely up in the air. He reigned at Roland Garros because he could go sideline to sideline past ten o'clock on fine late spring nights in Paris. He was said to have lungs the size of a blimp. There were articles written in medical journals about his otherworldly aerobic capacity, claiming he once ran on a treadmill without stopping for nearly three hours and didn't get off until someone tapped him on the shoulder and a trainer asked him whether he needed a break. "No, it's up to you," he replied.

He was said to have a regular pulse rate of thirty-five, and his blood pressure registered seventy over thirty. His countryman Ingemar Stenmark, the Olympic gold medalist slalom skier, placed second to him in a European health institute's study of the strength in athletes' legs. It was said that Borg could doze in airports or locker rooms, and before matches could easily sleep for ten hours.

Even if other players worked as hard as he did—and that was certainly the case of his practice partner, friend, and rival Vitas Gerulaitis—Borg had a fathomless reserve. But he still had to learn to measure his mind in the big moments on all surfaces. The grass of Wimbledon did not demand a marathoner's body but precision on a slick surface. Quick hands, keen eyesight, and the ability to push one's opponent off the net and away from the center of the court were paramount to success.

"Coming to the net is like being at the frontier," Bergelin said. "You're fighting the unknown."

Borg worked and worked on adding a few elements to his relentless defensive game, but still could not keep the chip-and-charging Ashe off his back in the quarterfinals and fell in four sets. Ashe, considered the ultimate sportsman, would go on to post his greatest victory when, at thirty-two years old, he shocked the heavily favored Connors to win the title in what is still seen as *the* breakthrough moment for African American men in tennis.

Borg was frustrated with his Wimbledon defeat, but he was still relatively young and clearly improving. Strangely, he lost a claycourt tournament in Båstad, Sweden, a couple of weeks later. While Borg was an incredibly successful Davis Cup player at home, he might have felt too much pressure out there all alone with his childhood peers watching, because he bizarrely fell to the lefty Brazilian Thomaz Koch, 6–2, 6–3.

He flew to North America for the summer season and began to make substantial progress, battering Vilas for the Boston title. This time, he felt a little more comfortable in zany Forest Hills, and why not? The United States Tennis Association had switched the tournament from grass to green clay (called Har-Tru), which should have played in his favor.

He knocked out Laver and then the combative American Eddie Dibbs, before falling in a rough 7–5, 7–5, 7–5 semifinal to Connors, who was still at the height of his powers and unlike Vilas could rip his two-handed backhands anywhere in the court. Connors felt that he was tougher than Borg, could overmatch him from the backhand side, and when called for could more efficiently close out points at the net. Plus he liked the consistent pace that Borg fed him.

In the finals Connors fell to the savvy left-hander Orantes, who enjoyed ebullient support from the crowd—they clapped for some of Connors's errors (a no-no in the still somewhat civilized world of tennis sportsmanship), perhaps because, as some of his peers said at the time, he exuded hate when he competed and the classy Orantes was much more lovable.

Recovering from his Wimbledon loss, Borg led Sweden to its first Davis Cup title, winning all twelve of his matches against Poland, West Germany, the Soviet Union, Spain, Chile, and Czechoslovakia in the final. That run certainly inspired some positive feelings toward him at home, which was still smarting from his move to Monte Carlo.

Given how it appeared in 1975 that the Swede was on the verge of taking over the tour, Borg had an odd and erratic first five months of the 1976 season. He still wasn't driving the ball the way he needed to on hard courts and took two losses to Connors, but he did manage to win Toronto indoors over Gerulaitis and Dallas over Vilas. Injured, he didn't play the Italian Open, but he easily won Düsseldorf on clay and looked in prime position to defend his French Open title. But in the quarters, Panatta came straight at him and pulled off a 6–3, 6–3, 2–6, 7–6 victory, the last time Borg would lose at the French Open.

"I think sometimes something magical happens and you don't know why," Panatta said. "You just have it. You say to yourself that you are going to put the ball right where you want it and it happens all the time. Something that I cannot describe. It just happens. Everything becomes easy."

Something else was going on in Borg's life in Paris. A Romanian woman player, Mariana Simionescu, had caught his eye. They were introduced by Borg's Swedish girlfriend from the junior competitions, Helena Anliot. At the French Open, Borg asked Mariana to dinner with Bergelin and his father, Rune, to celebrate Rune's birthday. Afterward, they talked all night in Björn's room and a romance began.

While love was in the air, there was much work to do on the courts of London. Simionescu had gone off to play a tournament in Scotland (which she won), while Borg and Bergelin practiced at London's Cumberland Club, focusing on adding speed and placement to his serve, driving his return of serve, and increasing his comfort level at the net. A couple of days after Simionescu came to London, she moved in with Borg at the Grosvenor Hotel and became a regular fixture in his life.

Borg's transition from a born-and-bred European slow court player to one who could successfully attack at Wimbledon fascinated analysts. He hit heavy topspin groundstrokes with both his forehand and his backhand, which is difficult on grass, as the ball skids low and it's tough to get enough racket head speed to be able to properly come over the ball and keep it in the court. But Borg's fast hands and quick feet were adaptable almost anywhere, and he had a long and rapid follow-through, which is mandatory if a player is attempting to dip balls.

Again and again, Borg would say that his return of serve was the key at Wimbledon, not just his own much-improved first serve. He couldn't care less what the surface was if he got into a rally from the backcourt, because once there he felt that he could dominate. It was getting into the points that was crucial. On his own serve, he didn't need to nail an ace, only to prevent his foes from attacking him with a well-placed ball. From there, he could string them around like yo-yos from the baseline. On his opponents' serves, if he could get in a good enough return, he'd tempt them to come into the net off a mediocre approach shot and then would whiz a passing shot that they couldn't touch.

"I knew I could play well once in a while, but I would have to improve my game a lot if I wanted to win Wimbledon," said Borg. "I knew especially I had to improve my serve, so I was working a lot on that—the whole year, but mostly the two weeks right before Wimbledon. I was practicing the serve an hour every day, which I had never done before, and Lennart made a change that was very important. He told me that my position was not exactly right."

Borg's left (front) foot was almost parallel to the baseline, so Bergelin made it a little more straight, pointing it to the net, which allowed Borg to aim his body more at the net and be able to toss the ball up in front of him. His previous stance had him tossing the ball more to the right, and he didn't know exactly where it was going and would at times mis-hit serves. Now he felt that he was able to hit through the ball with his body moving forward toward the net and, most important, could smack it with more power.

That fortnight in the London suburbs began with what Simionescu described as a Wimbledon routine of room service, practice, room service, practice, room service, and little to no sex (as it might affect Borg's stamina). He marched through 1976 Wimbledon without losing a set, an incredible achievement for a player who had struggled so much in the past. Some said it could have been the unusual heat that aided his title run as the courts baked and the balls bounced higher.

In the first round, he thrashed British Davis Cupper David Lloyd 6–3, 6–3, 6–1. "The kid was playing a different way than I've seen it," Lloyd said of how Borg could hit the ball so high over the net because of his enormous spin and then watch it drop deep inside the court. "I thought here was a kid who was going to change the game." In the next two rounds, he crunched Marty Riessen and Colin Dibley.

But Borg had developed a muscle strain because of all the time he spent practicing his serve and was unsure how he would hold up, so he took one painkilling injection after another. Nonetheless, he bested a frustrated Brian Gottfried, blasted a despondent Vilas, and managed to get back enough of the hard-serving Tanner's big blasts to reach the final against Nastase, who had won the U.S. Open in 1971 and the French Open in 1973. Nasty was thirty at the time he faced Borg in the final, but he was still regretting his five-set loss to Stan Smith in the final in 1972 and was itching for the title.

Simionescu had told Borg before the tournament how much she wanted her fellow Romanian Nastase to win, figuring that Björn wouldn't make it past the round of 16. But when the final came, she had a decision to make: pull for her national hero or her newfound love? Love conquered all, but she sat on her hands during the match and left during the third set. "Ilie's brother, Cotica, could read it on my face, otherwise he wouldn't have asked me so bluntly, 'Which side did you choose?'" She didn't reply and he parried, "Here at least I see a Romanian who is not rooting for Ilie."

According to Nastase, Borg took a painkilling injection prior to the match and was rubbing some kind of cream on his sore muscle in the locker room. They went out on a steamy court where temperatures reached above one hundred.

A nervous Nastase got off to a 3–0 lead and held break points to go up 4–0, but in his words, "The Ice Man Cometh."

"Had I won the first set, anything could have happened, but he got into his stride while I seemed to lose my momentum. My serve was neutered and he was benefiting from the slower court and higher bounces to slug great returns at me as I made my way to the net. He also served unbelievably well."

At one point, with Borg at the net, Nastase smashed a ball straight at his head. Borg let it go and it flew out. The Swede looked Nastase's way and the Romanian turned around and faced him. "What the bloody hell you looking at?" Nastase spat out.

Borg let him know with a cold stare that he wasn't pleased that Nastase had gone at his noggin. Nastase also mocked the Swede by rubbing his stomach.

Nastase recalled Borg running down everything he threw at him, and even in the third set while he tried to hang in there, he just couldn't find a way around him. Borg hit a service winner on match point, threw his racket into the air, and knelt on the grass, securing his first Wimbledon title with a 6–4, 6–2, 9–7 win. He became the youngest male Wimbledon champion of tennis's Open Era at twenty years and one month (a record later broken by German Boris Becker, who won Wimbledon at age seventeen in 1985).

"Borg just knelt to offer a pagan prayer to thank the Swedish wood fairies who made his triumph possible," Simionescu said.

Arthur Ashe was more than surprised, he was a little flummoxed. "Most of us thought it was kind of a fluke the first time he won Wimbledon in 1976. Hell, nobody in thirty years had been able to win on grass from the baseline hitting topspin the way he does. But his serve made a quantum leap—at least a 50 to 75 percent improvement—and his return of serve is tailor-made for grass, because he stands about two or three yards behind the baseline and just lets the topspin take its natural course. His hands are quick enough that he can change grips and handle the fast, skiddy bounces on grass, which is unusual for a European, and his shots just come over the net and dip. Anybody who tries to come in and volley against him is hitting up all the time. It's tough to put the ball away that way, and he runs everything down and is in a position to hit a passing shot. He also moves incredibly well on every surface. It's tough to move fast from side to side on grass, because there isn't much adhesion between the sole of the shoe and the court, but he can do it."

It has been said that artists should not be asked to describe their works because the meaning of their pieces is clear if you take a close look at them. Vilas said the same of Borg's inability to speak to the reasons for his success.

"It's the same if you go to Van Gogh and say, 'Oh, but you know, Mr. Van Gogh, you are the best painter in the world, but why don't you play soccer?' It's enough that Björn is the best at what he is doing. I don't think he has time to do a lot of other things; to be number one, to win Wimbledon at his age, he's never had free time. When I was his age I did because I was losing early at a lot of tournaments, I started writing because I was feeling lonely and depressed. Maybe he didn't pass such time, so that's why I write poems and he reads comic books."

That summer, Richard Raskind, a forty-one-year-old doctor and former captain of the Yale tennis team, came onto the tour as a woman, Renee Richards, a year after undergoing a sex change operation. After a reporter discovered that Richard was a transsexual, the

United States Tennis Association denied her entry into the 1976 U.S. Open because she could not pass an Olympic-style chromosome test.

"If I was allowed to play," she later wrote, "then the floodgates would be opened and through them would come tumbling an endless stream of made-over Neanderthals who would brutalize Chris Evert and Evonne Goolagong."

Encouraged by what she said were thousands of supportive letters, Richards successfully challenged the USTA's sanctions against her in court and was allowed to play in 1977, where she lost in the first round. But there was no question that she struck a chord with disenfranchised groups. "I heard from blacks, convicts, Chicanos, hippies, homosexuals, people with physical handicaps and, of course, transsexuals," she wrote. "My god, the whole world seemed to be looking for me to be their Joan of Arc."

While the Richards issue dominated hallway discussions at Forest Hills, Borg still could not get comfortable in the loud and often chaotic environment of Queens. Given his extraordinary record on clay courts, it's stunning that he was unable to win the U.S. Open on green Har-Tru. In the final, he still could not find a way to face down the grittier Connors, who hadn't won a major that year and was upset by Tanner at Wimbledon. At Forest Hills, Connors rediscovered his strike zone and bested Borg 6–4, 3–6, 7–6 (9), 6–4.

Borg was still young and working at smoothing the rough edges of his game, while Connors was nearly as fleet and had more self-confidence when it came to going for big shots at critical moments. Connors would stand inside the baseline and push the points, while Borg camped well behind it, preparing for counterattack.

While Connors was still ranked No. 1 going into the match, Borg's ascension at Wimbledon and domination of the French Open made him the sexy pick going into the final. Plus, he had pulled off two incredible five-set victories, over Gottfried in the fourth round and defending champ Orantes in the quarters, and then had pasted Nastase in the semis.

Connors knew that Borg was coming, and despite the fact that claycourt tennis demanded patience, he decided to go on the attack.

Borg could very well have won that match had he managed to win just one of four set points he held in the third-set tiebreaker. Down 6–4, Connors displayed his guts, while Borg lollipopped balls to Connors's forehand and wished that Jimbo would make a critical mistake. Connors pounced and hammered two winners. Down 8–7, he rushed the net and put away an overhead. Down 9–8, he crushed another forehand and delivered an overhead. Connors then won a marathon rally, and Borg deflated to lose the tiebreaker and then the match. The Belleville Basher had kicked Borg's balls in once again.

"The tiebreaker is probably the best tennis I've ever played under such pressure conditions," Connors said. "The New York crowd is a tough one to play in front of. They come to see blood. I didn't want to give them any of mine."

Connors ended the year with a 3–0 record against the Swede, but the tide would begin to turn in 1977, when Borg brought out a sharper pick and began to chip away at the American's thick wall of concrete.

Borg, Connors, and Vilas fought long, hard, and heavy to secure the top rankings in 1977, but the Swede made a terrible decision that year, deciding to play World Team Tennis for the Cleveland Nets, which cost him a chance at his third straight French Open title. The International Tennis Federation banned all the players who competed in the U.S.-based competition from playing in Paris, which was why neither Borg nor Connors participated, and one reason Vilas was able to march to the crown.

"If I regret something, and if I could change it, is when I didn't play '77 here," Borg would say after retiring. "I think that was the most stupid thing I did. We all do stupid things."

Once on the lawns of Wimbledon, Borg came in with much more confidence and was able to stave off amazing efforts by his rivals. He needed to come back from two sets down to defeat Aussie serve-and-volleyer Mark Edmondsen 3–6, 7–9, 6–2, 6–4, 6–1 in the second round. It would not be the first of Borg's early-round troubles as the defending champion at the Big W, but it held significance because his lungs and legs enabled him to run past the swaggering Aussie, a mustachioed former janitor who had won the Australian Open the year prior.

Borg then cracked Niki Pilic, Wojtek Fibak, and Nastase before contesting one of Wimbledon's greatest semifinals ever, his instant classic, 6–4, 3–6, 6–3, 3–6, 8–6 victory over his friend Vitas Gerulaitis in the semifinals. "Every time I play Borg I come out with some thirty ideas that should get me victory," Vitas said. "And each time Björn breaks each one of the thirty to pieces, like a clay-pigeon shooter."

Journalist Mike Lupica, a friend of Gerulaitis's from New York, wrote, "Vitas had his best shot when he was up a service break early in the fifth set. He had a point to go ahead 4–2. The score was 40–30. He had been coming in hard behind his weak second serve all day and getting away with it. This time he hesitated. It was one of those small openings in the fight that the champion sees and knocks you down. Vitas stayed back, Borg took control of the point and won it, broke back and won the match."

"That fucking second serve," Gerulaitis later told Lupica at dinner. "I could have won that. Imagine that, me winning Wimbledon."

In the final, Borg would have to face Connors, who had taught the teenage McEnroe a lesson in the semifinals. McEnroe was in many ways the story of the event, as he had graduated from high school and, unknown, worked his way out of the qualifying to reach the semifinals, but he was mentally unprepared to do battle with the U.S. legend Connors in a 6–3, 6–3, 4–6, 6–4 loss.

Borg knew that if he was ever going to get Connors's goat, he had to do it on the lawns. Unlike in New York, he could not play as passively and amped up his first service speed. Bergelin convinced him that he had to be more aggressive.

"I had to work on developing that kind of game—not serve and volley all the time, because that is not me, but just to come in to the net more, so that the opponent never knows exactly what I'm going to do," said Borg. "I worked on that until I was comfortable playing that kind of a game, too, and by coming in more I improved my volley a lot."

Connors caused quite a stir at the Championships, which was celebrating its centenary and had invited all the former titleholders to come in for a parade on Centre Court. No lover of ceremonies that were not all about him, a selfish yet keenly focused Connors—who was nursing a right thumb injury and claimed he needed to practice with a splint on—decided to skip the proceedings.

In the final, their baseline rallies were full of fire and sprints, but Borg was getting better depth on his strokes, served wonderfully, took away Connors's vaunted return, and was able to get numerous short volleys to fall below his opponent's outstretched metal racket.

Borg danced out to a 4–0 lead in the fifth set and held three break points to go up 5–0, but then Connors regained his form and aggression and roared back to 4–4. But oh so calmly, Borg broke serve as a clearly nervous Connors inexplicably folded, committing three unforced errors, including a dreaded double fault. "I played the ninth game like a dummy," Connors said.

The cool king of Wimbledon served out the match at love, and Wimbledon crown number two was Borg's in a 3–6, 6–2, 6–1, 5–7, 6–4 victory. Connors's spell was broken; Borg, after losing six of his first seven matches to him, would win fourteen of the next sixteen. Borg would never again think that Connors was too tough for him. He knew that if he could combine a hard-to-read offense and a tireless defense he could tunnel his way to victory.

"Connors hits the ball harder than I do, but his passing shots sometimes are not as effective as mine because they have little deception and no margin for error," Borg said. "When Jimmy is on, he is devastating, because even if you know where he is going to hit the ball, he hits it so hard that anticipation doesn't help. But day in and day out, my results may be better because my passes are more consistent, and it is difficult to volley my ball dipping at your feet. Connors's drives rise as they go over the net and a good volleyer prefers this to hitting below the net. On a passing shot I don't care whether the ball lands close to the baseline or the service line. If the ball passes the man at the net, it doesn't count more if it lands on the baseline."

The win propelled Borg to the No. 1 ranking on the computer, albeit for just one week in August.

The rest of his summer went to hell, as did life in New York prior to the U.S. Open. On the scorching night of July 13, 1977, the lights went out in New York City. New Yorkers responded with resilience as well as violence. In Harlem, Brooklyn, and the South Bronx, some folks came to their neighbors' aid, while other neighborhoods exploded into violence as stores were looted and destroyed and buildings were set ablaze. Many New Yorkers took to the streets with candles in search of friends, and in Greenwich Village some streets became an improvised festival. The police made 3,776 arrests, while 1,037 fires burned throughout the city.

Some called the season the worst summer in New York's modern history, as the streets were filthy and dangerous, while the subways were graffiti-ridden and totally unreliable. Even Central Park, that great expanse of green in the concrete jungle, looked barren and near dying.

The city was choked with fear as terrorist bombs linked to Puerto Rican nationalists exploded at Manhattan office buildings and department stores and a serial killer who called himself Son of Sam led a reign of terror over the nighttime streets. The murderer, whose name was David Berkowitz, killed six people and injured seven, mostly in Queens and the Bronx, before being captured. He scared the living daylights out of city denizens as he sent horrifying taunting letters to the police and the press. He was said to be hunting women with long dark hair, so some women took to wearing wigs or hats and the city's youth avoided parking on quiet streets, since several victims had been shot while sitting in cars.

Ed Koch, who would become a popular New York mayor, attributed his election in 1977 to the paralysis partly created by the string of murders. "The reason I believe I ultimately won was because of the fear in the city—and what should be done about it," Koch said. "The fear was palpable."

Jimmy Breslin, then a well-known columnist for the *New York Daily News*, who received some of Son of Sam's letters, described his early correspondence as being full of "the fear, the blood and the cracks in the sidewalk of the city."

Anyone who walked into Forest Hills, Queens, that summer could smell the fear just around the corner, but the U.S. Open, dusted with green clay and the hopes and dreams of all 128 participants in the men's draw, felt a bit like an oasis. Berkowitz had been arrested on August 11, two weeks before the Open began play, but still, the hangover from his reign rang on in Queens like the blood-curdling howls from his neighbor's dog that used to haunt him.

A few weeks later after winning Wimbledon, Borg lost to Connors on clay in Florida at the Pepsi Grand Slam exhibition, and then at the U.S. Open he was forced to retire against Dick Stockton in the round of 16 when he was overcome by a shoulder injury that he was said to have gotten waterskiing. He couldn't hit an overhead. "Some people just aren't meant to win certain tournaments," Swedish player Anders Jarryd said. "There was something there that Borg didn't take to."

In the U.S. Open final, Connors failed once again as Vilas's incredible form that he had begun after Wimbledon carried him to the title. He put together a forty-six-match winning streak, and Connors was no match for him, on court or in the hearts of fans. The atmosphere had a distinctly Latin flair to it as Vilas spun Connors all over the court in a 2–6, 6–3, 7–6 (4), 6–0 victory. After the final point, fans stormed the court, and some raised the triumphant Argentine on their shoulders, which effectively supplanted the traditional end-of-match handshake between the two players.

"It was crazy," Vilas recalled. "I thought the people coming [down to the court] were from Argentina, so I also kind of went to them. But then nobody was from Argentina, they were from Puerto Rico, they were from all over, Mexicans. It was a very amazing feeling. They made a big thing out of it, that he couldn't shake hands. You know Jimmy, he was not going to follow all the jumping [people] and try to shake hands with me. He said, 'He's not here, I'm going.' I understand the guy."

Connors was furious after the match, threatening to fight a fan, spitting on court, and taking off in his Pinto without speaking to the press.

Borg would never experience the same joy as Vilas in New York, but the Swede shook off his shoulder ailment and had a brilliant fall run, winning five European tournaments in a row. But back in New York, at Madison Square Garden, he still couldn't bring his best. He reached the final, only to have Connors best him in straight sets.

"I really think that something about New York bothered him," said Dennis Ralston, who coached Roscoe Tanner at the time. "Some guys just can't function as well in that environment."

6

"I Can Do Anything with a Tennis Ball"

The 1980 Wimbledon final is knotted at one set apiece. The color has returned to Lennart Bergelin's face and Mariana Simionescu is so excited that she asks for a cigarette from the John McEnroe camp.

"This July 5 seems endless to me," she recalled. "Yesterday, on American Independence Day, Yankees Connors and McEnroe crossed swords. These Yankees who come to Wimbledon claim that Europe has said all it has to say about tennis a long time ago. Borg seems to have appeared in the battle to ruin their plans."

Mac takes a deep knee bend before the third set begins, and Borg has an extra skip in his step. There is a spark of white light in his eyes and his long hair bounces off his shoulders.

Borg is on the ball. No longer just sitting three feet behind the baseline and waiting cautiously to return, he's moving forward and looking to crush McEnroe's second serve. Mac double-faults to open the second game. At 30–15, two chirping birds fly over his head and he stares them down. The crowd breaks into laughter, but this is no laughing matter. He can't handle a hard Borg forehand return with a backhand volley. He's straining, and he walks back to the baseline with his hands on his hips at 30–30. Mac's serve out wide means little as Borg murders a forehand return. On break point, Mac serves out wide again and Borg is too far out in front of his reply. But the American is dissatisfied with his stick and changes rackets. It doesn't make a difference as he dumps an easy volley into the net. On his second break point, Borg takes a McEnroe second serve and whips an inside-out forehand return for a winner to go ahead 2–0 and never looks back in the set.

Every serve seems significant, every groundstroke deep, every net rush meaningful. Now it's very sunny and fans can see the dust spewing upward from the court's dead spots.

McEnroe has five break points in the seventh game down 4–2, but Borg is as quick as a cat and fends off one after another. McEnroe's long dark curls seem to pull his headband down over his thick eyebrows, and he comes into the net off a little too much junk. A beautifully struck backhand volley finds the corner and he fights off one. A service winner at the backhand solves another, and then Mac takes his eye off a hard forehand and finds the net, screams, "No!" and smacks his head with his strings. A rapid-fire exchange with Borg at the net sees McEnroe miss a backhand, and the Swede seems to ask, "Who has the fastest hands on the court?" as he's fought off the fourth break point. A backhand pass and a brilliant chip and charge earn McEnroe his fifth break point, but again his backhand return fails him as it dips into the net. It's a delightful, marathon game with plenty of quick exchanges, but Borg finally holds when a McEnroe lobs flies long, and he has a 5–2 lead.

All humans have nerves, but not everyone gets frazzled when they are asked to perform at their best. Borg rarely showed fear of the big occasion, except in New York, a city that didn't suit his skin. At Wimbledon, he'd go for his best shots at crunch time, a frequent mantra of a tennis champion's success. He wouldn't push the ball around and hope for mistakes, but instead would write his own ticket. He would plunge mentally and then come back to the surface faster and with more ferocity than the great white shark in *Jaws*. He'd briefly lose a lead, gnash his teeth, and then snap his foe in half. During major championships, he'd let his beard grow so that he resembled a tough Swedish fisherman who was willing to battle the elements in order to feed his family.

Borg believed that his ability to step up when the tension was highest was innate, a curious sentiment, considering that most psychologists believe that performing well under pressure is a learned behavior. Maybe what Borg really meant was that he learned how to do it before anyone else.

"I think probably I was born with that," Borg said. "I remember when I started to play the circuit, I was more nervous because I was not used to playing big matches. But not for the last five years. I have been playing so many big matches, when maybe one ball makes the difference, that I got used to that. It's very difficult to tell a player that he has to be more relaxed, because he is the way he is. If he is tight or nervous at 30–40 on his serve, there's no way he can change that, because that's his personality. I feel more relaxed when it's 30–40, or a crucial point in the match. I'm not tight or anything when I'm tossing up the ball and making my swing. Maybe that's why I get my first serve in most of the time at 30–40. I know a lot of players might get tight because they're thinking, 'I'm break point down; I have to get my first serve in or I'm in trouble.' Their arm gets heavy, they have trouble to make a good toss. But I am thinking that for sure I will get my first serve in, so I'm very relaxed. When I'm behind, I always think that I'm going to lose, so I decide to go for my shots, to try to make shots I didn't make before. I always try to play a safe game, to make the other guy take the risk, but when I'm behind I take more chances. I gamble more, go for winners, and because I'm so relaxed I usually win those points."

McEnroe makes the Swede serve out the set by holding to 5–3, but Borg does it competently, hammering an overhead smash and then watching Mac push a forehand return wide.

Borg pockets a 6–3 third set and is clearly in the driver's seat. The Swede has entered the zone, and it will take a ninth-circle-of-hell effort from Dante's McEnroe to cool him off.

"When I go out on the court and I sense I am playing well," Borg said, "I feel there is no way a guy can hit a winner, because I am going to be there. I think I can do anything with a tennis ball. It is the best feeling. Then I will try something I have never done before, and that works too. I don't really know what I'm doing out there because something strange is going on. I think I am Superman, and I start to try all kinds of things, because suddenly I know I can't miss the ball. I make an unbelievable shot, and it feels just like all the others. So then I want to show the people even more, give them these most fantastic shots that maybe they have never seen before in their lives. But I want to show them these shots because suddenly, I know I can. I cannot miss, not even one shot. It is like I am dreaming. It is wonderful."

7

France to Stanford

In 1977, while Borg prepared for his title defense at Roland Garros, McEnroe set out on his high school senior project: to compete in Paris, London, and the U.S. summer hardcourt season. Many of his friends and foes from the juniors had already gone off to college: Billy Martin went to UCLA, Bill Scanlon to Trinity University in Texas, Peter Fleming to Michigan and then later UCLA, and Peter Rennert to Stanford.

During the last semester of his senior year of high school, Mac did get a couple of wild cards into two pro events—one in Maryland, where he lost to the loony Ilie Nastase in three sets, and another in Virginia Beach, where he scored wins over the aging but competent Charlie Pasarell and the hard-charging Bob Lutz. He then pushed Nastase to three sets again. (The U.S. hardcourt tournaments, along with most lesser tournaments, are best of three sets.)

Guillermo Vilas, who would achieve the No. 1 ranking that year, and his business-savvy manager, Ion Tiriac, told a story about the impetuous "redheaded" Mac—who incidentally wasn't redheaded at all. They said that the bold teenager approached them while they were hitting and asked to practice with Vilas, who was too nice to say no.

After five minutes, Mac asked Vilas to launch him some lobs so he could practice his overhead, an incredibly presumptuous request that early in a hitting session with a star who was working on his groundstrokes. Tiriac noted how odd McEnroe's choppy strokes seemed, and at that moment, on that day, he couldn't imagine that he'd ever become a big-time player.

"Lobs to Mr. Vilas! No please, no fuck you, no anything," Tiriac said. "Then he said after five minutes, 'Okay, that's it for me, see you guys.'"

But Tiriac did notice while watching the Nastase match how Mac, despite his unorthodox strokes, just always seemed to be where the ball was.

In May, Mac was handed five hundred dollars to travel to Europe to play in the junior Grand Slam draws, but since he had already earned a few ATP points, he was able to get into the qualifying in the French Open main draw. He was forced to check into a cheap Paris hotel and what seemed like a lot of money when he left New York all of sudden didn't look as if it would last for up to six weeks at respectable European hotels.

But he quickly grew excited about the prospect of qualifying for the French and dug in, chewing on his fingernails all the while. Gerulaitis had told him that his first on-court Parisian experience would entail confronting some dirtballer he had never heard of running him ragged, but once in his matches, Mac, who had plenty of training on clay in the United States, knew he could stick with his foes if he mixed up his lefty strokes enough.

That he did, but off court he had yet to groove into the Parisian way, and knowing not a word of French and staying in a cheap hotel, he was concerned that he would not receive a wake-up call for his second-round match. What else is a high schooler to do but pull an all-nighter, just as if he was cramming for an AP history final?

No matter, Mac won his qualifying matches, got into the main draw, and received a per diem, so he headed over to the more respectable (although not luxurious) player hotel.

Mac whipped Aussie journeyman Alvin Gardiner in the first round but faced a much more difficult test in the second round, going up against Aussie veteran Phil Dent, a real gamer without incredible skills but with plenty of know-how when it came to suffocating greenhorns. Mac contends that he consistently attempted to give back points to Dent because of the atrocious line calling, and after the 4–6, 6–2, 4–6, 6–3, 6–3 loss the Aussie came up to him, stared him in the eyes, and said, "Sonny, this is the pros now. You play the calls, and if you have something to say, say it to the umpires."

Mac took the advice to heart and never stopped taking any minor or major issue straight to the umpires. Mary Carillo fondly recalls what happened next: she ran into her old friend McEnroe from Douglaston in the players' lounge, and they decided to enter the mixed doubles.

"John is looking at the list of people who'd signed up and is like, 'Oh, geez, I mean we should win this thing,'" she recalled. That they did, skidding their way through a less than spectacular draw. In the final, they bested the obscure Florenta Mihai and Ivan Molina in front of just a handful of fans, as most folks had left Court Central after Vilas destroyed American Brian Gottfried for the title.

"I'm a rookie pro and he's a high school amateur and we win it," Mary said incredulously with a smile.

John's mother, Kay McEnroe, recalled, "Those were giddy days and stupendous. I remember I walked down to the Douglaston Club, and Mary's father was playing, and I said, 'The kids won the French!' And he said, 'What?'" McEnroe too was pleased with the win, but said he felt horrible about playing in front of a tiny gallery. That feeling would soon go away as his notoriety grew.

Although he had zero grasscourt experience, McEnroe went out to the lawns of Roehampton for the Wimbledon qualifying, a respectable but not royal nearby locale where the All England Lawn Tennis Club sends the men who are as yet unworthy of setting their toes on well-manicured lawns to fight it out for eight qualifying spots. Mac handily qualified, winning his last match in a downpour. He was warmly welcomed to the soggy summers in stodgy old England.

Even today, despite massive modernization of the grounds, Wimbledon's old guard is still partly in charge. Some five hundred men and women from the British army, Royal Navy, Royal Air Force, and London Fire Brigade take fifteen days of leave and travel to the All England Club to volunteer as stewards.

The armed forces began volunteering at Wimbledon in 1946, as the club wanted to reward the soldiers for their heroism in World War II. The UK's armed forces are given thirty days of leave a year, so for a soldier to give up fifteen of those to stand near a stairwell and direct fans takes a special commitment. The volunteers come from as far as Cyprus, Germany, and Belgium to make sure that spectators are comfortable making their way through the grounds.

Dressed to the nines in crisply pressed uniforms and wearing cheery smiles for up to twelve hours a day, this family of some of England's best-mannered men and women ensure that Wimbledon is a well-ordered place to visit. Safety is paramount. "This is the most high-profile sporting event in the UK," said David Jones, the head of the Service and London Fire Brigade at Wimbledon. "It's an opportunity for the taxpayer to see and interact with the men and women of the armed forces and the fire brigade who they are supporting throughout the year. The volunteers are attracted by the prestige of the tournament and the camaraderie and friendships that are built here."

Bob Bray, a London Fire Brigade station commander in Bromley, heads the Fire Patrol Safety unit at Wimbledon. Bray has been coming to Wimbledon since 1974 and agrees that the friendships built at the site are a big attraction for returning stewards, who represent up to 60 percent of each year's group. The fire brigade began working at the club in 1967, after a series of blazes at sporting facilities across the country prompted the club to ensure that no such tragedy would befall Wimbledon. Bray and his group work diligently to make sure that the kitchen crews take the proper precautions, that fans haven't dropped lit cigarettes in the trash bins, and that the fire exits are clear.

Volunteering at Wimbledon is no cup of sweet tea. Some days, the stewards are forced to stand for hours during a marathon match with empty stomachs. Plus, they must contend with temperamental superstars. "That's when they're under a lot of pressure," Jones said. "We ask them to be pleasant, polite, professional, smart, and alert. That's not easy after standing for so many hours. We try to make sure that their standards do not drop."

It is one thing to stand at attention on the upper tier at Court 1, but it is completely another to guide royalty into the Royal Box. "They have to put on their best uniform and be aware at all times. It doesn't suit everyone," said Jones.

Many of the Wimbledon staff are former military officers, and members of the fire and police departments are on site. Order is put at a premium. But getting the rebellious McEnroe to stand up straight, press his trousers, and pay attention was a little like asking an octogenarian steward not to straighten his tie before he goes to work.

At Wimbledon, McEnroe moved into a house with Robert Van't Hoff and Eliot Teltscher, his old foes and buddies from the juniors, who hailed from Southern California. The laid-back Van't Hoff would later become a noted coach of the women's star of the 1990s and early 2000s Lindsay Davenport, while the thinking man Teltscher would head up the United States Tennis Association's Player Development Department for a long stretch at the beginning of the twenty-first century. Mac seemed to be walking on the thick air that blew into SW19 and feeling no real anxiety about the enormous significance of the occasion.

On court, he threw the pressure to his foes, as he waltzed past Egypt's Ismail El Shafei (Borg's conqueror at 1974 Wimbledon), the stiff Briton Colin Dowdeswell, the German Karl Meiler, and then Sandy Mayer, a smart ex-Stanford player with just as much attitude as McEnroe.

Peter Fleming remembers sitting with McEnroe at lunch before he went out to play Meiler and warning him that his opponent could be a dicey matchup. Mac's straightforward response: "If I lose to Karl Meiler, I'm quitting the game."

Fleming added, "John saw the game differently than most of us and he was never lacking confidence."

Then, surprise, surprise, it was time to face Dent again, this time in the quarterfinals. The final eight players were moved out of the crowded and shabbier locker room B, and the clean carpets, polished wood, spacious showers, and roominess of the main locker room impressed even the rebellious Irish American.

Mac frequently said that once he had played an opponent, he knew what to do to beat him, but strategy and execution are two completely different things, especially against someone as driven as Dent was that year. After dropping the second set, McEnroe lost a little confidence and was clearly peeved. On the changeover, he bent over, put his wooden racket under his foot, and tried to snap it in half. Mac, who would be raked over the coals time and again at Wimbledon during the next fifteen years for his boorish behavior, then got struck with his first chorus of loud boos. Sportsmanship was still put at a premium in London in those days, and for most of the fans in attendance, watching a long-haired, red-faced punk from New York throw a fit against a veteran Australian was frowned upon.

But Mac did stir something in the hearts of some of the younger folks who sat on hard wooden benches that summer day, a few of whom were surely fans of the Sex Pistols, violent punk rockers who were revolutionizing London that season with their in-your-face album *Anarchy in the UK*. Graffiti scrawled on the concrete walls on Church Road in Wimbledon Village read JOHNNY ROTTEN RULES. Just for fun, McEnroe got into Sid Vicious mode and kicked his racket across the court. The boos rained down harder.

"I felt really amused," McEnroe said. "As impressed as I was by Wimbledon and its tremendous history, I found England to be strange, stodgy, and quaint. When I saw those dozing linesmen I thought, 'This is not what Wimbledon should look like.' The club was beautiful, but the whole atmosphere was set in its ways and the self-importance was beyond belief. I couldn't help resenting how badly the organizers treated the lesser players and how they genuflected to the stars. I was incredulous at all that bowing and curtseying to royalty and lesser royalty. I was a kid from Queens, a subway rider. How could anyone expect me to take all this strawberry-and-cream malarkey seriously?"

That day against Dent on Court 1—Wimbledon's second-most-important court after Centre Court—Mac was playing in front of the biggest crowd of his young life. He was a bit nervous and found himself down two sets to one and a break of serve in the fourth set. But he had no intention of going out. He sensed that Dent, who had never reached the Wimbledon semifinals before, might get tight and reasoned that with his success in the main draw, he didn't want to lose that day, because he would then have to play the junior tournament and might possibly suffer a defeat, which to him would stain his progress against the big boys in front of the ever-watchful tennis world.

Still questioning calls and intense as ever, Mac finally prevailed 6–4, 8–10, 4–6, 6–3, 6–4 (Wimbledon did not begin to use tie-breakers at 6–6 in the first four sets of a match until 1979). Dent was peeved, and McEnroe couldn't believe that he had made the final four: his boyhood idol Borg against the King of Queens, Gerulaitis; and the Prince of Queens, Mac, against Jimmy Connors, another antiestablishment American, but with midwestern roots and Grand Slam titles already in his pocket. Mac recalled looking at the odds the next day: Borg 2 to 1; Connors 3 to 1; Gerulaitis 7 to 1; and McEnroe 250 to 1. He knew he had hit the big time, low odds or not, as his name was among those that mattered.

Yet McEnroe was still looking up to Connors and Borg as the gods of the game, so in the semifinals he played as if in a daze. He had never met Connors before, and in the locker room Jimbo wouldn't even look his way. Mac went on court with his head down, his bushy hair flying in the breeze, wearing a skintight Fila shirt, shorts that looked like they gave him a wedgie, and a colorful ban-danna. At that time, he wasn't hosting his own talk show or gaining small roles in Jack Nicholson movies; he was an unknown, and one of the local announcers pronounced his name as "MA-CAN-row" or "Mc-KEN-row."

Nor was he the attacking player who would win the title four years later, as he spent way too much time behind the baseline. He was intimidated and wasn't able to let his game hang out, more wor-ried about being crushed than actually winning. McEnroe fell in four sets, stealing the third by taking away from Connors's enor-mous pace, but losing nonetheless because he couldn't get his legs moving. Connors, under obvious pressure himself to win the match against the American up-and-comer, didn't play particularly well, but noted Mac's talents.

"This kid is difficult to play; he makes shots from impossible places," Connors said.

McEnroe became the youngest man up to that time ever to reach the Wimbledon semifinals, and also began to develop his reputation as one of the sporting world's "bad boys" along with Connors and Nastase. "He is a young man who raised perfectly placed strokes to a high art form, only to resort to tantrums that smear his master-pieces like graffiti," wrote Pete Axthelm in *Newsweek*.

Mac never saw the historic Borg vs. Gerulaitis semifinal, as he and Carillo had to play a mixed-doubles quarterfinal against the grizzled Dennis Ralston and Martina Navratilova (the eventual nine-time Wimbledon singles champion), a much more formidable pairing than any they had faced in Paris. They went down 10–8 in the third set, and McEnroe was steamed at Ralston, claiming that he hit Carillo on purpose with an overhead. "I felt like killing the guy," he said.

Ralston was a quintessential California tennis success story. Born in Bakersfield, raised by tennis-loving parents, a Southern Califor-nia junior standout and star for a USC team that had been called by many the best collegiate team ever, the intelligent all-courter made his mark on all levels of the game. A former Los Angeles Open champ, Ralston also reached the Wimbledon singles final in 1966, but played a desultory match and fell to Manolo Santana 6–4, 11–9, 6–4.

He was a Davis Cup hero, and would go on to coach Wimbledon finalist Roscoe Tanner, eighteen-time Grand Slam champion Chris Evert, French Open winner Yannick Noah, and U.S. Open champ Gabriela Sabatini. A prideful, outspoken man who is deeply concerned about the sport's history, Ralston completely discounted McEnroe's version of what occurred in the 1977 Wimbledon mixed doubles and is still angry about it.

"They had just won the French, and Martina was a little heavy then and still a heck of a player, we are out there on Court 2 and we knew they were good. At the start of the match, every time I'd get a lob from McEnroe, Carillo would face me straight on and move around like she could knock off my overhead with a volley, and I thought, 'What is she doing?' I never hit a woman in my life and you can ask anyone I ever played with, Billie Jean King, Martina. I was taught not to hit the lady—it's disrespectful.

"So I'm moving my overhead around the whole match trying not to hit her. So in the third set, it's 2–3, my serve, break point, and I knew if we got broken it would be very tough to win, because you never want to lose the guy's serve and it's so hard to break back. I served a big serve to McEnroe, he makes the return, I stick a volley deep and I'm on the opposite side of the court near where the tearoom is and he's over near where the road is, and he backs up, hits a forehand scoop lob, a hell of a lob. I back up five feet and if the ball lands it's going to be about three feet from the baseline. I see Carillo dancing around again and I thought, 'If I move this overhead anywhere else, I'm in trouble.' So I think, 'Mary, look out, that's where I'm going!' We're break point down and I was sick and tired of her messing around on my overheads, and I crushed the thing and it hit her right in the knee, knocked her right down. I had nowhere else to go. She's lying on the court and I walked over and said, 'I'm really sorry, but you were the only place to hit it.' McEnroe then walks up and says to me, 'You tried to hit her!' And this is exactly what I said to that jerk: 'Shut your mouth, you punk!' He looked at me, turned around, and went back and shut his mouth, finally."

Ralston said that later McEnroe claimed he ended Carillo's career, a charge he resents (Carillo actually wouldn't retire until the fall of 1980), especially when McEnroe recounted his side of the story at a banquet in front of Ralston's friends and business associates some twenty-five years later, completely embarrassing him.

"McEnroe sees things exactly the way he wants to," Ralston said. "I never got along with McEnroe. I don't have any respect for him as a person. I realize he was a tremendous player, but like 99 percent of the old players, I think he got away with murder and the game would be different if they disciplined him at the All England Club."

But that attempt would not be made by Wimbledon officials in 1977. Mac was still a kid who had come out of nowhere, and no official could have known how consistently ballistic he would become on court.

After Borg won his second Wimbledon title over Connors, reporters were banging on the McEnroe family door in Queens, as he had made the front pages of the *Daily News*, the *Times*, and the *Post*. He wouldn't be able to sneak around Manhattan for much longer.

"Nobody knew how to react to me, the Wimbledon semifinalist," he said. "And you know, to this day that's been a big part of my job—putting everyone at ease."

His younger brother Patrick, who had just turned eleven, recalled, "It's incredible, but we actually invited reporters into our house then—how times have changed. John was the sensation coming out of qualifying. He was over in England all by himself and not one of us expected it. From then on it was par for the course, but I didn't realize how good he was. We knew he was a great junior and all that, but playing Jimmy on Centre Court was a whole other thing. I guess I didn't realize until I grew up how good he was or realize how tough it was to play at that level until I got to the pros myself."

Mac had another thing to contend with when he got home: the girl he had been dating since he was sixteen, Californian player Stacy Margolin, had returned from Europe early because of the death of her father. She didn't let John know until after he returned stateside.

"I felt numb," he said. "That put things in perspective in a hurry."

As the U.S. Open was still played on clay—it would switch to hard courts the next year when it moved to Flushing Meadows from Forest Hills—Mac didn't have much of a chance to make a big impact when he set off on the summer trail to the Open, not winning a title and losing to the likes of Vilas, Dent, the heady Australian John Alexander, as well as Connors again. He and Fleming had begun to hang out together a lot then, and it put the younger McEnroe at ease.

"He called me Junior then [in their days at PWTA] and that was what he called me now. It had a slightly different spin, now that I came up in the world, but it still felt affectionate," McEnroe said.

In New York, Mac crushed his friend Teltscher in the first round of the Open and scored impressive wins over two fine clay-courters, the steady Chilean Hans Gildemeister and squirrelly Eddie Dibbs, but another lefty, 1975 champ Manuel Orantes from Spain, could junkball with the best of them and defeated the kid from Queens 6–2, 6–3.

Mac was proud of his effort over Dibbs, as he managed to maintain his focus even though a spectator was shot by a stray bullet in the stands during the match. But he knew that Orantes played teacher to his still wet-behind-the-ears student. "He gave me an absolute claycourt lesson," Mac said.

The country would elect Jimmy Carter, a Georgia peanut farmer, to the presidency a few months later, but pop culture still had a distinctly New York feel. Punk rock raged in the Bowery with bands like the Ramones, Iggy Pop, the Clash, and the Sex Pistols drawing in teens who were reacting negatively to the dominance of disco in the nightclubs, while the Bee Gees hit the top of the charts due to their participation in the soundtrack for *Saturday Night Fever*, the successful film starring John Travolta. But while Mac and his boys heard plenty of the disco that was dominating the airwaves, they were still rock and rollers at heart who may have picked at air guitars when the Eagles released their mysterious and thumping rock ballad hit "Hotel California."

After losing in the second round of the U.S. Open doubles with his partner Bernie Mitton, Mac decided to team up with Fleming, whom he was becoming closer to, for two September tournaments in San Francisco and Los Angeles. They wanted to put themselves out there a little more before settling down for the rest of the school year.

In San Francisco, Mac came up against Cliff Richey, who was ranked No. 1 in the United States in 1970. Cliff and his sister Nancy formed one of the best brother-sister combos in history. An opinionated, tough-talking Texan, Richey couldn't believe McEnroe's antics and publicly scolded him in front of the crowd, saying he was a disgrace to the game.

"I was probably over the edge that night," said McEnroe of the match, which he ended up winning. "But I was incredibly embarrassed."

That embarrassment wouldn't last for long.

That fall, McEnroe headed out to the Farm, otherwise known as Stanford University in Palo Alto, California, on a tennis scholarship. Set on hundreds of well-groomed acres among swaying eucalyptus trees in a summery climate, Stanford offers a near-perfect tennis culture. Its surrounding community is full of thousands of recreational players, and plenty of former top pros lived in the Northern California area.

Mac nearly joined Fleming at UCLA (he was tempted to live close to Margolin), but when he went on a recruiting visit and sat down with the coach, Glenn Basset, he opted out. Mac asked Basset what the Bruins' daily routine was, and when the coach answered four hours of practice a day, Mac said no thanks.

Then McEnroe met Stanford coach Dick Gould, who would eventually become the most successful collegiate tennis coach in

U.S. collegiate history, coaching teams to seventeen NCAA titles. Gould is as civilized a man as they come: soft-spoken yet authoritative, a great listener who remembers everyone's name and has a firm handshake, a real motivator of men, and not a bad tactician.

He took the program by the horns in 1969 and recruited Roscoe Tanner, who led them to their first NCAA title. The Cardinals hadn't won a single NCAA team championship before Tanner enrolled in the fall of 1969. The team won its first title in 1973, when he was a senior. "Tanner put us on the map, and McEnroe was the best we ever had," Gould said.

By the time Mac arrived on campus, Stanford had a stocked lineup, but as one of the other players said, everyone knew who had reached the Wimbledon semis that summer and who hadn't. The players included McEnroe, Bill Maze, Matt Mitchell, Perry Wright, Lloyd Bourne, and Peter Rennert, McEnroe's old foe from Port Washington. The team went 24–0 and captured the NCAA team title that year, which is not stunning, considering that every one of the men on the team eventually had some sort of pro career.

"There was a ton of talent on that team," Gould said. "That team was a great team at every position. It was the same four guys who could have alternated at number one throughout the year. They ended up having to play each other to determine the order. That was a good and a very deep team. We could have self-destructed. It turned out that John was a great team player."

Given that Stanford was a high-level academic institution that featured geniuses in every walk of life, Mac wasn't as well known outside of the athletic facilities, but tennis fans knew who he was. Stanford's indoor facility, Maples Pavilion, was said to be nearly full well after midnight with a deciding doubles match against UCLA still in progress. In 1978, UCLA's Teltscher, who later would become a top 10 player, had a match point in the second set against McEnroe and scorched an approach shot deep that looked to be the clincher, but McEnroe hit an incredible forehand passing shot to stay alive and break Teltscher's spirit. "It was one of the best shots under pressure I've ever seen," Gould said. "His style is very unique and distinct, so I had to learn how best to complement his style of play, which was well developed at the highest level. I think John has a lot of respect for me in terms of how I did that. He was a genius with the racket."

Mac couldn't completely contain himself on court or off, but boys will be boys in college. Gould said McEnroe represented Stanford well the vast majority of the time, and yet he had his questionable moments. "You wish everyone were an angel on the court and looked like they were respecting the honor of the game, but sometimes that's hard for an eighteen-year-old kid to do," he said.

Mac said his first priority was to enjoy the college experience and he didn't feel prepared to turn pro. He needed to get into the right mind-set, where as the team's main man he had to deliver under intense pressure. He wanted the challenge, met it head-on, and in the long run it helped him grow up and be accountable.

McEnroe did not excel academically that year, dropping his harder classes for more of a jock's type of fare, with courses such as "Sleep, Narcolepsy and Politics," a subject that he claims he was able to get an A in by playing a charity tennis exhibition.

Richard Lyman, an expert in contemporary British history, ran the university at the time. Student activism had rocked the campus since the late 1960s, and Lyman was known as an outspoken communicator who enjoyed the give-and-take of argument. While Mac offered his blood, sweat, and tears on court, other Stanford students composed a position paper on Stanford's investments in corporations operating in apartheid South Africa, which led to a direct action campaign for university divestment. It culminated in 294 arrests for civil disobedience and helped spread the campus divestment idea across the country. In 1985, after McEnroe's most dominant (and last significant) year on tour, many universities across California would divest from South Africa.

On weekends, Mac would occasionally drive down the coast to L.A. in his Pinto. "He never had any money," said Margolin. "My mom would have to give him fifty dollars to buy gas."

Most of the guys on the team enjoyed having the Wimbledon semifinalist as a teammate. He did have a temporary problem with one teammate, but that was not of his own making. McEnroe fit in well off court and on.

"He hasn't changed that much," Bill Maze said. "He has the same intensity to challenge every call and fight every point. I read about him in the paper that summer during Wimbledon, and I knew he was supposed to come to Stanford, but I thought he'd turn pro. I was excited that he decided to come for one year. Stanford tennis got a lot of attention in those days due to the titles we had and got more due to Johnny Mac. It didn't seem to bother anyone on the team that he got the lion's share of attention. I thought he was special with his hands. I feel lucky to have played doubles with him, because he seemed to put the ball in the right spot every time. He just made me look good. He was also a team guy, and it was interesting that he became a great individual player, because he made me feel like we were in this together. He was very supportive. I never felt he was ticked off at me. The only time he'd be ticked was if another guy was not giving it all. He was an easy guy to play with."

The team had some memorable road trips, including some frat-boy-type drinking binges, but Gould never came down on them hard, which the players appreciated. One night they were up late on a road trip and Gould walked in. Mac said there was a pungent odor in the room, but Gould only said, "Guys, can you keep it down?" and then walked out.

McEnroe thought, "I've got to play my heart out for this guy. He was my kind of coach."

Gould has never claimed to be a disciplinarian and says he teaches responsibility by leaving it up to the kids to be on time and to learn to make their own decisions. He doesn't tolerate excuses or alibis, but trusts his players to make the right choices. He tries to make men out of boys. "If I prevent them from making the wrong choices, then they don't grow," he said.

Mac did not go undefeated in the 1977–1978 season, losing to the collegiate standout Eddie Edwards of Pepperdine and his old foe and former doubles partner from the juniors, Larry Gottfried, but he had a tremendous run at the NCAA championships in Georgia, played in May 1978. The tournament is a true grind—team matches, singles matches, doubles matches, one after another, day after day.

UCLA's Billy Martin won the 1975 title, and Bill Scanlon of Trinity took it in 1976 over Fleming—all guys whom Mac had played with at Port Washington. Stanford's Mitchell beat UCLA's Tony Graham in 1977, a hard-partying guy who would turn out to be one of Mac's touring buddies.

Mac, the Wimbledon semifinalist, was feeling the heat.

"At the NCAAs John was wound tighter than a drum because he was a heavy favorite and really wanted to win and the pressure kept building," Gould said. "He exploded a couple times, and until then I hadn't seen that and I thought, 'The guy has done so much for me all year, what good is it going to do me not to let him play after his first outburst?' I decided to weather the storm, let it go."

In the semis, Mac came up against his friend and Stanford teammate, the senior Bill Maze, who was from a long line of fine California players, had been his frequent practice partner, and would be his doubles partner during the tournament. It was not a comfortable position for either of them. Things got heated during the match as Mac questioned calls, which delayed the proceedings and sapped Maze's concentration. Mac even stared down Maze on a few occasions in a 6–4, 6–7, 6–1 victory.

"Winning was the number one thing on court, not the relationship or friendship," Maze said. "I probably needed to be less sensitive to it. When I played him there was no love lost. I felt like I played pretty well, it went three sets, and he didn't play horrible either. I knew his game. But I think he does direct a little bit at his opponent, and he does whatever he needs to win the match, within the rules that were set, and the umpires in those days were not setting guidelines clearly and he took what he got. He likes to compete and do whatever he has to win, and if it's done within the framework of the match, he'll take whatever he can get, just as any great competitor would."

Mac would later say that he felt bad because he stepped on their friendship, but added that he was delighted with the victory. The New Yorker was able to put his friendships behind him on court and rarely cared whether his tantrums were having an adverse effect on his buddies. It's clear that he couldn't care less what his enemies thought, but it's striking that he didn't tone it down against guys with whom he would share a six-pack.

He and Maze still had the doubles to play, and Gould thought that the sore feelings after the singles semifinal affected their play, as they lost to Texas's Kevin Curren and Gary Plock 6–2, 6–4. Gould said that Maze and Mac were still boiling and "were in essence still playing singles."

Maze disagreed, saying that Curren played extremely well that day, but admitted it took him more than a few minutes to get over the singles debacle.

"It was tough after that, but eventually it blew over," he said. "John was good at blowing off steam, and then he'd like to go out and have a beer later, but for the guys on the opposite side of the net, it was tougher."

However, Mac and Maze made up once they hit the pros and eventually won a doubles title together. Maze now coaches at UC Davis, and a few years back McEnroe came out and did a successful fund-raiser for him. At another event, a friend laughingly introduced Maze as "having the dubious distinction of playing with the greatest doubles player ever and not winning the NCAAs."

"Over the years we have had a great relationship and no long-lasting problems," Maze said. "He was just pretty damn good mentally and a tough cookie on court despite the ranting and ravings. He's become a great friend over the years."

In the NCAA singles final, McEnroe came up against big-serving John Sadri of North Carolina State, who was a dominant collegiate player and would eventually reach the world top 20 and the final of the Australian Open. Sadri came on the court wearing a blue blazer and a ten-gallon hat, and the southern crowd went crazy. Georgia's coach at the time, Dan Magill remembered seeing Mac play three months prior at the Collegiate Indoors. "I wrote that he was the most gifted shotmaker since [Hall of Famer] Bill Tilden," Magill said.

The match against Mac was viewed as East Coast vs. West Coast, and the stands were packed. Charged up by the 3,000-strong hostile crowd, Mac served brilliantly and survived, but only barely, 7–6 (3), 7–6 (3), 5–7, 7–6 (4), in four hours and twenty-five minutes. He won only a single point more than Sadri.

"I felt I could fly," Mac said.

Just before the awards ceremony, Mac rushed over to Magill and asked where the nearest phone was. The Georgia legend recalled: "A few second later I heard a voice, exhaling, 'Daddy, I won!' The new NCAA champ was a kid at heart."

8

A Four-Hour Match

At the start of the fourth set, BBC commentator John Barrett remarked, "Borg just needs the one chance only. He can raise his game when it matters."

Not even two hours have transpired, but Lennart Bergelin says to Mariana Simionescu, "As I told you, this is a four-hour match." He's right.

Mac is down two sets to one but keeps charging forward. So does Borg. The Swede is showing superior confidence, even swinging a little with his normally lifeless backhand volley to give it more juice.

The crowd is enjoying the bull's mad rushes at the matador Borg, but it seems as if the American is being blinded too often by the Swede's parries with his red cape. Mac isn't angry, but he begins to hold his bruised head. He not only has to serve as well as he did for the better part of the first two sets, but must return and pass with more acumen.

He cranks up his first serve to open and easily holds, but his task is to threaten the Swede on the latter's service games and he can't seem to develop a dependable and threatening return, even on Borg's second serves. Borg takes a high bouncing forehand from McEnroe and laces it down the line for a winner to hold to 1–1, and all Mac can do is admire the majesty of the shot. McEnroe is imploring himself to do more damage with his volleys as he finds himself 0–30 after a leaping Borg overhead. He spits into his hand after he hits an ace that skids off the line under Borg's racket. He's pushing himself to fight, and after he holds to 2–1 with a slamming volley, Johnny Mac puffs his chest out and preens. After he crushes a forehand return to go ahead 30–15 on Borg's serve, he confidently slaps his hand on his racket. But his one-handed backhand is vulnerable and the Swede keeps going there. McEnroe knows this and takes some practice swings, but it doesn't matter and it fails him again. Borg holds to 2–2.

Serving at 40–15 at 2–2, Mac grows irritated with the chair umpire after Borg flips a pass by him. He queries "No let," as he thought his serve had hit the top of the cord, but to no avail. He grunts as he slices a serve way out wide that a sliding Borg can't do anything with and wipes his upper lip as he strides back to his chair, up 3–2.

McEnroe is rubbing his thighs, and it's possible he's stiffening up. He takes a couple of bites of food and walks back on court, only to be overwhelmed by a deluge of Swedish service bombs. Borg appears untouchable on serve now and is doing whatever he pleases from the forecourt and backcourt.

It's 3–3 and McEnroe is fighting himself on his service games. Nothing is coming easy now as his serve is lacking a little bite, but he wills himself to a hold to 4–3. His fight will surely matter. If McEnroe can just do a little more with his backhand returns, maybe he can grab the necessary break, but on the opening point of the eighth game he pops up a slice serve from Borg that lands before the net, and he wheels around in a 180 in disgust. Borg is in a bit of trouble at 15–30, but he anticipates Mac's pass and pokes a backhand volley winner. Then his legendary speed comes into play as he tears to his right after a deep McEnroe forehand and passes the bewildered American to his left side. The crowd erupts and McEnroe pinches his lips. Borg holds to 4–4 as he scurries into the net and smokes a forehand swing volley.

At 4–4, 15–30, an anxious Mac takes a simple backhand volley and floats it three feet wide. As he walks back to serve, he squints hard. Then he dumps a dipping return into the net and grabs his ear. He fights off one break point with a fine forehand half volley, but then Borg crunches a two-handed backhand crosscourt that Mac can't handle on the full stretch to gain another one.

Mac can't seem to close quickly enough. The American lasers in a wicked slice serve on the chalk into the ad court. It flies off to the right, but somehow Borg's eyes zoom in on the ball and his wrists snap quickly enough. He pounds yet another two-handed backhand pass, this one careening off Mac's frame.

Mac is broken to 5–4 and it seems that Borg will close him out. The Swede can feel his fifth straight Wimbledon title touching his fingertips. But he knows there is still reason for concern.

Before the championships began, Borg could see McEnroe coming. In an essay discussing the contenders for his top ranking, he wrote, "Jimmy Connors has been my most intense rival for six years. But at the moment, John McEnroe has the game to give both Jimmy and me sleepless nights. His style is flexible while Jimmy's is rigid . . . but the fury of a McEnroe/Borg rivalry has not yet had a chance to boil over. It's still simmering."

McEnroe nearly begins to boil over with anxiety at 4–5, while Borg casually spits twice into the turf and towels off. Stacy Margolin and McEnroe's brother Mark are twitching behind Simionescu and Bergelin.

"It was a nightmare it all happened so quickly," McEnroe said. "Here I honestly thought I was going to win the match 6–1, 6–4, 6–3 and all of a sudden I'm almost out of the match. Which was when something magical happened. I got my fight back."

John Barrett says that we are just a whisper from immortality. Borg is just two points from the match after Mac can't hustle down a weak overhead. McEnroe keenly comes in and smooths a nifty forehand drop volley to close to 30–15. But then Borg holds his first two match points after smoking a forehand pass off a garbage approach shot down the middle by Mac. The crowd prematurely screams after a Borg first serve out wide to deuce court just misses the line, then McEnroe punches a backhand pass down the line. The American fiddles with his strings, spins his racket in his hand, and after nailing a couple of backhands deep, he watches Borg dare him to pass him again as the Swede slices a mediocre approach shot to his backhand. McEnroe goes down the line again, but this time Borg is there. However, Borg has to bend low, pops his volley up crosscourt, and Mac takes it out of the air and crushes a forehand swing volley winner to the open court.

Two match points gone, and Mac lifts his chin up.

At deuce, Borg nets a forehand passing shot attempt, and then Mac cracks an inside-out backhand return winner past the onrushing Borg, shakes his fist, and yells out, "C'mon!" Where in creation did he pull out that shot from? The American has evened the set at 5–5 and a tense Margolin rests her nose on her clenched fist.

Barrett says, "It was pure instinct that saved him."

Mac holds easily to 6–5 behind two aces and two return errors from the Swede, and he struts back to his chair. Since going down two match points, he's won eight straight points and is playing instinctually, seemingly without nerves. This time on the changeover, Borg towels off much more quickly. He also holds quickly, as he is cheetah quick at the net. It's 6–6 and Mac likes his chances. He reflected later, "By the time we got to the tiebreaker, I thought I could win the match."

9

"Borg Is Borg"

In some ways, 1978 was Borg's best year ever, but for the first time, in his last tournament of the season in Stockholm, he'd face the brash New Yorker McEnroe and, somewhat remarkably, lose 6–3, 6–4. After a long year, he might not have thought much of the result then, but during the next three years that defeat would ring true as Mac pursued him like Saint Michael in full religious fervor after Satan.

The Stockholm tournament was played on ultraquick indoor tile, so it obviously favored the attacking McEnroe, but still, it was played in Sweden, where Borg was mostly adored. Given that Mac worshipped his boyhood idol, it was stunning that he didn't get cold feet the first time around.

"I think he felt pressure playing me in his hometown," McEnroe said. "That was a huge victory for me—I was the first player younger than Borg to beat him—but it didn't make me think one bit less of him."

For the first five months of the season, while McEnroe partied and sweated hard at Stanford and remained confused about how the bruising Leon Spinks stunned his hero Muhammad Ali for the heavyweight crown in fifteen rounds, Borg went about his early-season normal routine, playing six U.S. tournaments to open the year, winning three titles, but taking an odd loss to Tom Gullikson in Miami on carpet. Gullikson would go on to captain the U.S. Davis Cup team, most memorably tutoring the great Pete Sampras and his teammates to an extraordinary upset of Russia on hated clay in Moscow in 1995.

Unlike in America, Borg was utterly dominant on European clay, the surface on which he faced Adriano Panatta in the finals of the Italian Open. Two months before the tournament began, the notorious Red Brigade had kidnapped five-time prime minister of Italy Aldo Moro and killed five of his bodyguards. He was later assassinated by the terrorists.

While the raucous and in-your-face Italian crowd in Rome undid other players, Borg adeptly navigated the bloody waters. Even as his colleagues sweated and strained on the heavy clay and with the labors of their profession, Borg appeared to be unfazed by the task ahead of him. He seemed to be born with a special type of confidence: he knew deep down that even in the most dire moments he'd be the better man of the day. Few knew him well and he volunteered very little to the press, but everyone had the utmost respect for him.

"He comes and goes silently, almost stealthily," wrote tennis journalist Peter Bodo. "There is a touch of Howard Hughes about Borg, from his ineffable manner right down to his compulsive privacy."

In the semifinals, Panatta faced José Higueras, a gentle and steady Spaniard who would later become one of the game's most respected coaches, tutoring Americans Jim Courier and Michael Chang and Switzerland's Roger Federer to Grand Slam titles. As a player, however, he was not considered the genius that he is today, as he had a longshoreman's type of game.

Panatta and Higueras were Davis Cup rivals, so the crowd that day was already familiar with how José could bob and weave, and they were out for his scalp early on. Panatta knew that if he was to win the event, he'd have to encourage the masses to do some of his dirty work. In an earlier victory against the tall and soft-spoken Californian farm boy Hank Pfister, he gesticulated to the crowd again and again, whipping them into a frenzy.

"I thought he was playing the hero kind of heavy," Pfister said.

Panatta fell behind against Higueras, but as he began to play better, the crowd dug into Higueras's ears, screaming, chanting "Buffone" and throwing coins at him. The chair umpire was unable to control the crazed fans, nor would the attendants listen to Panatta's coach's pleas to stop the yelling during points. Eventually Higueras quit; he and later said in the locker room that he had to or he would have killed someone in the crowd.

Prior to the final against Panatta, Borg said that if the crowd went nuts like they did against Higueras, he'd stop too, but after a first set where Panatta dominated play by serving and volleying beyond his capability, Borg cooled the crowd down with his efficient game. He cast no sideward glances, spoke no loud words, decided not to engage outside the court. His sole goal was a lockdown in the fifth set. At one point, a fan threw a coin to the court floor. Borg bent down, picked it up, took it over to his chair, dropped it, and quietly informed Bergelin that he would stop play if they continued. No one did as he promptly went out and wiped the floor with Panatta in a memorable five-set victory.

"Borg is Borg even when he isn't playing well," Panatta conceded, paying him the ultimate compliment. "Maybe it wasn't even the best Borg."

Paris is just a few hours north of Rome by plane, but the cities couldn't be more different. Both are full of warm-blooded, food-loving, theatergoing, art-appreciating denizens, but modern-day Romans take themselves less seriously and cherish a good joke as much as the Parisians value a hefty and biting criticism.

The Paris climate suited the Swede perfectly. He could eat well, take Mariana on long window-shopping excursions, and, if he was so inclined, sample the latest in haute couture nightclub fashion. Disco reigned supreme, but New Wave was also making its mark. While the Bee Gees' songs from the award-winning *Saturday Night Fever* soundtrack topped the charts and the 1950s-style musical *Grease* was displaying the quick-footed dancing skills of John Travolta and the girl-next-door cuteness of Olivia Newton-John, the art rock band Devo was pumping up crowds with its hit "Whip It," which is exactly what Borg did to the Roland Garros field—without wearing the band's trademark black-rimmed goggles.

France has been known for some time to be a liberal, permissive nation, but at times it has also been more than lenient in accepting a person's faults. France, the nation that once prided itself on being a mecca for disaffected writers such as Hemingway, Faulkner, Fitzgerald, and the brilliant African American homosexual novelist James Baldwin, was the center of controversy in 1978, when it took in the famous Polish film director Roman Polanski (*Tess, Chinatown*), who skipped bail in the United States and fled after pleading guilty to charges of engaging in sex with a thirteen-year-old girl. Polanski, the onetime husband of Sharon Tate, who was murdered by the notorious Manson Family, disputed the charges but didn't bother to stand trial and fight them in America, which has seriously tainted his reputation.

Borg had a few rough edges off court, which would be illuminated after he retired, but they were largely hidden from the French public, who watched him behave and play impeccably at Roland Garros.

How good was Borg in 1978? In seven matches, he didn't drop a set, was only taken to 7–6 once (by Roscoe Tanner in the fourth round), to 6–4 once, and to 6–3 twice. His three final matches read like this: a 6–3, 6–3, 6–0 stomping over Raúl Ramírez, a 6–0, 6–1, 6–0 throttling of Corrado Barazzutti, and a 6–1, 6–1, 6–3 dropkick of Guillermo Vilas in the final.

Ramírez had liked his chances going in, saying he was going to go all out and not get drawn into a Ping-Pong match. But he did, and couldn't manage to keep the ball on the table. Playing super-aggressive tennis can be anathema to a backboard game. If the Mexican didn't find the zone, he'd be sucked into Borg's Bermuda Triangle. "Why is he playing like that? Why so many balls?" he asked.

Vilas, the defending champion, had struggled at periods throughout the tournament, but he had worked very hard to get at Borg again. He was four years older than the Swede, and at one point they had become friendly practice partners. But once Borg took up with Simionescu, and Vilas and his coach Ion Tiriac began going full-bore together, their relationship waned. Tiriac wanted Vilas to get serious, to toss away the chatter with his locker room buddies, especially with those who might seize the golden chalice from him. Tiriac believed that Vilas was too nice, and in 1977, the best year of the Argentine's career, Vilas took on the role of a loner off court and was able to transfer that stark feeling of rugged individualism on court.

Due to his decision to play World Team Tennis in the United States, Borg had skipped Roland Garros in 1977, and now, if Vilas was to establish himself as the man to beat again, he had to overcome the Swede in Paris.

He never came close. Vilas tried to run with him, but his heavy legs chugged as if they were caught in quicksand. He tried to whale forehands at him, but Borg sent them back deep and with more pace. Vilas's backhand slice wouldn't bite and his drives were lazy, soft balls. Borg moved his serve around adeptly and caressed drop volleys. Vilas tried to play ultra-aggressive in the third set but was already out of rhythm. The Argentine bull went down in a flurry of the blond matador's lightning-fast parries.

"He looked a little bit afraid," Borg said. "I saw it in his face and his shots. He became very nervous when he made a mistake, like he didn't believe it."

Borg then took the next flight to Belgrade, where he scored three wins over Yugoslavia in the Davis Cup on clay. He was happy and appeared tireless.

Just before the 1978 Wimbledon began, a shootout between Pro-
visional IRA members and the British army left one civilian and
three IRA men dead, stoking flames in the Isles and in London.
After a yearlong cease-fire failed, the IRA had begun its strategy of
fighting a long war of attrition and it seemed there would be no end
to "the Troubles."

Borg had grown up in a society that paid homage to royalty, so
he was relatively unaffected by the incident and went about his business, while Londoners debated whether Ireland would ever truly
become part of the United Kingdom.

The Swede practiced relentlessly before the tournament, often
with Gerulaitis, as well as with Heinz Gunhardt, a midlevel Swiss
player who would later become the coach of the all-time-great
German Steffi Graf, and with Billy Martin, an American workhorse.

Gunhardt and Martin were recruited to practice with Borg by
IMG, the giant sports agency that represented all of them. Bergelin
was none too happy that Borg had skipped the French Open in
1977 to play World Team Tennis and wanted to make sure that his
pupil got in plenty of long sessions and had some regular playing
partners he could travel and bond with.

Martin, who played for UCLA and now coaches its men's team,
is the only person to capture NCAA team titles as both a player and
a coach, and is considered by many to be the best U.S. junior player
ever, winning the 1973 and 1974 singles titles at Junior Wimbledon, the Junior U.S. Open, and the Orange Bowl. As a freshman,
he led the 1975 UCLA team to the NCAA team championship,
posting a perfect 19–0 record and winning the NCAA singles championship.

During his playing days he married a Swedish girl, whom he
would later divorce. He was familiar with Swedish culture and
enjoyed his days practicing with Borg on his Nordic island, as well
as at London's Cumberland Club.

"He was a pretty quiet guy," Martin said. "But people don't realize what kind of fierce competitor he was. He played with this calm
and looked like he had ice in his veins, but on the practice court he

had the worst temper, maybe even worse than Mac, breaking rackets and all that. We'd play badminton or Ping-Pong, which he had set up in his barn, and he loved it. Both of us would be going nuts. But he was a good and loyal person from a close-knit family. He trained unbelievably hard, four hours a day on court, and then he'd run. It was a daily routine: food, practice, massage, and train; they were a little ahead of their time with their regimen, unlike Jimmy and Mac, who would practice for forty-five minutes max."

Borg also impressed Martin by being one of the first players he knew who focused on keeping his weight at the perfect level. "Lennart was adamant about that and not having Björn's weight fluctuate at all," Martin said. "He was the first person who got me to believe in massage—Lennart gave the hardest deepest massage I'd ever had in my life. He'd dig those thumbs in. You were so sore afterward, but a couple of days later it loosened you up, you were more mobile and you really believed in it."

Martin said the relationship between Bergelin and Borg was a good mixture of mentor and apprentice finding each other's strengths. "Borg could always override Lennart, and that certainly happened with Team Tennis, but there was also money and agents involved. . . . The relationship was more than just a coach and a player. There was a real bonding there. Lennart was an older guy, not really a father figure, but he really cared about Björn. It was fifty-fifty and Lennart could put his foot down and sometimes Björn had to have his way. It was give-and-take."

Martin played Borg twice on tour, and was thumped on both occasions. He simply didn't have the weapons or speed to contend with him. But practicing with Borg was more than beneficial, as he felt completely in tune after their months together.

"It absolutely raised my level," said Martin, who reached the Wimbledon singles quarterfinals in 1977 and lost to Vitas Gerulaitis. "The intensity was there. I felt like I had to keep my level high in order to keep practicing with him. He was by far the fastest player I ever played against, the best-conditioned guy I played. I first played him at fifteen years old in the Orange Bowl and I considered myself to be in good shape. It was 5–5 in the third set and I had gone through three or four shirts, and I looked over at him and he was wearing the same shirt with a little sweat dot in the middle of his chest. He was fresh and I was bent. I could barely move my feet, and he never got tired."

Martin revered Borg's game and recalled a saying from Bergelin: "Borg's backhand is the best shot in the world and it's his weaker side."

Martin believes that Borg had to be attacked, because it was incredibly difficult to try and hit around him. "He could get to almost anything and still pull off a better shot," he said. "Björn wasn't the best volleyer but was still able to put the ball into the open court. His serve got much better too. The only weakness I saw over the years was against lefties, because he didn't like to return their serves from the ad court."

Borg was more than familiar with the monarchist traditions of Wimbledon, its overabundance of stuffy ushers, stiff-looking and stiff-talking security guards, overly deferential locker room attendants, and ladies, sirs, dukes, and duchesses from the far reaches of the once-dominant kingdom.

McEnroe, to put it simply, had huge problems with authority, whether they had been royally decorated over generations or were just a Joe Citizen who put on a linesman's green blazer for pro tennis matches.

He came into the historic Queen's Club tournament on grass, which is played in London two weeks prior to Wimbledon and the week after the French Open, as more of a known quantity and full of bravado after his NCAA victory. There he played Fleming for the first time as a pro in the first round, besting his buddy in an emotionally trying three-setter. It was a match that ended in angst. Mac would go on to reach the final, where he fell to the wily old Aussie lefty Tony Roche, but it was his first clash with his old buddy from New Jersey that would stick most in his mind.

"We had a huge argument on court," said Fleming. "It was over calls. It was stalling or complaining or who knows what. We're both pretty similar characters in that regard. We were both really angry, and although we shook hands afterwards, we sat side by side on a bench for an hour and a half without speaking. I said, 'We can't do this. We're doubles partners and best friends and we're trying to kill each other.'"

Even though they were close and Fleming knew McEnroe as well as anyone on tour, McEnroe could still irritate him. "He got under everybody's skin," Fleming said, who concurred that some other players thought that Mac's tantrums were a type of gamesmanship. But Fleming didn't buy into that wholesale. "A lot of people thought that. That's who he is, he's nuts. He's not faking that, what you see is what you get."

Fleming knew McEnroe well enough not to ask him to change, even if it would have spared him some grief in their singles clashes. "That always fell on deaf ears. I don't think he actually wanted to control that part of him. There is that part of him that says he's successful, and this is what he's always done. 'I don't want to change a winning game.' He wasn't going to listen."

In doubles, McEnroe was slightly more controlled and Fleming knew well enough to leave his partner alone unless he really got out of control. "He didn't do it that much in doubles; the atmosphere was always lighter . . . it did happen once in a while. I usually just waited it out. There were a lot of times I'd just say, 'No, no, no, no, that was out,' when he'd hit a serve that he could have sworn it was an ace, just to shut him up, so we wouldn't argue."

In the 1978 Wimbledon singles, Mac was stopped cold 7–5, 1–6, 8–9 (at the time they played tiebreakers in the first four sets when the score reached 8–8), 6–4, 6–3 by U.S. Davis Cup player Erik Van Dillen, a classic serve-and-volleyer from California who didn't have the New Yorker's overall talent level but knew his way around the net cords and came straight at him.

"All right, he played better than me, I finally admit it," Mac would later say.

Van Dillen, a preppy, old-school player from Northern California, was one of the heroes of the United States' 3–2 victory over

Romania in the Davis Cup in 1972, when the nations faced off in one of the most infamous finals ever in Bucharest, where the notorious Black September terrorist group issued threats against Jewish U.S. team member Harold Solomon, and Romania's Ion Tiriac was said to be determined to win the cup by any means. The matches were played on slow indoor clay in front of berserk fans and perhaps, as some contended, corrupt linesmen.

That was six years prior, and Van Dillen's singles career was on the decline. Before he went out to play McEnroe, Van Dillen had a sit-down with his occasional doubles partner Charlie Pasarell, who told Van Dillen in no uncertain terms that he better not try to win the match playing cute: "'You are going to play a real close match, one shot here or there, but you have to take it to him.' As only Charlie can do, he said, 'Just hit the ball, take charge, he's not going to lose. You have to win it.' For some reason it just freed me up. The defining moment was at 3–4 in the fourth. My natural instinct was to chip low, and I nailed one and he missed a volley and then I broke and served out the fourth. Your natural tendency is to go back to try your normal game, and the harder hurdle was to keep going for it, but I was able to do that. I was in the match, and he was serving at 3–5, and I'd thought I had to serve for it, and we got in a long point, and I hit an overhead at his feet, and he hit it in the bottom of the net. It was over, and I was thinking, 'Is this my court?'"

Even with the win, Van Dillen knew that Mac was a true up-and-comer, not in the traditional boom-boom style, but a special type of player. "He had a fabulous serve, it wasn't sheer raw power, and he was like [legendary baseball pitcher] Greg Maddux more than Nolan Ryan. Clearly he had great hands, but his strokes were a little unorthodox. I saw Connors play at eighteen at the Pacific Southwest and he beat Roy Emerson and a bunch of other top guys and just drilled them. He was hitting pure winners, and Emerson had a good serve. I said, 'Wow, this is a problem.'"

Van Dillen's sense was that Mac had more talent than anyone he had seen, but whether he would reach his full potential was a question of whether he would mature. "He had a Nastase type of talent.

It wasn't a clear path, but you saw the glimpses of brilliance. He learned to suck it up when he was down. It was a question of him growing into himself and then when he reached an important final, whether he had the talent to raise his level when it mattered. All the great champions have that."

With their relationship healing, the unseeded Mac and Fleming reached the doubles final. They overcame the U.S. Davis Cup duo of Stan Smith and Bob Lutz in the third round after being down eight match points. They split the first four sets, and during the changeover, McEnroe said, "Come on, these guys stink. How can we lose to these guys?"

Fleming realized that McEnroe was denigrating Smith and Lutz, Davis Cup heroes whom he admired. "I realized right then we were not in over our heads," Fleming said. "Everything was relative. We had become as good as them. We won in five. My self-worth changed for all time."

The next day they drove through the black steel gates at about 12:10 p.m. for their 2 p.m. match against Ross Case and Geoff Masters. "We noticed there wasn't an empty seat. It was packed to the rafters. Wow! John and I just looked at one another when it dawned on us that all those people were willing to sit in a cramped seat for two hours just to see us play doubles. For a player, the electricity at Wimbledon is like no other tournament."

While they beat Case and Masters in the semifinals, Fleming-McEnroe failed to show up mentally for the big dance. In the final, they were defeated by the cagey top-seeded team, South Africans Bob Hewitt and Frew McMillan, 6–1, 6–4, 6–2, the worst defeat in a Wimbledon final since 1911. "A sickening psych-out," Fleming recalled. "We were so impressed with them, so worried about their touch and angled stuff, we tried to hit impossible shots they couldn't reach. We played into their hands rather than playing our own game. We had too much power to piddle around. We should have just hit straight through them. We never forgot that."

Borg, like many champions before and after, was nervous for his first-round match. It's the contest where a player hasn't gotten the proper feel for the ball or the courts yet and isn't quite prepared to unleash his best stuff. The first round is the most perilous of first-week encounters; the pressure wraps tightly around a player's throat and heart, and his hands are prone to sweating and shaking. Borg needed to call upon all of his vast reserves against American Victor Amaya to reach a cataclysmic 8–9, 6–1, 1–6, 6–3, 6–3 victory.

The towering six-foot-seven-inch Amaya had him on the ropes. A former All-American player at the University of Michigan, Amaya led two sets to one and had a 3–1 lead in the fourth set and a point to go up 4–1, but understanding the importance of the moment, Borg charged hard.

"He looked as if he was spaced out, but all of a sudden he came to life," Amaya said. "Sometimes he seems to go into limbo, and then he wakes up before the end. . . . At 30–40 at 3–1 in the fourth set, I've never seen him hit a second serve like that on a point so huge. It was the best second serve you could imagine, hard, deep, with enough spin to keep it from moving away, but not enough to slow it down. It was a great serve—that's all."

Relieved, Borg then registered a routine straight win over Aussie Peter McNamara, and then dropped a set to clay-courter Jaime Fillol of Chile in the third round, but survived intact. Aussie Geoff Masters couldn't win a set in the next round, but did push him to 8–6 in the third, and in the quarters he pinned Sandy Mayer 7–5, 6–4, 6–3.

One of the sons of Alex Mayer, a former Davis Cup player from Hungary, Sandy had an encyclopedia of strokes and tactics in his head, as his father spent his life attempting to perfect the game. Before playing Borg in the quarters, Sandy thought he had the match nailed down. "My game is better suited to grass. I don't think Borg can stay back and be effective. God is my guru."

Borg won 7–5, 6–4, 6–3 and shouted his own amens and hallelujahs at the top of his lungs. "Today was the first day I enjoyed it," Borg said. "I was really going for my shots. The pressure only goes to you if you play bad. Tennis is not everything. If I think about the points when I get back to the hotel, I'll go crazy."

Mayer termed Borg a monochromatic player, limited in range in what he attempted to do, mostly because he had early success with a one-dimensional game and didn't change until he was forced to.

"One day Bergelin said to him, 'There's a kind of serve which isn't just starting a rally with,'" Mayer recalled. "'You are allowed to hit the first one hard because there are actually two serves.' He was so nonconfrontational and so nonaggressive, other than on passing shots, he didn't envision the need to be aggressive. His service motion was fine, and eventually when it came to the time that he felt he had to hit it harder, he was able to."

Mayer didn't fear Borg's return, but was stunned by the Swede's ability to get the ball back in play time and again, despite the force of the serve. "It was beyond belief," he said. "I never felt it was the first volley that was the problem against him, but it was the pass, when he said, 'Now I got you!' He hit that backhand crosscourt pass that most people couldn't even get a racket on, and then almost hit a one-and-a-half-handed backhand down the line. I looked at Borg as playing an average groundstroker, and that gave me an opportunity almost every rally to attack, and I was good at that, but my conversion rate was half what it was against other players. When he had to react to pass, he read you so well, and the quickness was there."

Borg then said good-bye to Tom Okker 6–4, 6–4, 6–4 in the semis. There would be no high kicks for the Flying Dutchman. "It is not so much fun playing this guy," said Okker. "Against him you feel you are always trying to hit shots better than you can hit them."

After Jimmy Connors had stopped Gerulaitis in the semifinals in front of Vitas's new friend Bianca Jagger (the ex-wife of Rolling Stones lead singer Mick), Connors seemed ready for a bruising final-round battle against Borg. He seemed totally in his element, lashing out at reporters, pounding his own chest, looking for someone to despise to get his juices flowing.

"I prepare for [Wimbledon] fifty weeks a year and then I'm in there on that crazy little court with birds flying over my head and fourteen thousand people leaning on me," Connors said.

Connors claimed that he was seeing the ball like a grapefruit and believed he could crack Borg's armor, but he almost inexplicably fell on his sword. "I never got into it mentally," he said.

Borg served wonderfully, barely missed a return, and Connors simply couldn't find a way into the match. He played as depressed a match as he ever had in a major.

"I know I serve better than Jimmy," said Borg. "I am not scared of his serving because I feel I can break every single time. If I am serving well, I know I can break, because he doesn't serve well then. For sure, that explains everything."

Borg blew Connors's cover, utterly embarrassing him and munching on the American's midcourt floaters. Borg was ebullient, as the backhand slice approach shot he had been working on bit sharply on the turf and he was able to swarm the cords successfully.

"The plan was to get to net," Borg said after the 6–2, 6–2, 6–3 victory. "The court was soft and the bounce was low. I want to slice and come in because Jimmy doesn't like that. He usually put the pressure on me—I have to do the passing shot; I have to do the lob. Today he'd have to do all of that. I win so many points because he can't do it all."

All that work that Borg and Bergelin had put into speeding up his serve had worked. On that day during a rainy and cold fortnight in London, Borg actually looked like a consummate grass-court player as he joined England's Fred Perry (1934–1936) in winning three Wimbledons in a row. He became the first player since his hero Laver in 1969 to go back-to-back in Paris and London.

Winning three straight crowns eventually paled in comparison to the five consecutive ones he ended up with, but at the time there were a slew of Hall of Famers who could never post the trifecta—Don Budge, Lew Hoad, Rod Laver, Roy Emerson, Laver again, and John Newcombe.

To say that Borg was confident, then, was bit of an understatement. In Paris and London he had so thoroughly thrashed his two main rivals—Vilas and Connors—that he spoke assuredly of being able to realize tennis's largest dream: winning the calendar-year Grand Slam and standing side by side with his boyhood idol, Laver, who pulled off the feat in 1962 and 1969.

"Before, I never even dreamed to win the Grand Slam," Borg said.

10

The Battle Begins

At the start of John McEnroe and Björn Borg's fourth-set Wimbledon tiebreaker, Mariana Simionescu feels as if she is part of an opera, and is hoping that McEnroe isn't playing the role of the phantom, dictating who is to sing the sweetest notes and who will conclude the performance.

The crowd stirs with a special feeling. Simionescu says it sounds like the drumbeating that met the tumbrel carrying convicts to their executions in the Middle Ages. Indeed, all the balconies in this scaffold square are booked because no one wants to miss the moment of the beheading.

No Wimbledon final has ever ended in a tiebreak, but the fans may be on the verge of statistical history.

McEnroe nails an overhead to go ahead 1–0, but then nets a return and misses an easy backhand slice into the center of the net. He wrings his neck with his hands. Overly excited, he failed to stay level to the ball.

Down 2–1, he's not yelling but is full of angst—that is, until he drops a forehand volley just over the net and lifts his chin, raising the score to 2–2 and signaling Borg to bring it on.

Mac then puts his chin up and confidently nails a service winner down the T, but with a terrific chance to gain a minibreak, he rushes toward the net and takes a lousy Borg pop-up volley and yanks it wide crosscourt. He gasps and most assuredly curses himself inside. It's 3–3, and they change ends.

The crowd is heavily breathing as Borg hits a right-handed twisting serve out wide and McEnroe misses another backhand crosscourt, this time long. Then Mac uses the same strategy, employing a can-opener lefty serve to Borg's backhand that the Swede floats long. It's 4–4.

McEnroe confronts the let cord twice on his first serves, finally gets one in, and rushes the net, but Borg smokes a backhand crosscourt that he can't quite catch up to and he slaps it long. Borg has a minibreak to 5–4. But McEnroe sears an excellent return at Borg's feet; the Swede pops up his volley, and the New Yorker closes quickly and easily passes him. It's 5–5, but the Swede has two serves to close it out.

The unfettered Borg nails a backhand crosscourt approach shot that skids off the grass, and Mac lazily pushes it into the net. Borg has his third match point, the first one of the tiebreaker. The stadium is deathly silent as Mac gets up to serve down 6–5. Does he have any more lives left? He's hanging on for dear life and needs to do more than just scowl.

Mac hits a high-bouncing kick serve. Borg nails a forehand return, but Mac sprints to his left and stretches way out for an incredible forehand volley winner. Margolin giggles in delight. It's 6–6.

"Björn must feel crushed," thinks Simionescu, but he's not as he whips another backhand pass to 7–6 and his fourth match point.

As if pushed back by a gust off the North Sea, Borg then hits a terrible soft first volley down the middle and Mac comes over a backhand pass to even it at 7–7. Borg ends up tumbling into the doubles alley and has to wipe some strands of grass off his white shorts before he walks back to serve.

After pushing Borg off the net with a nifty topspin lob, Mac gains his first set point at 8–7 with a running backhand pass and the stands erupt in a sea of heavy British colors.

But Borg isn't going anywhere.

Mac tries his standard slice serve to the Swede's backhand and ends up with his face in the ground after seeing a Borg backhand pass whiz by. He shakes his head. It's 8–8.

Mac gains his second set point with a vintage serve-and-volley foray.

With her beau down 8–9, Simionescu finds her nail clipper and bites at her nails until she sees blood. She looks up suddenly and sees Borg deny Mac with a backhand volley winner. It's 9–9.

Nearly every point is now a minitriumph or demise or sudden death, as both men continue to kick the dirt out of their caskets.

11

To the Ends of
the Earth

In July 1978, while Guillermo Vilas was still reeling from his Parisian pummeling at the French Open, Jimmy Connors, who had lost to Björn Borg in the Wimbledon final, acted like a caged, starving rat. He was no one's comfortable No. 2 and remembered the days when he could overpower the Swede. Within his own large and often oppressive ego, the only man who would achieve the Grand Slam during Borg's tenure would be the brash boy from Belleville, Illinois.

Connors was asked what he would do if Borg won the U.S. Open, and whether he would travel all the way to Australia to try to prevent such a moment. "I may follow him to the ends of the earth now," Jimbo said.

On occasion, Borg would return to Stockholm and wear down the young talented Swedish juniors. Anders Jarryd recalled being put through Borg's meat grinder along with future Hall of Famer Mats Wilander as well as Joakim Nyström. There was little small talk or words of advice, just a few exchanges about hockey and soccer. Borg led by example.

"We knew we would be there all day," said Jarryd, who would end up winning eight Grand Slam doubles titles. "He was so intense and played with such a high tempo. You were totally dead after just the warm-up. Then you'd start to play a match for two hours and the tempo was so intense. I was tired, because I had to concentrate every point, but I wanted to make a good impression. It wasn't easy. He was so fit and he just kept on going. When you practiced with him, you didn't rest too much. He would sit for a second, take a drink, and just keep going. If we wanted to be great, we had to work hard and be determined, not give up. That's what he showed us.

"It's a shame that he stopped when we all were starting to do well. It would have been fun to have him around, and I think he would have liked hanging around with the up-and-comers. He was the only Swede out there before our group, and I think he would have enjoyed the camaraderie with some guys from his own country. Maybe if he had stayed a little longer, having that might have encouraged him to play much longer."

McEnroe was not ready for prime time yet. The pre–U.S. Open tournaments were still played on clay (they would later transition to hard courts), and he was at his tantrum-throwing, racket-chucking best in Indianapolis, where he lost to Connors 3–6, 6–1, 6–1 in the quarters.

At the time Connors played the wise old sage, as he wasn't particularly threatened yet, but he clearly saw the New Yorker's potential. "I was that way once," Connors said. "But don't forget that kid's probably the future of American tennis for the next ten or so years, so I wouldn't knock him. . . . If he's modeling his attitude on mine, I'm flattered. But I don't think he'd do that. He's too good. A really good player doesn't model himself on anybody."

That wasn't quite true. Years later, McEnroe admitted that he was attracted to Connors's intensity, the way he would scratch and claw when down, bare his fangs with his back against the wall.

Connors added, "He's got to get his brains beat in a few times before he makes his move. Then he'll have a little smarts of his own."

Mac then attempted a little of his own teenage psychoanalysis, which didn't quite hit the mark, but at least he was attempting to be introspective, a feat many athletes rarely seriously attempt.

"I wanted most to play in a great match. It was only after I lost that I realized how much I wanted to win. I have to feel like it's right out there. Understand, it's not like I wasn't trying. The difference is 95 percent instead of 100 percent. But I'm always looking around. I don't have that killer instinct. I'm not into that Connors thing. If I hate someone, I play worse."

Unlike Connors, Borg was relaxed and moved on, but not stateside yet. No, he went back to the seaside resort of Båstad in Sweden, put his toes back on the clay, and lost all of fifteen games in five matches in winning the title. Then, for some much-needed R&R, he took an extended break until the U.S. Open, which, after fifty-four years, had been moved from the hallowed grounds of the West Side Tennis Club in Forest Hills to its new confines in Flushing Meadows, Queens.

Borg's chances of winning the coveted title on his beloved dirt had vanished, but still, he was confident enough on hard courts and in good enough form to think he could give it a go. Or so he thought.

When Borg arrived at the new site, he complained that the courts were too fast and claimed that the United States Tennis Association had fiddled with the speed because it wanted eight Americans in the quarterfinals.

Nonetheless, for most of the tournament it looked as if the title would be Borg's. He didn't drop a set until the quarterfinals, when Ramírez stole a first-set tiebreaker from him in a 6–7, 6–4, 6–4, 6–0 win. But he brutalized the New Yorker Vitas Gerulaitis 6–3, 6–2, 7–6 in the semis. All it would take was another win over Connors and Borg would be all but golden for a run at the Grand Slam. But Bergelin had been saying Borg looked slow, and for a man who relied on his foot speed, that was more than problematic.

Unlike Borg, Connors had pressed on after Wimbledon and had many more matches under his belt coming into the U.S. Open.

Flushing Meadows would end up being a grittier environment than Forest Hills, which was also in Queens but was more of a blueblood, old-money British-style oasis in a concrete jungle.

Not so Flushing Meadows, which was built between the massive parking lots of the New York Mets' Shea Stadium and a portion of Flushing Meadows–Corona Park, which hosted the World's Fair in 1939–1940 and 1964–1965. Despite the amount of redevelopment money that has been poured into the area, it remains a poor section, full of dingy housing projects and declining commercial strips.

It was a perfect locale for Connors, who saw himself as a man of the people, even if few folks outside of his camp had really taken to him yet. The red, white, and blue National Tennis Center was a $10 million, sixteen-acre, thirty-four-court (indoors and outdoors) megacomplex that would fit perfectly into the 1980s mentality of spend and spend more to impress.

"If people want tradition, I'll plant some ivy," said USTA president Slew Hester, an oilman most responsible for the transformation of the Open. "I think the National Tennis Center is as American as apple pie. It's not Wimbledon because we don't have royalty. It is American because we have all the people. Some of them, in my mind, are not ready for tennis; they're not entitled to be part of the tennis crowd because they're boisterous and don't wear shorts, but this country is a melting pot and this tournament is strictly American in the same way."

Connors had a relatively easy first four matches at the 1978 U.S. Open, and then crisis struck when the acrobatic Panatta kept coming at him in the quarterfinals. Down 3–5 in the fifth set, it looked as if Connors was due for another huge letdown, but his groundstrokes drew more depth, he began to play more creatively, and finally the crowd began to relate to his grit in a remarkable 7–5 fifth-set victory.

"Jimmy doesn't want to die," Panatta remarked.

It was an enthralling victory for Connors, who wasn't beloved yet as he would become in 1991 when he reached the semifinals as a middle-aged man at the age of thirty-nine, but he had begun to establish himself in the psyche of the crowd. "That's as good a match as I can play," Connors said. "I've been fired up all summer. They're going to have to take this one away from me. They all know that."

McEnroe was fully aware that Connors wasn't going to give him anything in the semis, but he was in terrific form coming into the match, having trounced Fleming, Britain's Colin Dowdeswell, and American Butch Walts. His bad back had healed, largely because he had changed his service motion from a more straight-ahead stance to one where he stood completely sideways to the net, which allowed him to disguise his serve better and leap completely into the court. The newfangled motion also lessened the amount of time it took him to get to the net.

Connors and McEnroe faced off for the first time at the U.S. Open, and it didn't really matter where Mac was delivering service bombs from—Connors was all over the nineteen-year-old kid, beating the hell out of him from the backcourt, reading his serve beautifully, and passing him at will. Connors found the corners and came away with a substantial 6–2, 6–2, 7–5 victory. He was so sure of victory that he spat water at Mac's feet during the third-set changeover. He spoke of loving the hungry crowds and played like a starving lion.

"I'm an animal," Connors once said. "Which one, I can't tell you, but I would say that's the way I played my game from start to finish. I went out there with one goal in mind, and that was to play the absolute best I could and give it everything I had; win or lose."

"Jimmy was still Jimmy," Mac remarked.

Borg once again couldn't get it right in New York, and this time he was truly under the gun. The idea of the calendar-year Grand Slam was on his mind, but he was in a negative mental state much of the way. His topspinned ball didn't penetrate enough on hard courts, and he couldn't slide into shots on cement the way he could on clay or grass. The crowd was in his ears. The stench of hamburger fat swelled up his nose. Loud screams of drunken fans pierced his ears. Trains from the Long Island Rail Road roared by, while the New York subway screeched and moaned. And hour after hour, he could hear the deafening roar of planes arriving and departing from nearby LaGuardia Airport.

The European claycourt aficionados complained early and often. Manuel Orantes defaulted in the first round, while Corrado Barazzutti of Italy said, "These courts are shit," after he was bounced out in the second. Many foreign players threatened not to return unless the surface was made slower. But as Victor Amaya, the "Incredible Hulk" from Michigan, said, "Let them go. We don't ask anybody to speed up the clay in Europe. Why shouldn't we play on a fast surface at home?"

Even though he scored decisive wins over Ramírez and Gerulaitis, Borg wasn't as confident as his foes believed. "The way I was today I would beat fifty other players," said Ramírez, "but I cannot beat this guy." Then he added, "Björn may be breakable here because of his doubts about the surface. If Jimmy gets on top of him, Björn may say to himself he can't play on this court."

Ramírez was correct, as Connors, the man Borg had jumped on at Wimbledon, was hungrier and more intense, knowing full well that his grit, guts, and flat shots should be an integral part of the New York haze.

At one point late in the second set, Connors yelled at himself, "This is Borg and he can get back into it anytime. Don't let up—rip that fucking ball!"

Just like the crosstown New York Yankees, who were completing a four-game sweep of their hated rivals the Red Sox in what was termed the Boston Massacre, and who then would come back from 14 games down to win the division, Connors had rediscovered what he considered his rightful place in his sport—the top of the heap. The result was a 6–4, 6–2, 6–2 pummeling of Borg, where Connors put himself firmly back in the elite mix and Borg came back to earth with a heavy thud heard at nearby Shea Stadium.

Connors had exorcised his Wimbledon demons, relentlessly attacking the Swede, leaping at his serves, carving sharp angles of the ground, stabbing volley winners. Borg came into the match with a blistered right thumb, and it clearly affected his game and confidence. He had taken an injection in his hand, but he couldn't control his racket, which at times flew out of his grasp.

Classy as always, he would offer no excuses. "The thumb didn't make any difference," he later said. "Jimmy was born on this stuff. This is his court. I saw he was on top of his game from the beginning. There was not much I could do."

Bergelin cursed the event. "How can you have a championship like this—these lights so bright and far away, everybody running in and out, the airplanes. This is not a tournament, but a circus!"

Connors put the golden heavyweight champion's belt back on once again, even if it wouldn't last long. "I played like that. Yeah, like a crazy man," said the new Jimbo. "Now I've won this tournament on three different surfaces. It feels good to know I can still play like No. 1. . . . I was taking care of business and business got done."

Before heading back on tour, Mac got a call from U.S. Davis Cup captain Tony Trabert, who asked him to make his debut as doubles player with Brian Gottfried in Chile. Connors rarely played Davis Cup, but McEnroe, weaned by former Aussie Davis Cup captain Harry Hopman and his patriotic parents, couldn't wait to play. Connors, Mac said, didn't play because the money wasn't good enough, and indeed in the years that passed, on tour and off, it was always hard to get Connors to show up for anything unless he was being paid a big sum or had a reason to promote one of his own products.

"Where do I show up?" Mac asked Trabert, who told him it would be Santiago for a tussle on clay in World Group qualifying competition.

An earthquake struck the city that week, but Mac slept through it, instead causing his own vibrations on court with the ferocity of his serves. Gottfried remembers McEnroe as a consummate team player, and one who was supertalented.

"He was incredible for a rookie," Gottfried recalled. "I don't remember him being nervous. He was great to play doubles with. I like to talk a bit, and he was very much a team person and more of a locker room guy than others. There are some others who like the individual side, but he excelled in both and was part of the crowd. He was easy to talk to. It was team out there and not two guys trying to show each other up."

Billy Martin, who traveled with the Davis Cup team as a practice partner, remembered much the same. "He was pretty easygoing off-court. A guy who liked to hang out after practice."

Gottfried and Mac hadn't practiced much together, but Mac's magic worked wonders from the ad court. They pulled out a four-set win over Patricio Cornejo and Belus Prajoux, and the United States eventually won the tie 4–1 in front of an incredibly hostile, boozed-up crowd. Solomon greeted Gottfried and McEnroe in the locker room and declared, "Awright, after five fucking years we have finally got out of this fucking zone."

Mac was reveling in his chance to play the pro tour full-time without the distraction of school. He didn't appear distracted by his loss to Connors and kept knifing his serves to success, winning Hartford over Johan Kriek, and San Francisco over Dick Stockton. While in San Francisco, he totaled a car, just as any other nineteen-year-old might when winding up and down the foggy city's treacherous hills.

He and Fleming then traveled to a tournament in Hawaii, where Mac lost in the semis to a man who couldn't stand him, Bill Scanlon, and Fleming went on to reach the final. Mac refused to watch the final, and when he discovered that Fleming had lost, he said that in a sick way he was relieved. "Then of course I felt bad about myself and then I didn't know how to feel."

What McEnroe later discovered was that he was jealous of Fleming's happiness, as his relationship with Margolin was on the rocks and Fleming had fallen in love with a British girl he would eventually marry, Jenny. "I was doubly jealous that he had somebody and that she had him. . . . I had been leaning on Peter emotionally, as my best buddy, now suddenly there was no one for me to lean on."

While Fleming and McEnroe maintained a fruitful relationship on court, they were no longer that close. "Our relationship really struggled for a while," Fleming said. "But there was always a part of us that didn't want to let go of it. There is always going to be a bond between us, however much we abused it. Hopefully that continues to grow. But we definitely weren't always close. During doubles, for a couple of years, it was great. It was like the world was our oyster. But then that thing with Jenny and Junior and me kind of threw the whole balance off. It just wasn't the same. It definitely affected our doubles."

McEnroe said that in later years, after they had both retired, Fleming called him early one morning to say, "I'm just calling to say I forgive you for trying to ruin my marriage." He added that he and Fleming are still trying to work the kinks out of their relationship. Fleming isn't sure they ever will. "We're not that similar now, we don't have as much in common, but we have that past in common."

The New Yorker was developing a reputation for making others feel bad about themselves. Another one of McEnroe's rocky relationships was with Bill Scanlon, a journeyman player with a decent amount of talent. McEnroe would beat Scanlon nine of twelve times, but many fans most vividly recall Scanlon's round of 16 upset of the New Yorker at the 1983 U.S. Open.

The two men had a bizarre relationship, beginning with their conflict as juniors at the Port Washington Academy. Scanlon argues that McEnroe's temper tantrums were calculated maneuvers to slow down his opponents if he was struggling or if they were on a hot streak. While there are other players who say much the same, the one thing that saves Mac from being unequivocally condemned for unsportsmanlike behavior is that he blew his stack even when he was way ahead, potentially derailing his own victories.

Scanlon claimed that the reason he had small success against McEnroe was that he bored him to death, hitting to the same spot over and over again and driving him crazy. Mac acknowledges that Scanlon had technical talent, but said his lack of athleticism kept him out of the top ranks.

Before their Maui grudge match, one of Scanlon's tennis-teaching pro friends arranged a reception for him. Another guy got up and gave him a pep talk based on the baseball movie *The Bad News Bears*, which starred Tatum O'Neal, soon to be McEnroe's first wife. The audience got up and yelled that a meeting with Scanlon would mean "bad news for McEnroe." Scanlon would later use that phrase as the title of his book.

Scanlon won the match, oblivious to Mac's explosions and delays. A few months later in Japan, the two walked straight into each other on a changeover and the blood feud became more sour. "Our relationship had been bitter, intense, and fiery," Scanlon said.

A bit put off, Mac flew to Europe, fell to Vilas in the Basel final and to Wojtek Fibak in Cologne. Even though he was still a youngster, he was proving that, as Swede Mats Wilander would say of the great champions, he had balls.

"I remember at Basel we were doubles partners," Fibak said. "John lost in the singles final, and he was in pain; his elbow hurt. He came to the dressing room, took two aspirin, did not change clothes; just lay down for twenty minutes. Then we went on the court, and I told him I would serve first because I knew his elbow hurt, but he said, 'No problem.' The first ball he hit was a clean ace. That's John . . . he can do it not just one hour or one match but for three and a half hours every day."

Then the big encounter came against Borg in Stockholm, where McEnroe served beautifully and kept the points short in his 6–3, 6–4 win. Borg's countryman Mats Wilander, who would later win seven Grand Slam titles, said that the ultraquick court played in Mac's favor. "You could see how Borg could lose; he was caught so far behind the baseline." Swedish journalist Björn Hellberg recalled, "He was completely outclassed. McEnroe was so fast."

For the New Yorker it was a milestone. "I just felt like I was with the big boys now and this was an official coronation."

McEnroe's year did not end there, but climaxed in the United States' first Davis Cup crown since 1972 in Rancho Mirage, California. The teen lost only ten games in six sets to Britain's John Lloyd (then the husband of U.S. women's star Chris Evert) and

Buster Mottram and helped lead his nation to a 4–1 win. His loss of just ten games was a record at the time.

"It's incredible," said Lloyd. "I have never played anybody, including Borg and Connors, who has been as tough and made me play so many shots. No one has ever made me look like that much of an idiot."

Gottfried had somehow lost his singles contest to Mottram, an old-school attacker who was born with blue tennis blood coursing through his veins. But then the oldies-but-goodies doubles team of Stan Smith and Bob Lutz came through in front of a small yet vocal crowd.

McEnroe raised the cup for the first time on Sunday by flattening Mottram. Gottfried was in awe. "On the first day, he lost about five points on his first serve against Lloyd, and in his second match, he lost about eight to Mottram. You never had a chance on his serve and that makes it very tough. He was unreal."

At the end of 1978, Ohio State dismissed the tough-as-nails, legendary Woody Hayes as its football coach after he punched an opposing player who had intercepted a pass. It was just one in a long series of controversial, temperamental incidents for Hayes, a no-nonsense man, but one who was called loyal and devoted to his friends. Hayes once opined, "Without winners, there wouldn't even be any god-damned civilization."

Mac, who on more than one occasion was accused of destroying civilization by laying waste to its manners and protocols, might have agreed. His character wasn't too dissimilar from that of Hayes.

"He had dual personalities on court and off," Martin said. "Off the court, he was much nicer."

12

Both Still Alive

After he cuts a sharp serve at John McEnroe's body, Björn Borg holds his fifth match point against the straining American at 10–9.

The Duchess of Kent smiles at Mariana Simionescu. Perhaps she feels that the king might die, the Swede's fiancée thinks.

Simionescu takes a deep breath. Mac's serve down the middle confuses the Swede, catching him flat-footed and he knocks a return way out into the doubles alley. It's 10–10, and Mac eases a slice serve down the middle. The Swede decides to run way around his backhand, catches a high forehand, and rotates it toward an onrushing Mac, who, off balance, pushes an awful backhand volley short. Instead of ripping his pass, Borg guides it down the line, but an overanxious McEnroe buries his forehand volley in the net.

Borg has his sixth match point at 11–10 and McEnroe walks back to return serve looking as if he might weep. But with the gods briefly on his side, Mac gets lucky when his soft approach shot clips the net and lazily drops over, giving the Swede no chance to scoop it up. McEnroe inhales deeply and tugs on his shirt, realizing just how incredibly fortunate he was.

Commentator John Barrett opines, "Surely there's nothing left to happen in this tiebreaker." He is dead wrong.

Borg nails an excellent backhand volley crosscourt, and McEnroe ends up running into the green tarp on the side of the court after netting a forehand. Now Borg has his seventh match point at 12–11, and the background noise is constant. Mark McEnroe, sitting next to Margolin, is anxious. He's seen his older brother in tough spots before, but never on such a grand occasion. Mac goes at the Swede's lithe body again with a heavy second serve and flies forward, punching a picture-perfect backhand volley winner crosscourt. As he quickly changes ends at 12–12, McEnroe thinks, "I knew something special was happening. The fans wanted me to win the tiebreaker. They just didn't want this match to end. And the match itself didn't seem to want to end."

Barrett says, "They've both stared down the gun barrel and they are both still alive."

Mac blows on his hand, scratches his nose, and then handles a Borg return with precise acumen and wrong-foots the Swede with a slapping forehand volley down the line to gain his third set point at 13–12.

Borg nails a huge serve down the T, charges the net, and adeptly places a low backhand volley right on the baseline. McEnroe is completely flustered with the backhand pass he just poked into the net and briefly stands with his hands on his hips.

But then Borg rushes and misses a low backhand volley crosscourt into the net. Mark McEnroe utters a "C'mon" to himself while Simionescu breathes a curse Bergelin's way. Mac will have another chance at 14–13 to close out the set.

Mark McEnroe, sporting an impressive pair of dark shades, can't stop twitching and must have foreseen something as his brother John pushes an easy forehand volley a fraction out. Mark coughs into his hand. It's 14–14, and if fans peered at that moment over St. Mary's Church at the top of Wimbledon Hill, they could see the future of this delicious breaker stretching far beyond the horizon.

13

In Search of the True Genius

Early in 1979, John McEnroe had begun to stalk Björn Borg in full, knowing that if he was to eventually rise to the top of the tennis food chain he had to begin to hurt his rival with crunching body blows outside of the majors.

The tennis calendar has been pockmarked over the last century with bizarre scheduling decisions, and for many years one portion of the men's tour played its Masters event, or year-end championships, at the beginning of the next season. (It is now played at year's end in mid-November.)

The 1979 tournament was held in January in a packed Madison Square Garden. The eight top-ranked men from the year prior qualified, but in 1979, Borg and Guillermo Vilas didn't participate because of disagreement over how many events they should be playing. McEnroe, just shy of his twentieth birthday, entered the season realizing that he had added a few more weapons to his arsenal toward the end of 1978. He was a smarter player with a still-developing serve and volley.

Yet he was still looking up at the twenty-six-year-old Jimmy Connors, who had reclaimed his elite status by winning the 1978 U.S. Open and had learned to peak again for the big events. At the Masters, Mac faced Connors in a contentious final between two lefties with a mean streak.

Before that, there was little visible hate between them, but jealousy and envy of the other's status crept into their heads, and thus began a growing, spitting rivalry that wouldn't rival Borg vs. Mac in majestic quality, but was certainly more bitter, of the highest quality, and much longer-lasting, until Connors retired from full-time play in 1992, with Mac owning a 20–14 career edge over him.

During the week of the Masters, President Jimmy Carter and his administration watched nervously as Shah Mohammed Reza Pahlavi, the ruler of Iran, went into virtual exile after some two million people marched through the streets of Tehran in a massive show of support for the Iranian revolution. Carter appealed publicly to the new man in charge, the hard-liner Ayatollah Khomeini, to give the U.S.-supported compromise civilian government in Iran a chance to succeed. That lasted all of one month, before Khomeini and his glassy-eyed followers took over.

While Iran entered a new era, Southeast Asia ended one of its bloodiest chapters, when the Vietnam-backed Cambodian insurgents announced the fall of Phnom Penh–governed Cambodia and the collapse of the Pol Pot regime, which was said to be responsible for up to 1.7 million deaths, approximately 26 percent of the population at that time. America was scraping the resin off one foolhardy and very costly war and about to enter another questionable conflict far from its shores.

While the tennis folks restrung their rackets, much of the American sporting public's mind was on the Super Bowl, where two of the NFL's most storied and popular quarterbacks, the Pittsburgh Steelers' Terry Bradshaw and the Dallas Cowboys' Roger Staubach, went at it in one of the most entertaining finales ever, with the upstart Bradshaw leading his team to a 35–31 victory.

As much as Mac loved other sports and surely watched this duel between two legendary quarterbacks, his mind was on "the Garden," a historic locale where he used to take in New York Knicks games and deeply inhale the glory of the likes of Walt "Clyde" Frazier and Willis Reed.

The Masters was a round-robin competition, and since it was just a quick subway ride away from home, Mac acted as if he was conducting his own garage band, playing lead guitar and belting out tunes. He got over Arthur Ashe 6–7, 6–3, 7–5 in his first match, to the partial delight of the crowd, which reveled in their shotmaking.

Ashe was overwhelmed: "He can hit any shot you can think of. I haven't seen anyone with that much talent in ages. He doesn't have a flaw. Within two years it will be Borg, Connors, and McEnroe. I think he already passed Vilas and Vitas. His potential is unlimited. Against Connors and Borg you feel like you are being hit with a sledgehammer. But this guy is a stiletto."

Then the blood match came against Connors, who wanted to keep him in his place. For Connors, every high-level contest against a main rival had to be seen as a war, which was the way he kept himself highly motivated. He would have made Pol Pot proud with his total lack of mercy. "Four great months by McEnroe doesn't make him the best yet," Connors snarled. "I look forward to these meetings. I like to play the young kids coming up trying to get me." Connors added that the match "would be good practice for me," to which Mac sarcastically replied, "I hope to give Jimmy some good practice."

In front of sixteen thousand fans, with McEnroe in the driver's seat, Connors retired down 7–5, 3–0, because of a huge blister on his left foot. It was the first time McEnroe had defeated him. Mac was pissed off that he didn't come away with a more legitimate win, but took it nonetheless. "A victory from Connors is a victory over Connors, and I won the match. . . . It's better than losing so I'll take it. . . . But I don't think one match changes that he's number one in the world."

Next up was Philadelphia, where the two were expected to meet again, but Roscoe Tanner served Mac off the court 7–6, 6–2, as the still-blossoming teenager couldn't take care of three set points in the first set.

The week before, Mac had been in Las Vegas for a bit part in the tennis movie flop *Players*, which was directed by tennis nut Robert Evans and starred Dean Martin and Ali MacGraw, along with a bunch of ex–tennis players, including the cantankerous Pancho Gonzalez. McEnroe delivered three lines, including, "Don't choke, Pancho."

That month, Bianca Jagger, who had dated Vitas Gerulaitis and hung out with Ilie Nastase, filed for divorce from Mick Jagger in Los Angeles, seeking half of the $25 million he made while they were together. Sadly, Sid Vicious of the Sex Pistols, whose band's thumping, screaming anthems were sung from London to Los Angeles, was found dead of an overdose in his New York apartment just a day after being released from city jail on $50,000 bail after being accused of killing his longtime girlfriend, Nancy Spungen.

Mac went off to Richmond, where he would face Borg again, this time after besting Nastase. Yet unlike in Stockholm, the Swede was able to back him off the net in a 4–6, 7–6 (8), 6–3 victory. McEnroe was very close to winning the match in the second set, holding a 6–2 edge in the tiebreaker, and he also had match points at 7–6 and 8–7, but he missed returns wide. McEnroe blew eight match points in the loss, the only time he would ever commit such a gaffe.

He was playing in his home country this time in front of fans and media who were measuring his progress more closely. After the Connors victory, he wanted to show that he was becoming a consummate closer and could coolly chop down the other elite players just like his idol Borg did in big moments. But he envisioned the rewarding handshake at the net too early and fell apart at the seams.

He was none too pleased with the way he comported himself when he got frustrated with his play. "The way I acted on a tennis court was more the way people acted in life," McEnroe would later say. "It's an extremely frustrating game, and difficult to do right. We all have situations every day that make us want to yell at people. What Borg did seemed unbelievably hard to do. It was weird. Every now and then I'd go on the practice court and say, 'Hey, today I'm going to act like Björn. I'm not going to say anything.' And it would maybe last like five shots. It didn't seem right."

Mac then lost to Connors at the Pepsi Grand Slam on clay in Florida, but Borg, the blond streak of wind, was happy to be back on dirt and sprinted right past Connors in the final 6–2, 6–3. Connors tried to attack and moved forward, but was too impatient and watched Borg scald balls past him again and again.

"I didn't make any mistakes, I was serving well and making good passing shots," said Borg, who ran his record to 7–10 against Connors and showed the American that despite his U.S. Open loss to him, he still had the keys to his mental vault.

Interestingly, the normally uncontroversial Borg was chafing to the other players at Connors's thin skin and the American's general lack of sportsmanship. "It always feels good to beat him. He has one weakness in that he can never say that the other player plays well. I think that everybody likes to beat him because of that."

At the Rancho Mirage, California, tournament on hard courts, Mac was taken out by his junior Davis Cup teammate, the resourceful Eliot Teltscher, 7–6 in the third set in a 36 mph wind. Teltscher noted that they had played about twenty-five times as kids and was by no means intimidated in a three-hour match that was filled with unforced errors. Borg flailed in the wind too, going down to Bruce Manson.

Mac then headed to west Los Angeles to vegetate with Margolin—two young tennis sweethearts with their whole lives waiting to be played out. "At first it was good to have him in my corner because he understood the pressures of the tour," said Margolin, who now runs an outdoors company in Ojai. "But he wanted me to watch him play, while I needed to practice for my tournaments. There was also the East Coast–West Coast thing. He was so New York and I was so California. I always rationalized his bad-boy [attitude] because he treated me and my family well. But after a while, as I was getting older, I wanted to be with someone who respected people as much as I did."

The Borg-Mac rivalry began to take off in smaller venues, where they continued to feel each other out like boxing sparring partners, similar to former heavyweight champs Larry Holmes and Muhammad Ali, who had once battered each other inside small gyms.

In New Orleans, Mac again squeaked past Borg, this time 5–7, 6–1, 7–6 in the semis, but not before blowing his stack. Obviously, the residual effect of the Richmond loss got to him, for as well as he played for most of the match, he couldn't contain his demons when things got tight. But then his hero did him a favor, consoling him toward the end of the match and telling him to keep his head clear. That's how Borg won his matches against the other top-drawer players, and knowing how much McEnroe admired him, he decided to set the rookie straight. McEnroe never forgot that, and the man whose poster was slapped on his bedroom wall grew in stature.

"It was five-all in the third set and I was getting all worked up and nutty, and Björn motioned me to the net. I thought, 'Oh, God, what's he going to do? Is he going to tell me I'm the biggest jerk of all time?' And he just put his arm around my shoulders and said, 'It's okay. Just relax.' This was at five-all in the third set! But he was amused by the whole thing. 'It's okay,' he told me. 'It's a great match.' It made me feel really special. He didn't look at what I was doing as something I'd done to affect him. It was just my own nuttiness. Plus—and maybe this was the main point—he was still number one. Borg and I never had a problem, on or off the court: he understood. He thought I was a little crazy, but it didn't seem to bother him. The way I saw it, he even went out of his way to show me respect."

Mac was on a real roll, taking out Tanner for the title. He then skipped over to fashion-conscious Milan, where he blew out Vitas Gerulaitis and John Alexander for the crown. It was there that he got his first real taste of Borg's and Gerulaitis's abilities on the nightlife circuit. All of them would pay for going overboard in later years.

"I marked the occasion by indulging in something I never tried before (never mind what)," McEnroe recalled, "and the next thing I know Vitas and Björn were carrying me back to the hotel. I felt sick but wonderful: I had passed the initiation. I was part of the gang. Broadway Vitas and Björn! To me they were like elder statesmen. It was so exciting to be running around with the best players in the world. I still pride myself on being energetic, even a hyperactive guy, but I didn't have the energy that these guys had. They would run me into the ground on a consistent basis."

Mac noted that on court, Vitas imitated Borg, but off court it was Borg who was the follower. Vitas would set up which restaurant they would eat at, which club they would go dancing at, which women they would pursue.

Even though Borg would be married the next year, like Gerulaitis he had an amazing ability to recover from late nights and enjoyed life after hours. "No one deserved to party and have a good time more than Borg," said Billy Martin. "He worked his butt off just like anyone else. He needed some time away."

While Mac was winning in Europe, tension gripped the United States when a nuclear reactor on Three Mile Island outside of Harrisburg, Pennsylvania, had its cooling system fail, which raised serious fears of an explosion and dispersal of radioactivity. Thousands of people living near the plant left the area before the nearly two-week crisis ended, during which time some radioactive water and gases were released. The accident also seriously increased public concern over the dangers of nuclear power and slowed construction of other reactors. Later, some locals wore antinuclear power buttons that read THEY LIE.

While President Carter sought to calm the nation in his cool and measured southern drawl, McEnroe went to Rotterdam and lost only fifteen games in four matches to reach the final. Once again, Borg was waiting for him. The contest was played on slick indoor carpet that should have been more to McEnroe's liking, but Borg's much-improved first serve and handiness at the net propelled him to a 6–4, 6–2 victory over the now twenty-year-old McEnroe. After New Orleans, the Swede knew that the kid was a serious threat, and this time there would be no older-brother-type talks to his growing rival at key moments in the match.

Then Mac bested Fleming in the final of San Jose and traveled to Las Vegas, and in what was becoming a sorry trend for the head-strong American, he lost to Connors in the semifinals 7–5, 6–4. The older and prideful American had no intention of allowing McEnroe to negate his significance so early in the New Yorker's career, and while he was clearly troubled by McEnroe's frequent change of pace from the baseline and swarming net game—which by now was the best in the business—he could still murder returns and take it to him off the backhand side when he was in top form.

At the time, outside of the Grand Slams, the men's circuit was split between the Grand Prix circuit and World Championship Tennis (WCT), which was run by Texas oilman Lamar Hunt, with most players competing in both series while the competing owners tore at each other to grab total control of men's tennis. Hunt was a cofounder of WCT in 1967, which lasted for twenty-three years before the Association of Tennis Professionals (ATP) took over and stands to this day. Hunt, the only person to have been inducted into three major Halls of Fame—the Pro Football Hall of Fame (1972), the Soccer Hall of Fame (1982), and the International Tennis Hall of Fame (1993)—helped build the American Football League as owner of the Kansas City Chiefs. He was a tremendous force in helping professionalize the men's tour, but his constant fighting with the Grand Prix caused divisions in the pro ranks.

So 1979 crazily began with the Grand Prix Masters at Madison Square Garden, and then in May WCT held its eight-man round robin in Dallas. Promoter Hunt added glitz to the event by inviting Dallas Cowboys head coach Tom Landry, Princess Caroline of Monaco, and crooner Frankie Avalon to attend.

Borg, Mac, Connors, and Vitas were among the field. Before the tournament began, it was revealed that Connors had secretly married Patti McGuire (who was also from the St. Louis area), a former Playmate of the Year, and that the couple was expecting their first child. But the honeymooning Connors was already upset upon arrival, as he claimed to have had an infected callus on his left hand from the Las Vegas event. He asked for a late start, which was granted. That meant that McEnroe's match against Aussie John Alexander was moved up to Tuesday

"McEnroe is the equal of anyone I've ever played," an already impressed Alexander said. "I've played them all now, and he's the toughest."

An angry McEnroe was peeved that he wasn't getting two days' rest and demanded that his match start on Wednesday as originally planned. Connors's problems were not his. "It's not my fault he's got a blister," he said. "I've got things wrong with me, but I'm not going to hope people feel sorry for me. I've got a callus on my hand. I've got blisters on my feet. I'm calling my father. He'll handle it with the WCT people."

But Mac didn't get his wish, which perhaps fired him up even more. He beat Alexander in the first round and Connors bested Gene Mayer. The two snarling lefties would go at it snort-for-grunt again. Mayer didn't think that Mac was ready for Connors, but he was off the mark, as McEnroe volleyed, lobbed, passed, and, of course, served beautifully.

In the third set, both men complained about calls, but Mac was getting the better of Connors in that department. McEnroe was yelling and stalling and Connors was none too pleased. "You going to let this keep up?" he asked. McEnroe screamed at the chair umpire, which prompted a fan to yell out, "Call your daddy," a remark surely heard by J.P. McEnroe, who was in attendance.

Johnny Mac didn't need to contact his pop on speed dial as he raged to a 6–1, 6–1, 6–4 victory. The elder lefty Connors was so upset that he hired a private plane to race him out of town. "I had a game plan against him," McEnroe said later. "For the first time I felt totally in control. I don't think I've ever served better."

Connors was furious and refused to talk to the press. Said WCT public relations man Rod Humphries, "Jimmy is an angry young man. He will not talk to the press. He asked Patti, 'Who's got the keys?' He has left the building. Maybe the city."

Borg had bullied Geoff Masters and Gerulaitis to reach the final, where of course Mac stood once again in a period that could be called the Prague Spring of their rivalry, with Mac playing the role of sniper and Borg the tank commander.

Borg was not surprised that McEnroe would be the man across the net in the final. "No," said Borg. "He has all the shots. You have to be quick in the legs to play against this guy and his serve. It all depends on him."

Mac found every angle and placement and won going away 7–5, 4–6, 6–2, 7–6 (5). He served slightly better, which made the difference in the fourth set, when Borg owned a 5–3 lead, but serving at 5–4, the Swede pushed an approach shot long and then saw Mac wallop a forehand winner. McEnroe broke back and rattled Borg in the tiebreaker. There would be no throat-clutching gag like he experienced in Richmond. "I felt slow and always too late," Borg said later. "When you play John you have to be absolutely on top of your game, or you lose immediately."

The two wouldn't face each other again until just before the U.S. Open, at the Canadian Open in early August. Mac missed the French Open due to an injury, while an unaffected and still determined Borg flew to Paris to don his Grand Slam best.

Northern Europe was going through a cataclysmic change at the beginning of May, when Margaret Thatcher became Great Britain's first woman prime minister and set out to dismantle Britain's postwar welfare state. The conservative Thatcher would serve longer than any British prime minister in the twentieth century, and with a stern face and sharp tongue, she worked diligently to impose her own "Thatcher Revolution," focused on reducing the influence of the trade unions and combating inflation. Like her future friend Ronald Reagan, she was a pure free marketer.

While Thatcher's moves pleased the well-dressed financiers who strode around London's financial district, the world at large took a collective sigh of relief before the first specks of dust were kicked up on Stade Roland Garros in Paris as Prime Minister Menachem Begin of Israel and President Anwar Sadat of Egypt announced that the former enemies would open their borders to each other for the first time since the birth of Israel thirty-one years earlier.

Borg knew no borders within his relentless game at Roland Garros, but he did wheeze a bit early, dropping sets to Tomas Smid and Tom Gullikson in the first two rounds. He picked up steam, not losing another set until the final (including a 6–2, 6–1, 6–0 stomping of Vilas in the semis). On the final Sunday, he overcame surprise finalist Victor Pecci of Paraguay 6–3, 6–1, 6–7, 6–4 to win his fourth title.

"What Borg has in common with Rafael Nadal [the young Spaniard who won four straight French Open titles from 2005 through 2008 and a fifth crown in 2010] is that they have the two best heads I've ever seen on clay," said the legendary Spanish coach José Higueras, who as a player was 1–9 against Borg. "They have the unique ability to play every point the same, and that's remarkable. I beat Björn once when he was about fifteen and then he got stronger. If you couldn't come in and take time away from him, serve and volley and not give him rhythm like Panatta once did in Paris, you had no chance. I didn't have the weapons to do that. I'd play the best I could and he'd beat me 6–2, 6–1. His footwork was incredible. Anybody who played from the back had no chance on clay."

While Borg and Simionescu celebrated once again on the sleek Champs-Élysées, it appeared that world was moving into a more peaceful stage. In his last significant and praiseworthy move as president, Carter and the stone-faced Soviet premier Leonid Brezhnev signed the SALT II treaty in Vienna, which sought to reduce the manufacturing of strategic nuclear weapons and banned new missile programs. Huge sighs of relief blew across the Great Plains of the American Midwest and the vast Soviet wheatlands, where the missiles were ready for launch. Although the U.S. Senate failed to ratify the pact, both countries honored its contents until 1986.

Recovered from his injury, McEnroe made his way to the fine lawns of the Queen's Club Championship, where he bested Charlie Pasarell in the first round. Pasarell, a close friend of Arthur Ashe's at UCLA and the finest male player ever to come out of Puerto Rico, once lost the second-longest match in history to the forty-one-year-old Pancho Gonzalez at 1969 Wimbledon 22–24, 1–6, 16–14, 6–3, 11–9 in five hours and twelve minutes. (The record was surpassed at 2010 Wimbledon when American John Isner defeated France's Nicolas Mahut 6–4, 3–6, 6–7 (7), 7–6 (3), 70–68 in eight hours and eleven minutes.) After he retired, Pasarell became one of the sport's most successful promoters, as the tournament owner at Indian Wells and one of the powerful board members on the men's ATP Tour.

While Pasarell won numerous boardroom battles and had a stint in the U.S. top 10, he couldn't come close to matching up against McEnroe. "He was the best I've ever played," Pasarell said. "He might not have as many Grand Slam titles that Borg had or was at No. 1 as long as Connors, but he was a pure, one-of-a-kind talent with what he could do with the ball. No one was like him, could create shots like he did."

Mac then pasted Sandy Mayer, Tanner, and Britain's Mark Petchey to win the Queen's title and looked to be in vintage form to take on Borg at Wimbledon. "There is only one true genius in the game, and his name is Junior," said Mayer.

Even though his rivalry with Borg was growing and some analysts thought he was ready to make a major impact at Wimbledon, Mac was still too uncomposed and immature, which could both fire him up and jangle his nerves. "That's the way I was then," McEnroe later reflected. "You regret it but you don't dwell on the past. I did what I felt like. I'm growing and maturing. Look, I don't want to do things that are different. But I'm not an everyday person. I'm an individual. I know I piss a lot of people off. There are thousands of people who don't think I'm a nice guy. They think I'm an asshole. If someone called me an asshole on court, I'd challenge them. I'd ask why. They have to explain it. It seems all people want to do is talk about my temper."

After knocking out right-handed Tom Gullikson in the third round, he lost to Tom's lefty twin, Tim, 6–4, 6–2, 6–4, who would later become the coach of 14-time Grand Slam winner Pete Sampras and die prematurely of brain cancer in 1996.

Mac was shocked and embarrassed at the loss, and as the popular new rock band Supertramp sang that year in a high pitch, he was forced to "take the long way home."

Borg never flinched, knowing full well how to negotiate the hurdles of Paris to London. For some reason, despite the long points and claycourt wear of Roland Garros, he never felt so put out that he couldn't put his blinders on again and get his legs pumping on the final turn in London.

"Of course you're mentally tired after this tournament," Borg said. "Paris is the toughest tournament mentally and physically to win, because it's on clay, you have to stay out there for many hours, many matches. Of course I was tired after this when I went to do England and prepare myself for Wimbledon. Every player—to say you're not tired, I mean, the players are lying. But the thing is that at Wimbledon, if you survive—I mean, I had always problems the first couple rounds, my first or second round of Wimbledon. If I survived those matches, then I started to play good tennis. . . . So that's a crucial thing."

That year, he had problems at the All England Club early, middle, and late. After besting Tom Gorman in four sets in the first round, Borg faced Indian Vijay Amritraj, the regal sportsman from Madras with a classic serve-and-volley game who had Borg all but left for dead. Amritraj won the first set in twenty-five minutes, but in the second, Borg rediscovered his nerve, serve, and a few key passing shots. In the third set, Amritraj broke Borg in the final game when the Swede uncharacteristically double-faulted.

Amritraj broke for a 2–1 lead in the fourth set, and after Borg broke back, Amritraj broke again to 3–2. But then Borg shook off the cobwebs, nailed winner after winner, and Amritraj completely collapsed in the tiebreaker. The Swede then sped away 2–6, 6–4, 4–6, 7–6, 6–2. "This man is a genius," Amritraj said. "Any man who wins a tournament four times on a surface he plays once a year is an absolute genius."

Borg then took a straight-set win over Hank Pfister, but in the fourth round, Californian Brian Teacher bombed big serves, crisp volleys, and fine returns. Still, Borg seized the big points in a 6–4, 5–7, 6–4, 7–5 win. No surprise there. "I'm not mad that I played so well and lost," Teacher said. "I'm mad that I played the whole damn tournament so well and had to meet up with him."

Borg then wasted Dutch ladies' man Tom Okker and again faced Connors in the semifinals. The American wasn't exactly brimming with confidence against Borg. In fact, it could be said that the Belleville Bulldog was feeling lower than at any time during his career. He was smarting from his off-court problems and angry at the seeding committee's decision to place him third, so he decided to stay away from the players' tearoom and wouldn't talk to the officials or the media.

"F—— the press," Connors allegedly said to a club official after Borg had trounced him 6–2, 6–3, 6–2. The Swede was making mincemeat of their recent rivalry. "Jimmy doesn't walk around like he's going to win anymore," observed McEnroe.

Although he had dismissed his main elite rival, the final was torturous. There he faced Roscoe Tanner, another lefty with a faster serve than McEnroe, the fastest on tour at the time, and armed with a reconstructed one-handed backhand and a stiff yet competent volley. Borg observed that he never knew what Roscoe was going to do—nail aces and winners all over the place, or skyrocket balls into the bleachers. But Tanner had a pretty good idea of what to expect from Borg: "He's pretty instinctive. He's machinelike in the way he plays. I don't think it requires too much thinking. Not that he couldn't think or doesn't sometimes have to, but he'll always play his game. His style is dominating, like Connors most of the time, but he is dictating the pattern."

Tanner had a fairly easy road to the final, stinging Mac's conqueror, Tim Gullikson, and then Pat Dupree in the quarters and semis. He did not fear Borg, not with that flamethrower of a serve. But he had not only to hold but to break him, which would be no easy feat given the relative weakness of his return and ground game.

The child of wealthy parents, Tanner was a pure southern charmer who some thought had an inborn sense of entitlement. A congenial yet manipulative, hard-to-read sort, Tanner would later serve time in German and U.S. jails for theft and the failure to pay child support. He played by instinct and lived much the same way, rarely thinking through his decisions off court.

"Roscoe's greatness was that he saw the glass overflowing—never half full," said Dick Gould, his coach at Stanford. "He just couldn't understand that other athletes might be his equal. It was pure confidence." Dick Stockton, who played against Tanner as a junior, added, "He was kind of like the Pied Piper. He just drew people to him."

Tanner was very outgoing, while Borg rarely spoke to those he didn't trust and know well. "You don't see him very much," Tanner observed. "The times I've talked to him, I like him. You never used to see him at all. Now that he's older, he's found his place, and maybe that's one of the reasons he played so well. But he keeps to himself."

The final would have major significance, as it was the first time that NBC decided to broadcast *Breakfast at Wimbledon*, live tennis in the early hours of the U.S. morning. Producer Don Ohlmeyer had requested an adjusted start on Centre Court, a mere five minutes back, which would allow the network to insert an introduction. The club's response: "'Not on, old boy. Not on.' Why? 'Never been done.'"

Broadcaster Bud Collins recalled that Ohlmeyer was worried that Tanner would play scared and that by the time they went on air the first set would be over. "They thought he was crazy," said Collins, who broadcast the match. "They said, 'Nobody will watch a tennis final early on a Saturday morning.' Don said, 'We've got to try.' We wanted McEnroe or Connors against Borg, but what we got was Roscoe."

So they hatched a plan. Donald Dell, one of the NBC commentators and also conveniently Tanner's agent at the time, was asked if he could pull off some kind of delay. So he asked Tanner to head for the bathroom and stay put.

"I hid out in a toilet stall, looking at my watch while Peter Morgan searched the dressing room, calling out, 'Oh, Mr. Tanner?

Where are you, Mr. Tanner? We're ready for you. Mr. Borg is ready,'"
Tanner recalled.

Eventually Tanner came out of the closet—the water closet,
that is.

"I told them I hadn't felt well. And the show went on. I'll never
forget stepping onto that court. I had played on Centre, but this was
the final. I was stepping into history."

History dictated that Borg would pass Tanner at all the key
moments, but the rugged Tanner didn't fear him. He was planning
on belting the Swede with left-handed hooks and tiring him out
with body blows.

"When a guy stays back as he does, he should be more vulnerable
on grass," Tanner said. "Looking at him, you wouldn't say his game
is suited to grass. But he plays well on all surfaces, and that's what
you have to do to be number one. Technically, he's one of the toughest guys to play against. A lot of times he hits a return off-center and
the ball just goes so high, with nothing on it, and it comes back to
the baseline. It works out perfect, and that's kind of irritating,
because you figure there's no way he can plan that shot. I'm sure he
doesn't practice mis-hits, but that's the way he plays, and it works.
Otherwise, he hits with so much topspin that the ball comes over
and dips, which makes it difficult to handle. His shots are tough to
volley. You can't establish a good clean rhythm against him like you
can against Connors. His passing shots are good because he takes a
little topspin off. You can get more penetration, more forward
movement and speed through the air, when the ball has less topspin.
He just picks a shot and holds it; it may be the wrong shot, but he
makes it work. He doesn't think, 'Should I go crosscourt or down
the line?' Boom. That's confidence."

The well-built twenty-seven-year-old rushed the net on everything but a loose thread of Borg's headband, and by improving his
backhand by adding topspin to his more solid flat and slice strokes,
he stood stronger from the backcourt. He played fairly cleanly at the
net too, forcing Borg to come up with one brilliant pass after
another—thirty-two in all.

Borg broke Tanner in the opening game of the fifth set, and as well as he was serving, it looked as if he would easily hold another five times and grab title number four. But then Tanner briefly enjoyed the fruits of his reconstructed backhand. He held two break points in the eighth game, but missed an easy forehand pass and then saw Borg kiss the line with a backhand winner.

"I played it too fine," Tanner said of the first opportunity. "The match might have come down to that point . . . basically . . . probably."

Tanner saved three match points with some huge shots, but Borg was more consistent and determined to hold the trophy once more. He scored a 6–1, 6–7, 3–6, 6–3, 6–4 victory. "I've never been so nervous in my whole life. I could hardly hold the racket," Borg said. "If he takes that game from 0–40, no way I win. In the fourth and fifth sets I win all the big points, every single one. I don't know. In this tournament I am always winning those points. It is very strange."

Borg compared his achievement of four straight titles to that of Eddy Merckx, a Belgian cyclist who won five Tours de France. It was well beyond that for Tanner. "I don't think the rest of us in tennis can even relate to four Wimbledons in a row," the American said.

McEnroe didn't go home early, though. He stayed to win the doubles with Peter Fleming in a thoroughly convincing 4–6, 6–4, 6–2, 6–2 victory over the stellar team of Ramírez and Gottfried.

Fleming was there for McEnroe once again, not as the better player but as the steady anchor in their improving doubles partnership. Today's game rarely sees a top player compete in doubles, but back in the 1970s and into the early 1980s, a few leading lights were willing to share the court in pursuit of success. One of those was McEnroe, arguably the greatest doubles player ever, and another was the six-foot six-inch, sandy-haired Fleming, who reached the top 10 in singles but never won a Grand Slam title in individual play or was a consistent threat to the top men.

In a down moment, when he was injured in 1982, Fleming said that the best doubles team in the world was "John McEnroe and

Borg's coach,
Lennart Bergelin,
encouraged him
to be a workout
animal.

Borg worked on his
serve for years before
it became a major
weapon on grass.

Borg rarely displayed outward anger in matches but was capable of busting a few rackets in practice.

McEnroe and Fleming
were one of the best
doubles team ever, but
their off-court
relationship had its
ups and downs.

Both Borg and McEnroe
admired the Aussie Rod
Laver, who won calendar-
year Grand Slams in
1962 and 1969.

McEnroe's parents, John and Kate, knew they had a genius on their hands.

McEnroe (left), seen here with junior rival Larry Gottfried in 1973, could never settle for second place, even as a kid.

Jimmy Connors dominated the tour before Borg and McEnroe came along and stole his thunder.

Johnny Mac vowed that lack of conditioning wouldn't be an issue in the 1980 U.S. Open final.

While Borg was said to have ice running through his veins, he didn't entirely lack a sense of humor.

Mary Carillo and McEnroe were the toast of Douglaston after they won the French Open mixed-doubles title in 1977.

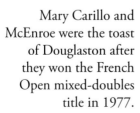

McEnroe's vintage serve-and-volley routine fit snugly into
Wimbledon grass.

The walk onto Wimbledon's Centre Court for the 1980 final was full of
tension and anticipation.

anyone," but that wasn't quite true. Not every player could contend with Mac's volcanic personality, nor earn his trust. Fleming did, although the relationship consistently evolved off court.

The duo won an amazing fifty-seven doubles titles together, including four at Wimbledon (1979, 1981, 1983, and 1984) and three at the U.S. Open (1979, 1981, and 1983). Fleming could serve a ton, had great reach and fine touch at the net, and knew that his good buddy had as much talent as anyone out there, or even more. Like McEnroe, Fleming had a temper. Like McEnroe, Fleming could talk. Like McEnroe, Fleming had an independent streak.

Years after they first faced off at the Port Washington Tennis Academy, the two teamed up for good in the summer of 1978, after McEnroe turned pro. Although they would occasionally play with different partners, they stuck together through thick and thin. After they lost in the U.S. Open quarterfinals, former U.S. notable Ham Richardson told them they were keeping too far away from the net. They heeded his advice and never looked back.

"I moved up five feet. Junior practically climbed on top of the tape. We won seven of our next eight tournaments."

In the fall, they faced the excellent duo of Hewitt-McMillan in the Cologne final, the same guys who had crushed them at Wimbledon that summer. Early in the match, McEnroe smashed a sitter toward Hewitt's face. Hewitt, a bald-headed confrontational type, screamed, "You want to die?"

McEnroe countered, "What? You want some more, old man? Next time I won't miss!"

On the next point, Fleming hit a winner down the line and the Americans ended up winning in a cakewalk. "It was all over for them," said Fleming, "and they knew it."

14

The War of 18–16

Mythologists say that there are dozens of ghosts that float around the Wimbledon grounds, hiding cans of balls under chairs, slashing net cords in the most hard-to-find spots, dampening a linesperson's chair with the sweat of their foggy brows. The tournament has hosted kings and queens, dukes and duchesses, knights in thousand-pound suits of shining armor, and damsels in distress, like Princess Diana, who would later leave a McEnroe match because, it was said, he was poisoning her royal ears with curse words.

The British have no players they can really champion as title hopefuls. In 1978, Borg's friend John Lloyd, who was then married to Chris Evert, reached a career-high ranking of No. 21, but despite his classic style, he never had the gusto to cut down major foes on the lawns, always failing to pass the third round on his home turf. After falling in the first round this year, he supported his wife while she upset the reigning Martina Navratilova in the semis and then somewhat shockingly fell to the graceful new mother Evonne Goolagong of Australia 6–1, 7–6 in the final. Former champion

Virginia Wade, now very much in decline, was hustled out of the tournament by U.S. teen phenomenon Andrea Jaeger.

Now all eyes are on Borg and McEnroe, who are locked at 14–14 in their epic fourth-set tiebreaker. Borg has already wasted seven match points and McEnroe has lost four set points, the last one at 14–13 when he nudged a simple forehand volley just out.

Mac underhands a forehand volley to a dead spot over the net and the American has his fifth set point at 15–14, but then Borg powers a fine serve down the T and Mac returns wide. It's 15–15 and they change sides again. "I've never seen a tiebreak like this, and I've seen a few good ones," said commentator John Barrett, some twenty minutes into sudden death.

Mac scalds a great backhand return, and then off a fine volley by Borg he thrashes an extraordinary forehand pass with his racket taken back well below his hip. The crowd roars as the peasants once did in the English countryside when the lords prepared Christmas feasts for them.

It's another set point for Johnny Mac, number six at 16–15, but he muffs an easy backhand volley and sends it so far long that Mark and his dad are beside themselves in pain, twitching.

It's 16–16. The BBC calls Borg the calmest man in the place, but they are wrong. Mac twists a serve into Borg's body and the Swede just misses a forehand crosscourt pass. It's 17–16 McEnroe, and he takes a deep breath, as Borg can't shake off his last error.

Seemingly upset, the consummate stoic then misses an easy forehand volley. Mac has stolen the set 18–16 in the tiebreaker. Papa McEnroe jumps out of his chair and wildly pumps his fist, while Stacy Margolin rubs her neck and laughs.

On the BBC, Mark Cox calls it the most dramatic tiebreak in history.

Mac thought, "I knew I had won the match. I *knew* it."

Mariana Simionescu still thinks her Swede will triumph. "Bjorn carefully checks his racket now, like a violinist who tunes his instrument between allegro and andante, while the listeners seem forced to cough so that they will not be taken by surprise when the music starts again," she later wrote.

Before he retuned, Borg nearly tuned out. "That was the toughest moment in my tennis career, that walk back to the chair," he later said. "I knew John thought he would win the match. I thought he would win the match. I don't know how I regrouped."

15

"A Notch above Son of Sam"

In 1979, when Peter Fleming and John McEnroe won an Open Era record fifteen titles together, the big guy saw Mac serve them out of plenty of tight spots. They learned from each other and realized that although their major ambitions were still in singles, doubles victories could take the sting off losses in singles and add a little more sweet icing to the cake.

"I learned from Junior," said Fleming. "He was so into our doubles. Always. If he was beaten in singles, he'd try even harder in doubles. We would never tank just because one of us got beat. The dubs got to be 99 percent a lock if the other poor bastards had to play us after Junior had lost."

While Fleming could grow wild while returning serve, he could also be devastating returning from the deuce court, where the right-hander was able to wind up with a crisp swing from his backhand side and bludgeon the ball wherever he chose, a difficult shot for righties. And of course, returning from the ad court as a left-hander, McEnroe could chip his backhand low and come over the top on his forehand. Plus, he rarely missed a volley. Perhaps most important, they were two of the world's most feared servers—with McEnroe's twisting daggers and Fleming bombing flat grenades down the T.

"John and I have similar personalities even if no one believes me when I say that. My image was that of Mr. Docile," Fleming said. "One of the things that held back my career was that I was never in control of my emotions. I was off the wall. In doubles John was real good at helping me relax; in singles I was on my own. I also became very self-conscious later on. After all the injuries I felt more and more wooden, more and more giraffe-like. There I was playing doubles with the most graceful man ever to play the game and I'm this stick figure stumbling around the court."

The freckle-faced McEnroe returned home after losing to Gullikson at Wimbledon. He was growing up, but at times he still acted like a teenager let loose from the dorm rooms of the tennis tour. He didn't care about how he looked, mixing up colors and patterns of his clothes at tournaments.

"Nice outfit," one player yelled to him at a Davis Cup tie when looking at his red headband, green sweater, and blue shorts. He also showed up to a regal Davis ceremony wearing ragged blue jeans and a blazer. "That's all I can afford," Mac replied with a sheepish grin.

Mac was a lover of rock and roll, but he was also influenced by the new pop culture, going so far as to say that he was thinking of taking disco dancing lessons, a big no-no for hard-core rockers. While trying to impress the black-jumpsuit-wearing partygoers at Studio 54, he still was putting ice cubes in his milk and downing six-packs of soda. That year, he bought a Mercedes 450, but on occasion he still flew coach. He was also generous, buying his brother Mark a new Camaro.

After his disappointing Wimbledon, Mac was able to get his head straight. Some pre–U.S. Open tournaments were still being contested on clay, where McEnroe crushed John Lloyd in a final at South Orange, New Jersey, on dirt, and lost to Vilas at Indianapolis.

Then in Canada, Mac had a chance to go at Borg again after beating Gerulaitis 6–3, 6–3. The tournament was played on hard courts, but the Swede still had his way with him in a 6–3, 6–3 victory. McEnroe littered the court with errors and didn't keep his first volleys or approach shots deep enough. He didn't serve particularly well and Borg simply punished him from the backcourt. Borg was thrilled after his eighth title of the year, believing that he was in prime form to win his first U.S. Open. On that day, it appeared that the young McEnroe was wearing down after a long season.

"I returned low, and I always got a second chance on my passing shots," Borg said. "It was the first time I've ever felt good against him and the best I've played against him."

Instead of wallowing in defeat, McEnroe shook it off as simply a lousy serving day and a poor day at the cords. It would be at the U.S. Open in New York that he would finally cut his teeth as an elite player, and it couldn't come in a more appropriate locale. But before he tasted Grand Slam glory, he appropriately traded barbs with Ilie Nastase in the second round of what is still considered the ugliest men's contest in tournament history.

"It wasn't a tennis match, it was more like a riot," the volcanic Romanian said.

There could not have been a better example of anger management gone awry than these two facing off—one a notorious Romanian with hot Latin blood flowing through his veins and the other a hotheaded Irish New Yorker.

Quick-tempered men do not know how to resist the anger of the moment. They hate losing control, being bothered, or being taken out of their comfort zone. Both Nastase and McEnroe have been asked a combined million times why they can't calm down on court, and perhaps the simple answer—which neither has ventured—is that they are genetically incapable of doing so without some type of medication.

"McEnroe fits into a category which a lot of great tennis players do, which is being a natural warrior," said Allen Fox, an author, a psychologist, and a former pro tennis player. "That's his genetic makeup. Humans are a social species and when they were evolving had an unfortunate tendency to fight each other. In group cultures, we need people with different functions. If a tribe didn't have some natural tough warriors they would be wiped out. The warrior type will react with aggression rather than retreat. In primitive times, someone had to be able to pick up a club and hit someone over the head with it. That's where McEnroe comes from."

Mac and Nastase tended to say that for the most part the reason they exploded had to do with the injustice of line calls, but many other players were able to object and get back to playing without degrading the person who made the call or the one who was overseeing the match. Not Mac. Not Nasty. They could be extremely vicious.

The aging Nastase had hired twelve-time Grand Slam champion Roy Emerson to coach him before the tournament, not because he thought he would win but because he wanted to perform respectably. On a hot August night, their match spiraled out of control. McEnroe began the contest behaving well, but the thirty-three-year-old Nastase, who was well past his prime, pulled every trick in the book, stalling, sweating, yelling at linesmen, kicking water coolers, and launching in on the respected umpire Frank Hammond, who attempted to discipline him but couldn't stop the melee. The Romanian spat obscenities at Hammond—whom he said he liked because he treated players like real people—but the umpire opted to default him.

The drunken crowd erupted, throwing beer cans and cups and garbage on court. "What happened was a threat of a mob take-over, mob violence," the noted British tennis writer Rex Bellamy wrote.

Nastase was defaulted by Hammond, and then an eighteen-minute free-for-all ensued in which Nastase was reinstated by tournament referee Mike Blanchard, who then replaced Hammond on the chair for the remainder of the match. "The crowd wanted his blood and they wanted to see the end of the match," Nastase recalled. After midnight, McEnroe won the match 6–4, 4–6, 6–3, 6–2.

"When the match ended," Mac's father recalled, "I asked my middle son Mark, a strong six-three and in good shape, to go on court and escort John to the locker room. Who knew what some crazy fan might do?"

In the locker room, Nastase invited a stunned McEnroe to dinner; Mac, amazingly, agreed. They went to a local watering hole on Northern Boulevard in Little Neck called Patrick's Pub, where they grabbed a few beers and hamburgers, and even shared a few laughs together. Years later, McEnroe and his new wife, the rocker Patty Smyth, attended Nastase's third wedding.

But there was some collateral damage: Hammond would never be the same. McEnroe's father claims that the match all but ended Hammond's career. He died not long thereafter, some say a dejected man.

"Of all the umpires out there, Frank Hammond was one of the few I liked," John McEnroe Jr. recalled. "I always thought of him as a player's umpire: he knew everyone by name; he treated you like a person. He'd say, 'Come on, John, you're over the edge. I'm going to have to penalize you now unless you pull it together.' I felt he was trying to get me back on track so I could play my best tennis."

That was McEnroe's only serious emotional crisis of the tournament. He received a walkover and retirement in two of his next three matches and blitzed Tom Gorman. Then he had to confront Connors again, this time in the U.S. Open semis.

Mac crushed him 6–3, 6–3, 7–5, winning a battle between two bloodthirsty lefties who both wanted the New York crowds to adore them but hadn't earned their affection yet. They were American gladiators before the TV show of that name was invented. Connors had real trouble returning serve and passing Mac, who anticipated where Connors was going with his passing shots. The artist in him allowed him to mix up the placement speed and spin on his volleys. McEnroe was not a straight-ahead serve-and-volleyer that Connors could easily dissect; he was a slightly crazy one who was difficult to read. "What the hell? He had an off day," said McEnroe. "He hits the ball so flat it has to rise. If I'm at the net I've got it."

"It was only a few years ago that Connors was beating up on Ken Rosewall," said former U.S. Open champ John Newcombe, who was commentating on the match. "Now he's got a young guy putting him in all sorts of trouble."

Interestingly, McEnroe was still exploding inside his head and berating linesmen even though he was clearly in control of a match. "I know I've got a problem," he said. "When I walk out there on court, I become a maniac. . . . Something comes over me, man."

Something came over Borg too, who by all rights should have won the tournament when it was played on clay, but now had to contend with the truer bounces on slick hard courts. Plus, he had to adjust his mind and eyesight for a new phenomenon in Grand Slam play—night tennis, where despite high-powered lights it's never as easy as in the sunshine to pick up zooming balls.

In the quarters, Borg had to face Tanner again, and during the entire fortnight his coach Lennart Bergelin had again complained about the noise, the heat, and the impossibility of night play. He even harried U.S. Open officials before the tournament began, asking that his pupil be declared exempt from nighttime play. "It's not tennis. It's not tennis. Cannot see at night," the Swedish coach complained.

His request was denied and Borg's clash with Tanner was held during prime time. "I imagine that Bjorn felt he was being led to the guillotine—and I was wearing a black hood—as we marched on court on Wednesday night," said Tanner, who added that despite his blinding serve he was no fan of night tennis either, because he had astigmatism. However, he didn't tell anyone because he wanted to maintain a psychological edge over Borg.

Tanner served as hard as he could during the match and blunted Borg's return game. Trying to serve out the match at 5–3 in the fourth set, he hit a serve somewhere in the 140 mph range that nailed the tape and actually caused the net to collapse. It took the grounds crew ten minutes to replace it. Tanner quickly gained a match point, but choked it, careening an overhead into the seats on a straight line. Borg then forced Tanner into a forehand volley error on the southerner's second match point and then broke him with two brilliant passing shots.

But "Hurricane" Tanner, as he was nicknamed during the tournament, stayed cool in the tiebreaker and won it 7–2. The Swede's run was ended decisively past midnight 6–2, 4–6, 6–2, 7–6 (2), as Tanner smoked eleven aces and seventeen service winners. He broke Borg five times, but Fleming believed that it was Bergelin who had already shattered his steed's psyche. "Bergelin psyched out his own guy," Fleming said before the match. "Björn will be negative. I guarantee he'll be out of this tournament."

Tanner believed that he was playing well enough to win his next two matches, against Gerulaitis, whom he outranked, and over McEnroe, who he believed would take out Connors but was still too young to win his first Slam. Fleming thought differently. "Vitas will get to the final," he said. "But McEnroe will be there, and then it will be all over."

Having four Americans reach the semis was enough to give the CBS network a broadcast orgasm. Gerulaitis was more in his element than any of them, as the kid from Howard Beach had the eyes of the world firmly on his beak and that's just the way he liked it.

Gerulaitis was always popular, always the man-about-town, perhaps the best-liked player of his era. Nothing was ever dull, not his transcontinental excursions to nightclubs between tournaments, not his nights before key matches, when he was known to stay up around the clock and then go out and score a win fresh as a daisy. He hung out with the Rolling Stones, and dated supermodels like Janet Jones, who eventually became the wife of hockey star Wayne Gretzky. In 1991 the English rock band Half Man Half Biscuit released a song titled "Outbreak of Vitas Gerulaitis."

Nastase recalled spending nights out with Vitas at Studio 54 in the company of the zany icon of the pop art world, Andy Warhol, whom Nastase grew close to for a time, partly because Warhol was also an Eastern European—he had Slovakian roots—and also because Warhol was a sports fan. Warhol made himself famous painting iconic American products, and Gerulaitis was one of those.

But Nastase, a notorious womanizer, claimed he didn't indulge in hallucinogens like Vitas did.

"I never got really into the whole scene like Vitas did, going there every night, doing drugs, going to each other's apartments afterwards to do more drugs," Nastase said. Tennis was part of popular culture, and Vitas wanted to cross over. The Romanian also remembered going to the designer Halston's opulent Park Avenue home, where he usually encountered an interesting group of partyers. But he claims that he never overdid it, while Gerulaitis took a high dive into the deep end. "I knew my limits very clearly," he said. "Vitas's limits, though, were completely different."

Gerulaitis lived hard and played hard. He was seduced by the glamour and saw it as a rite of passage. As early as 1979 he was appearing in Warhol's diaries as a sidekick at Studio 54 and Xenon. By this time, Gerulaitis, Warhol noted, had taken to "wearing his gold coke-cutter razor blade around his neck during matches."

McEnroe recounted that he was initiated into drug-taking by Gerulaitis, but was much less of a party animal than his friend, and when he was hanging out with Keith Richards or Jack Nicholson he felt a constant sense of guilt and exhilaration that was all mixed up. "You could be out with these guys, and you'd be having a wonderful time and you'd constantly be thinking you had to get your head back to the tennis. . . . I'd like to think I'm an athlete at heart, and I knew you can't burn both ends of the candle. You realize pretty quickly that it is going to interfere with things. . . . I don't know if it's being brought up a Catholic. In a sense you feel as though you are doing something wrong."

To some degree though, Mac was sucked in by Vitas's personality. "In terms of drive, talent, and charisma, Vitas was clearly a star. Even early on, when people used to joke, 'Vitas Gerulaitis—what is that, a disease?' it looked as though he was going to be tremendously famous. I admired him like crazy, but he wouldn't give me the time of day when I was fourteen or fifteen, and why should he?"

Writer Pete Bodo, who hung out with Gerulaitis at times, described him as "frank and accessible, but with a hunger for stardom that makes him seem vain and self-absorbed. He's materialistic as only an immigrant's child can be and his taste for the finest cars, expensive boots and budding starlets is flushed with the innocence of a hungry child in a sweatshop."

Despite his questionable off-court habits, Vitas could still play well, and in 1979 his youthful body was of Superman quality, regardless of what he was ingesting. He did not have a money shot, a killer shot, a major weapon as they say today, but he was fast and dogged in his pursuit of balls. He owned lightning-quick reflexes and was a good thinker. He was a risk-taker and would follow serves and even weak approach shots to the net, believing that by forcing the action he could coax his opponents into committing errors.

He was a close friend of Borg's, whom he would end his career 0–16 against. While he was a decent friend of McEnroe's, their relationship was still evolving. "We aren't very alike, or close. Studio 54 is Gerulaitis's place. I'm a McDonald's guy," McEnroe said during the event.

But Vitas kept his boogie nights in check during the U.S. Open and in the semis pulled off one of his greatest comebacks ever. He dropped the first two sets to Tanner 6–3, 6–2, completely overpowered, but began to will himself back into the match. Early in the third set, after a bad call, he smacked a ball at the baseline judge and missed, striking a female fan. "Excuse me," Vitas said to the spectator, "I was aiming at this asshole." He pulled out the third-set tiebreaker and then wore down Tanner 3–6, 2–6, 7–6, 6–3, 6–3. "It was my most devastating defeat," Tanner said.

For the first time, two guys in tight shorts and frayed headbands from just around the block and a few subway stations over had reached the U.S. Open final. But they weren't as beloved as Borg or Connors, two known quantities.

"They hate us," Gerulaitis said. "Popularity-wise, I'm a notch above John, and John is a notch above Son of Sam."

McEnroe added, "It isn't every day that two players who live ten minutes from the Open reach the final. New Yorkers should appreciate this. It may never happen again."

The final wasn't even close, as McEnroe served and volleyed and chipped and charged one of his boyhood idols off the court 7–5, 6–3, 6–3. He threw in every shot he had learned at the Port Washington backcourts, plus another hundred or so around the cords that he had learned at Stanford and on the tour. He kept Vitas guessing and was no longer the kid who had to follow the neighborhood star around. He won five service games at love, four others at 15. It was a good old-fashioned Queens-style butt-kicking.

"This is the best feeling I ever had in tennis. I volleyed well in the clutch," McEnroe said.

At age twenty years and six months, he had become the youngest champ since Pancho Gonzalez in 1948 and won his local and most important crown. He was the king of New York and the world. But his first Slam title felt strange. "For a couple of years, I'd been working to hang out with Vitas, wondering if I could keep up with him off court. I'd been trying to be his friend. I looked up to him. And now that I'd blown by him, the victory felt hollow. I had taken something from him. He was still a legitimate number four in the world, but now he was off the mountaintop. Now it was Borg, Connors, and me. Things were never quite the same between Vitas and me after that."

As good as Fleming and McEnroe were together on court, things were still a bit testy between them, even though they won the U.S. Open doubles, crushing Smith and Lutz in the final. A large portion of the New Jersey native's heart was still with his girlfriend, Jenny, and for all his success with McEnroe in doubles, his career pursuits didn't quite fulfill him.

Mac had tremendous respect for Fleming's spirit and was generous in complimenting him. He thoroughly rejected Fleming's famous remark that the greatest doubles team in history was "John McEnroe and anyone."

"The second he gave that answer I turned to him and said, 'What are you saying? That's not true,'" McEnroe recalled. "And I meant that from the bottom of my heart. I was really shocked how wrong that was."

Mac believed that in singles, Fleming didn't have the same merciless focus that he needed to be a top 5 player and lacked McEnroe's own take-no-prisoners attitude. Fellow American player Victor Amaya agreed. "Flem is one of the few guys out here who on a good day can manhandle anybody around—Björn, Jimbo, anybody. He can streak-return a guy off the court. He can serve a couple of aces every game, and then airmail a couple of winning returns a game. I've seen him beat guys in forty minutes. Wham. It's over. When he's on, he's awesome. Then I've seen him go totally in the dumper."

Mac took that same attitude on court against friends and even family. His brother Patrick, who just ended an eleven-year run as the U.S. Davis Cup captain, said that John always wanted his friends to win, just not against him. "He was great with me, but when we played, I was just another opponent," Patrick said. "When he gets on court his temper can get worse, but that's what makes him great because he was so passionate and driven. When I played him in Basel, he beat the crap out of me and gave me a staredown because he thought maybe I could beat him, and I was shaking in my boots."

Perhaps more than any other man on tour, Sandy Mayer resented McEnroe. Some think it's because they were of similar ability and Mayer could never achieve what McEnroe did, and unquestionably they were both type-A personalities. But Mayer, who was seven years older, made it his business to get in McEnroe's face, as he felt the New Yorker disrespected the game and, to some degree, most opponents. Mayer never beat McEnroe in 11 matches, but four of them were well-contested three-set matches and one went to four sets.

"Half the matches he killed me, half the matches that were tight he basically cheated me out of them," said Mayer. "I have absolutely no respect for the game that allowed him to do it. I can't tell you how many times I was threatened with defaults because I went to the umpire and said there was a thirty-second rule and I'm timing how long he's taking and we are going to a minute to a minute and a half. If you can't control the match, then get out of the chair. Then the umpire would say to me, 'I'm going to fine you for unsports-manlike conduct for talking like that.'"

Mayer pulls no punches when he says that Mac won numerous contests by gamesmanship, using every trick in the book to mentally tweak his foes. "The most benevolent thing I could say about John in a strange way is that I think he got into a shtick that worked for him, and then he got good, and there's always latitude given to top players and there shouldn't be. He realizes, 'This works, when I control the match and slow it down.' So did Connors at times, but Mac could take three minutes. I played him in L.A. one time [a 6–7, 6–3, 6–3 win for Mac in 1981] and Johnny Carson was sitting in the stands. . . . I was beating him badly, up a set and break, and he went off for the next thirty minutes and my back got so stiff I couldn't hit a serve. I was so ice cold."

During the summer of 1979 at the grasscourt event at Queen's in London, when McEnroe beat him 3–6, 6–2, 6–4 in the quarter-finals, Mayer was incensed at his foe's tactics. "I said you should be banned and I said a player like you should be banned. I was talking about the game and you are the vehicle."

An attacking player, Mayer quickly found out that he had met his match at the net. McEnroe was quick, could cover the cords and put away a volley. Plus, he was a resourceful defender from the base-line. "When you attack the net on a consistent basis it's 50 percent bluff," said Mayer, who would win 11 singles titles and reach a career high ranking of No. 7 in 1982. "You come in against Nastase and Stan Smith on their backhands and they couldn't pass you one in ten times. Mac was fantastic because he knew that just because you are down in the point doesn't mean you are going to lose it. Just because he's taking a beating, he knew how to hang in there. It wasn't difficult to get on top of him, but he'd find a way back in points. And at net, he had very quick hands and good timing and closed so well. He could come in on a bluff and it would work."

Mayer recalled a time at Forest Hills, after the U.S. Open had left but they were still running a pro tournament, that he and his brother Gene fell to McEnroe and Fleming in doubles. It wasn't a contest of gentlemanly gestures, as McEnroe was stalling and Sandy got into his face. "I asked him to stop quietly from across the court and then he would say something to me and then I said, 'Now you know why everybody in this stadium knows you are the biggest jerk to ever play in the history of tennis,' and I got a standing ovation. But nothing worked. It was cheating, but the game didn't enforce the rules. The fact that he now makes money on TV off his bad-boy image and saying he was somewhat sorry is a testament to today's world, because he was a flat-out cheat."

For all his complaining about McEnroe—and Mayer brought his opinions to the highest levels of the game—Mayer rarely approached him off court, although after that contest in Forest Hills, McEnroe came at him in the locker room, in the attic of the facility. "He came at me yelling. He said, 'You think my girlfriend and my parents like to read that stuff? Who do you think you are?' I said, 'Let's start with whether it's true, and then I'll explain, because guys are trying to get some justice.'"

"Finally he said, 'I don't give a damn what you think or anyone else thinks.' I said, 'Therein lies your problem. You started by saying you didn't want your girlfriend or parents to read this, and then concluded by saying you don't care what anyone thinks and you contradicted yourself.'"

Like some other players, Mayer felt that McEnroe wanted to own the locker room, which is supposed to be a common space. John's brother Patrick went so far as to call him combustible. "John liked to strut around, scowling, his body language demanding that you give him a wide berth," Patrick McEnroe wrote in his book, *Hardcourt Confidential*. "That could be intimidating."

Somewhat amazingly, Mayer claims that he and McEnroe had a few limited but very good conversations, despite Mayer's consistent emphasis on how McEnroe's antics were ruining the game.

"I was on a crusade to bring this guy down only as it pertained to the matches I thought I should have won. . . . I thought it was a bad stain on the game. Unlike Nastase, who really was out of control when he lost it, Mac was in complete control. He told Bill

Scanlon at the U.S. Open, 'Who do you think you are? You're not even supposed to be on the same court as me.' He was immature. You don't tell another sportsman that. He was so embarrassed by potential bad results that he resorted to something that was antithetical to all sports, which was, 'I don't lose because I'm Johnny Mac and you're Bill Scanlon.' . . . Johnny Mac would not have been nearly the player that he was if the rules were applied."

With all that said, Mayer believes that McEnroe was one of the best ever, regardless of titles, saying that he could change the direction of the ball better than anyone and had absolutely no limits. While many players know exactly which shot they have to employ at a particular time, most of them don't have the sense, hands, or technical proficiency to pull it off. Mac did.

"The thing that was so remarkable about John was that he could play angles without spin, he could play flat balls slow, he could put spin on the ball and control it, and his ability to absorb pace was incredible. He was remarkably gifted and talented and most times was able to keep his head in points and come up with innovative solutions. I put Gene and John in the same category when it comes to confidence, because they didn't know how not to do anything. They never felt uncomfortable, because if they needed to hit a shot they could think and react beyond belief. Other than that, I think he was emotionally a wreck, but he very much underplays his accomplishments and was one of the best in history."

Some twenty-seven years after they played their last match in 1983, Mayer, a renowned teaching pro in Northern California, is still seething, but says he doesn't dislike McEnroe. "He took advantage of a situation that was there. He probably understands that he needs to go to every player of his era, like he went to that German linesman in that American Express ad, and apologize. I'd have no problem having a beer with him, but I can't separate the fact that my pro career was affected by someone who was pulling that stuff."

A few weeks after the 1979 U.S. Open, Mac and Fleming met in the final of Los Angeles and the taller man was triumphant— the last time he would ever beat his friend in singles. "That was undoubtedly the highlight of my career," Fleming recalled. "He had sprained his ankle and wasn't moving too great, but that was probably the best match I ever played. Sadly, it wasn't an especially friendly match. We squabbled on court a few times over the years."

They would also exchange words in a tournament in Jamaica over a line call, where Fleming shouted, "Just because I'm your friend doesn't mean I'm the Salvation Army."

After Fleming's win in L.A., they met in the San Francisco final, and Mac came through with a victory. At that point, Fleming was playing well enough in singles to make some think that if he kept up that level the doubles partnership would never last.

"Listen," said McEnroe, "we've heard all that before. [Frew] McMillan predicted once that Peter and I had too similar personalities to last long. Where is he now? We both won over $150,000 last year in doubles. We win two-thirds of the matches without trying, for godsakes. We blasé a doubles match and still win. We blasé whole tournaments and still win. We're gonna give all this up? What are we, crazy?"

Not so much. Neither was Borg, who didn't play Stockholm, while Mac did, edging Gene Mayer in the final. McEnroe then went on to win Wembley, England, over Harold Solomon before taking a loss in Bologna to Butch Walts.

Borg traveled elsewhere, leading Sweden to a Davis Cup World Group qualifying win, taking the title in Palermo, and stomping Connors in Tokyo and then at the WCT Challenge Cup in Canada. His season was complete and he wouldn't have to face McEnroe again until January.

But the New Yorker had one more fish to fry in the Davis Cup final against Italy in San Francisco, where he won his 28th straight set in a 5–0 whitewash. "If the U.S. would play its fourth or fifth team this time, it would win," said Italy's Paolo Bertolucci.

In the first match, Gerulaitis ran over the injured "Il Soldatino" Corrado Barazzutti, a competitor known for his constant complaining. "Corrado doesn't think he can win on this surface," McEnroe said of the quick hard court. "I think Corrado is accurate, Junior," Gerulaitis replied.

In the second match, Mac had to face the colorful yet slowing Panatta, who was overwhelmed by the American's relentless net rushing and sleight-of-hand changes of pace. "It was my best match indoors," said Panatta in disbelief after his 6–2, 6–3, 6–4 defeat. Smith and Lutz then wrapped up the tie over Bertolucci and Panatta in a 6–4, 12–10, 6–2 victory. It would be Smith and Lutz's last as a the United States Davis Cup doubles pairing, as captain Tony Trabert had invited Fleming to join the squad for the next season to pair with McEnroe.

Trabert no longer felt that that he needed Connors to lead the U.S. squad, as he was comfortable with displaying McEnroe's scowling mug as the face of American tennis in international competition. McEnroe was here to stay, ending the year with 26 titles (10 singles, 16 doubles) and another Davis Cup crown. "He's the new phenomenon of tennis," Panatta said. But that phenom had yet to face Borg at a Grand Slam, and until he did and beat him, the Swede would be the most recognizable and admired face on the tennis planet.

16

Love and Sets

Björn Borg had ruled over London on four occasions, but he had never taken a substantial bite out of the Big Apple. When the world's best arrived at Madison Square Garden in January 1980 for the Masters, the first so-called mini–Super Bowl of the year between the top eight men in the sport, it was cold. In bundled-up Manhattan, the winds whipped down Fifth Avenue and folks huddled up near the railroad and subway tracks in Penn Station, which supports the massive weight of Madison Square Garden on its shoulders.

The 1980s would later become known as the "Me Decade," but at the outset of the ten-year period there was more sharing of grief than celebration of individual spirit. Little seemed to be working in either the Western or Eastern worlds, and the cold war took off again just as the year turned, with the late December 1979 Soviet invasion of Afghanistan.

U.S. president Jimmy Carter was furious, calling it the most serious threat to peace since the Second World War, but he could do little outside of placing a trade embargo on America's enemy, which it wasn't trading with much anyway. Carter had been funding covert operations against the Afghan communist regime since the summer of 1979, but at the time he didn't admit it publicly. His national security adviser, Zbigniew Brzezinski, later admitted, "We didn't push the Russians to intervene, but we knowingly increased the probability that they would. . . . The day that the Soviets officially crossed the border, I wrote to President Carter, 'We now have the opportunity of giving to the Soviet Union its Vietnam War.'"

January 1, 1980, opened with the fifty-seventh day of the Iran hostage crisis, and no one—not Carter, not Khomeini, not the hard-charging Ronald Reagan—knew it would last 385 more days. It was a miserable year of impotence for Americans, as they watched their countrymen held hostage while one attempt after another at securing their release failed. Inflation was out of control, unemployment was rising, and up-and-coming Japan passed the mighty United States as the largest automaker. In February, the FBI's undercover operation "Abscam" implicated key public officials in taking bribes. In April, Florida was overwhelmed by Cuban refugees. The next month, Mount St. Helens erupted in the state of Washington, the worst volcanic disaster in U.S. history. Then in June, a controversial law requiring draft registration for men eighteen and older came into effect, while wars raged in Central America.

During the summer, many folks in the United States were forced to crank up their air conditioners as a devastating heat wave struck the nation, claiming seventeen hundred lives and causing havoc in the agricultural sector totaling some $44 billion dollars in damage.

Björn Borg's Sweden was also going through changes as its social welfare economy began to disintegrate following the oil crisis of 1973. In 1976, after forty years of Social Democratic rule, the center-right Farmers' Party came into power and attempted to cut taxes and subsidies. Labor strongly objected, and on May 2, 1980, just before Borg went out and won his fifth French Open title, more than 700,000 Swedish workers were locked out by their employers, and a general strike ensued that paralyzed the nation for ten days.

Sweden's number one athlete-celebrity, Borg—who had escaped to Monte Carlo and was largely untouched by Sweden's economic woes—was none too pleased that he had fallen to Tanner at the U.S. Open some four months prior to the Grand Prix Masters at Madison Square Garden, but he was still the reigning French Open and Wimbledon champion entering the year, and, holding two 1979 majors in his pocket, was considered the world's best player, despite McEnroe's U.S. Open heroics and obviously rising form.

The streets of Manhattan were alive those days with tennis interest, and the crowds packed in to see not only the searing Swede but also its two homeboys, McEnroe and Gerulaitis, as well as gritty Connors and shaggy-haired Vilas. But it was the supermotivated Borg who sent out a signal that he was not willing to concede his king's scepter to anyone, not even briefly to his close friend Gerulaitis, who played one of the best tournaments of his life, just twenty blocks or so from the nightclub where he frequently held court, Studio 54.

The indoor court was playing very fast, so quick that after Vilas was outstroked in three sets in his opening round-robin match, the former U.S. Open champion (albeit on clay) said, "The Masters court gets faster every year. If I keep qualifying, someday I'll play the Masters on glass."

Borg knew he had to serve big, and this time, with the Garden lights cranked up to their capacity, he didn't have as much trouble returning Tanner's serve and scalded the Tennessee native 6–3, 6–3. McEnroe then gave his boyhood idol Gerulaitis hope in their section of the round robin by wasting Vilas in a match where he fell to the court chasing down a drop shot and banged his head hard. "Actually, that's the best part of me to hit," he said with a wry smile.

Borg then went out to face Connors, whom he had beaten six straight times. Connors had spent the off-season slimming down his already thin frame and said that he was in the best shape of his life, content that he and his wife Patti's new son, Brett, had taught him to be more patient. He also played more freely and attacked more, not allowing himself to get too caught up in monotonous rallies from the backcourt. The American brought the match to a third-set tiebreaker, but chucked in a few errors, while Borg played cleanly and walked away the victor once again. "I'm not out of this thing yet," Connors said, and somehow the next day he survived Tanner 2–6, 6–4, 7–6. He would await the winner of the semifinal contest between McEnroe and Gerulaitis, who contested their match on a hot-blooded Friday night.

McEnroe was tired, having won a doubles match with Fleming the previous evening that ended at 2 a.m. He was irritable and spent the night missing negotiable shots, yelling at officials, making ugly faces, and throwing his racket. It didn't matter that prior to the contest he had won seven straight sets from the Disco King Vitas.

Mac saved a match point in the second-set tiebreaker, but Gerulaitis served huge and eventually won the contest 7–4 in the third-set tiebreak. Mac was pissed off as, once again in Manhattan, Gerulaitis had shown his A-list credentials while Mac was left standing at the stage door. "John has got a lot more talent than I have," Gerulaitis said, "but now he doesn't own New York anymore. I got some of the Bronx back."

Those who knew Gerulaitis not only talked about him as being the life of the party, but a common thread that could pull all of humankind together. Two-time U.S. Open champion Tracy Austin, who won her first U.S. Open the year prior, said he was one of the nicest, most genuine men she ever met. "He connected with everyone from the janitor all the way up to a top businessman. He had a good heart and could find the good in everyone. People gravitated to him because he was so likable, so unselfish, so giving."

Former touring pro Ricky Meyer, a close friend of Gerulaitis's, told New York–based writer Cindy Schmerler that "of all the people I met in my life, I would say that Vitas was akin to Bill Clinton in terms of having this aura of energy and charisma that's unmatched by anyone else. You could feel it the minute he walked into a room. He was like the Pied Piper and there wasn't anything he tried to do. Everyone wanted to be around him. Connors, McEnroe, and Borg didn't have it and you couldn't create it if you didn't have one. Vitas had it."

Borg was much of the same mind-set, knowing that his great friend was the pilot in social situations and he was very much the calm and cool wingman. "When there were people in a room, you could always see and hear Vitas. He brought people to him. If someone had a problem, he helped. He would give rackets away, money, whatever it took."

Vitas's sister, Ruta, who had a decent pro career, put it bluntly: "He was the life of the party."

Mary Carillo recalled that when Gerulaitis played World Team Tennis for the New York Apples, he would consistently take the biggest bite of the forbidden fruit. One night, playing in Pittsburgh, Gerulaitis announced to the crowd that the party was on him and invited everyone back to his hotel room. He had to pay the beaten-up hotel for the replacement of the carpet and bathtub.

He was certainly the quintessential man-about-town and was never shy in picking up new dates. Chris Evert, who dated him in 1975, told Schmerler that one night, while they were sitting together at a disco in the city, a woman kept making eye contact with Gerulaitis, who told Evert that he must have dated the woman, but couldn't recall her name. "Then we realized it wasn't a woman at all, it was a transvestite who just wanted to meet him. . . . He was the most fun person to be around."

McEnroe gravitated toward Gerulaitis too, but they did not have the same temperament. McEnroe was a quintessential Irish-American brawler, brought up to throw a left hook if someone bloodied his nose with a right cross. Even though he and Gerulaitis would briefly fall out in later years, at the time McEnroe still itched to be included in his circle. The combination of being around the coolest kid in the area, Vitas, and the tennis god whose posters had adorned his wall, Borg, was too much to resist. "Borg and Gerulaitis had, shall we say, perfected the art of enjoying the fruits of tennis. They traveled together, practiced together, and then they had fun," McEnroe recalled.

McEnroe also had his amusing moments, but not on that cold 1980 evening in New York against Gerulaitis, when he couldn't cool himself off. There are many different ways to view why McEnroe went ballistic on court, but his varying degrees of temper and explosion were certainly the result of many factors. Tennis pro and sports psychologist Allen Fox saw the scowling Mac as a product of the evolutionary cycle, "a natural warrior." Call him a stern-faced, prey-seeking Cro-McEnroe Man. Some fled when the saber-toothed tigers approached, whereas McEnroe stayed and fought.

But why was McEnroe more of an alpha male than others? Every player who makes it to the pro tour likes to fight at some level. If they had failed to do so in every one of their thousands of skirmishes prior to making it as pros, they never would have gotten even close to earning a paycheck as pro tennis players. The sport does not tolerate weak-kneed men who aren't willing to wrestle with their foes until they are pinned to the floor. There are too many rickety ladders to climb, and every tennis player in the 1970s scaled one or another.

For a book he wrote, Fox sat down a bunch of 1970s pros for personality tests, and what stuck out the most were the aggressive, antagonistic, and suspicious types. McEnroe was one, Fox himself was another, and Connors, Pancho Gonzalez, and one of Mac's later nemeses, Brad Gilbert, who went on to coach Andre Agassi, Andy Roddick, and Andy Murray, also fit into the same category.

The icy Borg did not fit that stereotype, but what he did have in common with the other two members of the Big Three was that they were much more comfortable mixing with a small circle of friends and confidants than in large groups, as their friend Gerulaitis liked to do. As Fox pointed out, Borg, Mac, and Connors weeded out those people they didn't trust and kept close those folks who stood by them.

"They love their friends and are very loyal to them and they don't like their enemies—they don't like their enemies a lot," Fox said. "It's very useful on court because the other guys are trying to wrestle you down. The great players have enough inside to be able to keep fighting because they didn't want to yield."

Another preeminent sports psychologist, Dr. Jim Loehr, who has counseled dozens of top tennis players, went a little deeper, and while agreeing with Fox, said that McEnroe's use of temper was a learned behavior. McEnroe's father and mother would talk to him time and time again about his explosions, and John would concede time and time again that they were right; he could win without losing his temper. He would promise not to explode again, but a week later he would end up cursing a shivering linesperson up and down.

"This can happen to almost anyone, but in John's case he started playing and found out like everyone else does that he played terrible when he got nervous, and like everyone does, he hated getting nervous," Loehr said. "The chemistry of nerves comes from fight or flight and the species was designed to either get aggressive and attack, or . . . you got so afraid that you froze because predators picked up movement, or you just ran away as fast as you could. Nature was very exquisite in its ability to move you one way or another, and you can never do both. . . . Mac learned quickly as a junior that when his temper surfaces and brings the raging bull to the front, he learned unconsciously that it would chase nerves away. He began to develop a routine that when he would sputter, he would allow rage to surface and then it would quiet his nerves."

What many folks forget about McEnroe as they become so absorbed in watching his tantrums is how long he would take to prepare for points. Loehr believed he used that ritual to soothe himself after his nerves had disappeared. There was more work to do.

"The task is to learn to get rid of the chemicals that are associated with rage, so he would take more time, as opposed to others who would usually rush, he would walk back and forth. But very rarely did he attack himself. He was always fighting an enemy outside. Most athletes fight themselves, so he almost never had to fight two enemies. He always projected to a linesman or a ball boy or whatever. He'd get angry and cuss and swear then get into these long rituals before he would serve or return, and then he'd enter into his ideal performance state. Then it became his signature and he realized that he couldn't play without that and it was the only way to perform the best."

So it was in the Gerulaitis contest at the Garden—and many other times before or after that against lesser players—that McEnroe lost his cool, because by 1980 he knew he was a better player than Vitas and would feel awful if he lost.

"You very rarely get nerves when you play someone who you are better than," Loehr explained. "If you are playing someone better, or an equal, he didn't have as many explosions. When Borg and Mac played he virtually never got angry because he almost never had nerves. He was picture perfect. Nerves only come up when you have to play someone you have less respect for and you feel like an idiot and when nerves come up he would go AWOL. It became habitual and even today at age fifty-one on the seniors tour when everyone else is having a great time, he's throwing F-bombs around and can't figure out why the same patterns are occurring. This is survival-based, but it's also learned behavior. If he was taught early on to be another way, maybe he wouldn't have ended up that way."

Not only did Gerulaitis take a portion of the Bronx back in his win over McEnroe, but he earned a large portion of Illinois too, stunning Belleville native Connors 7–5, 6–2 in the semis. Jimbo was as flat as the island he stood on. "I had no zip," he said.

But Gerulaitis did, in his step and with his serve and groundstrokes. He had broken a 16-straight-match losing streak to Connors and uttered these immortal words: "Nobody beats me 17 straight."

A reporter then asked Gerulaitis whether he felt that he had entered the circle of the Big Three: Borg, McEnroe, and Connors. He begged to differ about the choice of the numeral. "I've always had this potential," he said, "but there aren't three. There are the rest of us. Then there's Björn."

Borg and Mac then met again in the round-robin tournament, and the big joint shook with anticipation. The thought then was that the Borg vs. Johnny Mac contest would be just one of many classics between the two during the next five years or so. No one in the building knew that they had to savor every last drop, as they would only compete against each other for another two years.

John McEnroe Sr., who observed the match, said that the rivals were like day and night. "Fire and ice, the stoic Swede against the crazy American. But John had enormous respect for him and never raised an issue when he played him."

Loehr attributes that to McEnroe's inner knowledge that if he lost to Borg, whom he considered the world's best, he wouldn't feel too badly about his own self-worth. But the way they went about contending with their emotions was vastly different.

"Borg's parents taught him early by taking tennis away from him when he lost his temper [so] that he learned to adapt to pressure in a different way that is oppositional to how Mac is, but they both accomplished the same thing—they kept their levels of cortisol [which is known as the stress hormone] below a certain point because you can't perform when it gets too high," Loehr said. "Borg loved it when his opponents went nuts because his foes would go crazy and he was unflappable and they would be thinking, 'What do you have to do to get this guy to look dejected? He's down 0–5 in the second set and he looks the same as when he was up 5–0.'"

As a result of his stoic demeanor, Borg was often termed as emotionless, a description that hurt him, not that he told anyone at the time. "It was just that I never showed my emotions and feelings when anyone was watching," the Swede said. "I would often let it out behind closed doors. I would go back to my hotel and scream and shout at my coach or my girlfriend at the time. I was often angry, and shouting at them, but they just stood there and took it. Lennart knew I had to get my emotions out and that it wasn't personal. . . . I wasn't as cool or calm as spectators thought."

Not only did Johnny Mac rarely lose his temper against Borg, but the one time that Borg did throw a bit of a fit during one of their matches—the very next year at the Garden in a three-set win for Borg—Mac was confounded, as was every other pro who observed the match. It's considered Borg's most notable fit, and for all intents and purposes, how he displayed his anger was to give the chair umpire the silent treatment.

In that match in 1981, Borg won the first set 6–4, and then came from behind in the second to serve for the match at 6–5. But McEnroe caressed a gorgeous lob and a drop volley to bring the set to a tiebreaker. At 3–3 in the tiebreaker, Borg's forehand pass was called good by the linesman, but umpire Mike Lugg, a stiff Englishman, overruled him, giving McEnroe the point and a 4–3 lead. Borg frowned, strolled to the chair, and disputed the overrule.

The crowd booed and whistled while, with left hand on hip, Borg demanded that Lugg—who was wearing a Fila sweater that matched Borg's attire—ask the linesman about the call. Lugg refused, told Borg to continue play, and put the thirty-second clock on him. Borg wouldn't move and Lugg awarded a delay-of-game penalty point to McEnroe. "I couldn't believe it," McEnroe said. "Just imagine what the crowd would have done to me in that situation."

Dick Roberson, the chief supervisor, came out to talk to Borg, but the Swede didn't move. Fellow pro Johan Kriek of South Africa recalls, "He just stood there and stared until a dead silence descended. It was about as passive-aggressive as you can get."

Lugg, a bit of a cad who sported a handlebar mustache, gave him a second penalty point and Borg was close to being defaulted. Then Borg looked for a piece of advice from Bergelin, who signaled that he should play on. "I was very mad, very disappointed," Borg said.

Down 6–3 in the tiebreaker, Borg flew a ball out to lose the set. In the third set after a bad call on Borg, McEnroe purposely nailed a ball into the crowd to give Borg a point back. The Swede regained control and went on to win. "John had enormous respect for him," his father said. "Borg went semi-ballistic that night, and actually for him, he went totally ballistic. John was astounded that night."

In 1980 at the Garden, there would be no awful overrules by the chair umpire in what was a delicious match. McEnroe climbed all over the net and won the first-set tiebreaker 7–5 with a sure-handed volley, but Borg kept coming, knowing that on a slick indoor surface he'd have to get on top of the ball, play closer to the net, make sure that his passing shots were true, and get as many balls in play as possible. Moreover, he decided to lob when he got a chance, to ensure that McEnroe wouldn't feel comfortable crowding the net. McEnroe would smile at times at the brilliance of his opponent's shotmaking, but in the final tiebreaker, McEnroe couldn't convert a few key volleys and fell 6–7, 6–3, 7–6.

"We made a great yin and yang," McEnroe recalled of the time period. "The contrast in styles was incredible. He was the first guy who took me under his wing and accepted me and showed me respect. It's pretty dog-eat-dog out there and to have the best guy in the world do that was an enormous boost to my confidence, and also that I was feeling that I belonged because a veteran would allow me into his small circle. . . . I could shut some other people up who were giving me a hard time, because if Borg was behind me, then it was like, 'The hell with everyone else.'"

In the final, Gerulaitis again had no answers for his practice partner Borg, who adeptly picked on all his weaknesses and was able to play to his own strengths in a 6–2, 6–2 victory. "Vitas was too human," said his friend Mel DiGiacomo. "That's why he couldn't beat Borg. In practice, he'd crush him."

Gerulaitis's onetime coach, former top-5 player Fred Stolle, added, "You play the cards you are given and you are who you are. Vitas wanted to be the nice guy."

Borg had never won the U.S. Open, but now after his win at the Garden, he poked a large notch in his belt and threw on a buckle that blared "NYC." "My career was not missing anything, but I put this title very, very high," he said in defiance.

Mac then traveled to Philadelphia, where he lost a vintage five-set final to Connors. The over-the-top Philly fans were all over the younger American, even cheering his double faults. McEnroe then won Richmond over Tanner, beat Mexico's Ramírez in the Davis Cup on clay, but lost to Gerulaitis again, this time at the Pepsi, which of course was won by Borg over the head-shaking Vitas.

Mac took out Connors in the Memphis final on carpet, and then had to travel with the Davis Cup team to play Argentina in Buenos

Aires. The tie, the Americas Inter-Zonal Final, featured four members of the world top 10, not a common occurrence in the Davis
Cup. There had been talk that Argentina might not consent to playing in the United States, because there were still residual anti-
American feelings from U.S. support of Britain in the Falklands/
Malvinas war. By then, however, many Argentine citizens had redirected their negative feelings against the incompetent and overly
aggressive military junta that had invaded the sheep-filled islands and
so quickly lost the conflict. Plus, playing America at home on soft
spongy clay gave the host nation a much greater shot at victory than
confronting the United States' top serve-and-volleyers on a fast court.

An extremely popular player, Argentine star Guillermo Vilas had
been arguing with his federation about his waning Davis Cup commitment, and, like Jimmy Connors, he spoke of the conflict for a
man who was used to competing day in and day out in an individual sport and then is asked to sacrifice all in a team competition for
the motherland. "All those people you meet in Davis Cup tell you
that you have to win because you're representing your country. People talk about a team. But when you get out there, you're all alone
between four lines, with only the ball. Then it's just you. A team is
not a marriage."

Vilas buried Gene Mayer 6–3, 6–3, 6–4 in the opening match,
and then McEnroe and José Luis Clerc took the court under a hot
sun. Mac complained frequently to captain Arthur Ashe that he
didn't have the right feel for the ball on that day, but nonetheless he
scratched and clawed and even mixed in some serve and volley
against his fleet and steady foe on dirt. After four hours, the match
stood at 6–4, 6–0, 3–6, 4–6, 5–2 for Clerc, before it was called for
darkness.

McEnroe came out on fire the next day and tied the fifth set at
5–5, but then lost the next two games and the match with indecisive
play. He and Fleming won the doubles 2–6, 10–8, 6–1, 3–6, 6–1,
but on Sunday he was pooped, easily going down in straight sets to
Vilas. Mac had won 11 straight Davis Cup singles matches going
into the tie and wasn't thrilled with losing two straight matches, but

the odds were clearly stacked against him on a surface where he couldn't shorten the points quickly enough. "In the long run the Buenos Aires situation probably did me good," he said. "I've had a few problems [including an ankle injury], but to give yourself excuses is the wrong approach."

Mac couldn't get enough tennis, winning Milan over Amritraj, losing to Vilas on clay in Monte Carlo, and then to the little backboard Harold Solomon in Las Vegas just before many of the sport's top men headed to Dallas for the WCT Championships—a mini–Super Bowl number two for the circuit's top eight points earners.

Lamar Hunt had moved his event out of the smaller Moody Coliseum on the Southern Methodist University campus and into the new Reunion Arena downtown. He wanted to jazz things up, as his circuit was losing the war to the Grand Prix. Borg didn't show, but Connors did for the WCT finale. The new dad Connors wanted back the mantle of being the best American, and while he didn't quite claim that accolade, he looked to be back in contention after besting his younger rival 2–6, 7–6, 6–1, 6–2 in the final, the third time he had defeated McEnroe in four meetings in 1980.

"I don't want to hear about number two," Connors said after he bullied his foe from the baseline. "I realized I could return his stuff. I waited for my exact shot. Then I took chances. Right away I lifted my game. I'm not exactly going into retreat formation. I was gnawing and clawing out there. Mac wanted to know what I was like in my prime. Well . . ."

While Connors felt his best stuff was returning, his level was nowhere close to that of Borg, whose business as usual that spring was the stuff of legends. He won the WCT Invitational exhibition in Salisbury, Maryland, over Connors and Amritraj, helped Sweden to a Davis Cup victory over Germany, and then easily won Nice, Monte Carlo, and Las Vegas, where in those three finals he remarkably lost only ten games in eight sets (two of the finals were three-out-of-five sets) to Orantes, Vilas, and Solomon.

His great victory at Madison Square Garden did his confidence a world of good, because he seemed to be lapping the field.

He took one loss—at the Nations Cup over Vilas—and skipped the Italian Open to prepare for another thunderous assault on the French Open. He had won thirty-two of thirty-three matches entering Roland Garros. None of his claycourt rivals, if they can even be called that, thought they had any real chance against him. "I don't know why anyone bothers," said Victor Amaya. "For most of us, Paris is a great tournament because of the city, the food, the Continental experience, the romantic trip with our wife or girlfriend. But some people don't realize this is the Borg Invitational. They think they can actually win the thing. What a joke."

Amaya was spot on. In Paris, Borg didn't lose a set, crushing Barazzutti (who opined that they should have two separate tournaments, one for Borg and one for the rest of the field), Solomon, and finally Gerulaitis in the final 6–4, 6–1, 6–2. He was never under a real threat, because he was too quick and struck the ball too deeply and with too much heavy topspin to allow foes to consistently try and shorten the court against him. "At Wimbledon it's very gambling," Borg said. "Here it is much more tiring. No cheap points. I have to work so very hard."

Borg's popularity continued to grow; the facility was full of shopkeepers hawking his attire, his face, and his image. By then, even though in some circles he was known as "Boring Borg," he was rolling in dough.

"In Paris, he was a player to be admired and respected not be enjoyed," wrote the notable British tennis journalist Rex Bellamy. "Cold blooded efficiency tends to lack charm."

But not all fans had their rose-colored glasses stained by watching too many of Borg's endless crosscourt rallies. The sports agency IMG and its CEO, Mark McCormack, who had made fortunes for golf legend Arnold Palmer, marketed their Swedish god to the hilt. Observed the Swedish player Anders Jarryd, "He was like a pop movie star and you don't have those anymore." Mary Carillo added, "Borg didn't have to affect a look. It was the way he carried himself, how comported he was."

Borg was now making millions and had some forty off-court commercial deals. "He deserves his one-million-dollar racket contract and three million a year and everything else he has, because since he was twelve years old he's worked harder than anybody else," said Gerulaitis. "The guy was out there practicing eight hours a day. I don't begrudge him a thing. I think he's earned it all."

In Paris, McEnroe hit a roadblock. After besting Patrice Dominguez in the first round and then the young but marginal Swede Per Herqvist (who ironically would later become Borg's agent), he went down 7–6, 6–7, 7–6, 7–6 to the scrappy Paul McNamee of Australia.

Mac's personal life had also hit a roadblock. He and Stacy Margolin were trying to maintain their romantic relationship, but they were rarely together outside of the majors, because in those days, unlike in the twenty-first century, the men and women rarely played at the same locale. When they did meet up at the Grand Slams, their relationship certainly had its ups, unless they were attempting to play mixed doubles together, which McEnroe couldn't emotionally handle.

On their last attempt as a team, at the 1979 U.S. Open, they lost to an aging Stan and not-related Anne Smith. Mac lost his serve twice during the match while no one else lost theirs. He was incredibly embarrassed. "I said, that's it. I'm never playing again. I can't handle this . . . that kind of pressure was beyond me."

Both members of the couple were feeling the strain of a long-distance relationship, but as McEnroe would admit, he liked having his cake and eating it too and ended up cheating on Margolin. A forthright person and ridden with Catholic guilt, he couldn't keep his tongue in his mouth and told her about it at the 1980 French Open. "It was such a disaster," he said. "Stacy was very upset. She didn't feel we could go on. And I can't say I blame her. It was obviously the wrong thing to do."

What Mac meant by the wrong thing was both cheating on Margolin and tattling on himself. "That was one of the worst weeks of my life," he said. "I felt so bad about unloading this bombshell on my girlfriend that I bombed out on court."

Possibly because they met before McEnroe became a star, the couple managed to stay together until 1982, and their partnership was considered a significant long-term relationship for both of them, but Margolin, a well-mannered and sweet person, was embarrassed by Mac's ongoing tirades and her career suffered as a result. Yet those who knew her said she was totally in love with the New Yorker, and the cultural conflicts that might have arisen between an Irish-American Catholic and an upper-middle-class Beverly Hills girl of Jewish descent didn't plague them. McEnroe would go on to play the field. Before marrying actress Tatum O'Neal in 1986, he also dated the model Stella Hall as well as Alana Stewart, rock star Rod's ex-wife.

Mac and Margolin's relationship lasted about as long as Borg's with the well-liked, charming, yet average Romanian player Mariana Simionescu, but in 1980 it was the Swede and the Romanian who had stars in their eyes every time they saw each other. Just before the French Open, the pair played a highly publicized $150,000 "Love Doubles" match against Chris Evert and her husband, John Lloyd.

Borg and Simionescu had met four years prior at the French Open, when Borg romanced her into accepting an impromptu dinner invitation. They stayed up until 5 a.m. talking, when Borg finally fell asleep while she was still chattering. She crept back to her room, where her mother was still awake, waiting for her. "I think I just managed to tell her how beautiful it had been before I fell asleep on the spot."

The Ice Man had melted her heart in just one evening.

17

The Genius Tested in London

Borg appeared so loose before 1980 Wimbledon that he was willing to sit down and publicly discuss his wedding plans with Mariana Simionescu, who by that time had put most of her tennis dreams aside and was already penning a long love poem to Borg that would later take the form of a book.

In later years, after his divorce from Simionescu, Borg would play the field like a utility infielder, marrying an Italian singer, fathering a child with a teenage Swedish model, splitting with her, and eventually settling down with another Swedish woman. But during that summer he spent a lot of off-court time with his Romanian sweetheart, planning to continue a long and illustrious career and begin a prosperous marriage. He was preparing to stick it out with a bouncy, good-natured young woman who willingly sacrificed her own modest tennis career for his. Simionescu was said by some to love the limelight and was willing to excuse Borg's transgressions because she was starstruck.

The two were to be married in a July 24 ceremony in Bucharest, a wedding that Simionescu spent a tremendous amount of time planning and photos of which were sold by Borg's sports agency, IMG. It was a high-level celebrity-athlete affair, but not one that gave Borg the jitters. He put his thoughts about the ceremony aside briefly, saying that he was happy and well balanced, aiming at a royal flush of five titles last achieved on fast Wimbledon grass by Englishman Laurie Doherty when tennis was little more than a parlor sport played in front of nobility.

"I know that Mariana is thinking more about the marriage than I am for the moment," Borg told the venerable tennis writer Barry Lorge before the tournament. "To me, it doesn't seem like such a big deal. We've been together four years, so nothing is going to change. I am not going to worry about the wedding much until after Wimbledon."

At the time, Borg maintained his godlike ambitions, and after winning Wimbledon for the fourth straight time the previous year he had said, "One of my goals in the future is to win maybe a lot of big titles and to make some records if I can, so maybe one day they will say, 'You have been the greatest player of all time.'" History was on Borg's mind, but he never boldly boasted. He was not Connors, a chest-pounder who also served as his own publicist. He was more like Laver, a "thanks very much for the applause" type of guy, "but I will leave it to you to shower me with accolades." He had a different sort of appeal, mellow and focused, but unerring on court, a sportsman who was all about winning, but not a person who lightly accepted defeats. "I hate to lose, I have always hated to lose at anything," he said—especially when a record was within grasp.

He entered 1980 Wimbledon having won twenty-eight matches in a row, not having lost on the All England Lawn Tennis Club grass since Arthur Ashe beat him in the quarterfinals in 1975. His mind was set on eclipsing the all-time record of thirty-one straight victories held by the Australian Rod Laver. Given his draw, surpassing Laver's mark was a reasonable goal, but tying Doherty was another matter, even though the Englishman's five titles came in the pre-1922 era of the "challenge round," when the defending champion sat out until the final and waited for a challenger to come out of a small pack. Doherty's five titles encompassed only a ten-match winning streak, which most historians consider to be a very modest mark, but it was a record nonetheless. Only a true master had a real chance.

"Borg is a genius, there is no question about it," said India's Vijay Amritraj, who nearly toppled Borg the prior year. "He has an uncanny ability to raise his game on the most important points. He is most dangerous when in danger. For a long time I thought Laver was the best player I would ever see, but I think Borg has surpassed him already, and he is still improving."

Borg said he was taking losing more easily than he did early in his career, but how was anyone to know that, when he had won 40 of 41 matches he played in 1980 coming into Wimbledon? "I hate to lose even more than I like to win, so I get very depressed right after the match when I lose," he said. "But then two or three hours later, it's over. I always look ahead and think, 'Okay, I might play the same guy next week.' As long as I have been trying my best, trying to win, trying to reach every single point, then it is all right. If I do that and still lose, I realize: 'Okay, the other guy was better than me today, so what can I do?' I never go to my room and scream or break the furniture, nothing like that."

True or not, Borg was known as a physiological phenomenon who had a regular pulse rate of only 35. Many called him the perfect athlete, especially after he overwhelmed the field during the European Superstars competition in Vichy, when some of the planet's best athletes from a variety of sports came out. He won the push-up competition—he simply didn't need to stop—and remarkably won the 400-meter hurdles over Guy Drut, who was the 110-meter hurdles champion. "I won because the problem in the 400 meters is breathing," Borg said.

He enjoyed discussing how well his body functioned, how in synch his legs and arms were when he was preparing to strike the ball with his tightly strung Donnay racket. "There is no other feeling like that, knowing that you have been working so hard, making sacrifices, and they are worth it."

When a man has dominated a tournament so thoroughly, has just come off another extraordinary French Open run, and there is no one out there clearly better than him, he's a substantial favorite to win the title. But a few of the British papers spoke of a threatening American coalition: McEnroe, Connors, Gerulaitis, Tanner, and Gottfried.

London bookmakers tabbed Borg a 4-to-5 favorite to win the title; after four years of hearing that only serve-and-volleyers should be able to win on a fast surface, it seemed that Borg's superior all-around play had turned the old tennis world on its head.

Just before the tournament began, eight tennis luminaries interviewed by the *New York Times* all picked the Swede. Laver, who had always been careful about choosing his words, said that Roscoe Tanner, John McEnroe, and Jimmy Connors had chances at pulling upsets, but still picked Borg. "He has every chance of winning again because he is a capable, proven player, and because many of his opponents feel beaten before they start a match against him. His game on grass is not as good as it is on clay, but that won't matter because lots of players today are not effective volleyers, so he can stay back and do what he does best—spray those forehands and backhands from the baseline."

Three-time United States doubles champion Billy Talbert said that despite his odd style, "Borg has made a believer out of me."

Pancho Gonzalez, who won the U.S. Open (then called the Championships) in 1948 and 1949, said, "I can see nobody beating him. Although he still lacks the volleying skills, the rest of his game has grown stronger. He has become a mature, knowledgeable player with a style that is almost unique. Nobody is fitter or concentrates better."

Jack Kramer, the 1947 Wimbledon champ, also applauded the Swede's know-how: "He is the outstanding favorite with a great record, even though he is not basically a grass player. The draw will have a lot to do with his chances; he could start slow, find the early going rough, and could be upset. I'd say McEnroe would have the best shot at him. Connors can handle him only once in a while, and Vitas Gerulaitis simply can't beat him at all. So who else is there? Tanner has a great serve, but the rest of his game is inconsistent."

Davis Cup captain and CBS commentator Tony Trabert, who won the 1955 Wimbledon title, sensed trouble but still thought that Borg would get through. "I make him the odds-on favorite, but he will be facing great pressure because everyone wants to bring down the top man. The players with the best chances to beat him are the serve-and-volley guys like McEnroe, Tanner, Victor Pecci, John Sadri or Vic Amaya. Why? Because on the grass the ball comes through lower and faster and he will not have much time to decide what to do with it. Connors, even though his serve and volley are not outstanding, has a chance because he has been playing well and has always been a fierce competitor."

Don Budge, who won the calendar-year Grand Slam in 1938 and was a vociferous critic of nearly everyone who came after him, reluctantly picked Borg. "He has been grinding down the same opponents over and over again. He is a marvelous player, but who is he playing against? I don't think much of the present crop. They just don't serve well or volley well. McEnroe might beat him, because he is the best of the lot. Connors can be dangerous, but has weaknesses. Borg seems to be a slow starter and I think the way to beat him is to go in on his short balls and punch them into the corners to break him out of his rhythm. Players like Kramer and Lew Hoad would be able to do it."

Allison Danzig, of the *New York Times*, was also unimpressed by the competition. "Borg is quite equal to do the job because he is a great player and at the moment neither McEnroe, Connors nor Gerulaitis is playing at his best. Something seems to have happened to McEnroe. He has lost his serve and his talent has gone awry. Connors, to me, has played his best tennis and looks burned out, and as for Gerulaitis, one never knows anymore what to expect from him; he can be great and then sloppy. So it will be Borg moving right through the field again."

Somewhat remarkably, even McEnroe's old tutor, Harry Hopman, went with the Swede. "Borg will win. He has beaten the same field too often before and it seems ridiculous to keep saying that grass is not his surface, not after he has won on it four straight years. To beat him, you must put him under pressure, hurry him, force him out of his rhythm. Connors and McEnroe have the weapons to do that, but there can be no easing up against him because he is so fit, so strong off the ground and concentrates so well."

Only Dick Savitt, the 1951 Wimbledon champion, picked against the legend in the making. "I don't think he can do it again," he said. "You need luck to win Wimbledon and he has had it. But I can't see his luck holding. Someone will break his streak, or the pressure will do it; it depends on the draw. The players with the best chance are McEnroe and Connors."

The fact was that outside of McEnroe, still a bold young player who knew he hadn't hit his peak yet, only Connors had the résumé, guts, and know-how to best the Swede, and he had hit a mental roadblock when facing Borg. Certainly there were other players who thought that on huge serving days they might have a puncher's chance to knock him off, but that would also mean that Borg would have to experience an unusually bad day at the office, and he hadn't done so in a five-setter at Wimbledon since Ashe schooled him when he was just nineteen.

"When somebody finally beats Borg at Wimbledon, it's automatically going to be one of the biggest single-match wins of the century," said American player Erik Van Dillen. "That works in Borg's favor, because when a guy gets close the pressure on him is incredible. Borg is used to it, the commotion and the tension and the hundreds of photographers who come running when they smell an upset. He's protecting the streak, but there's more pressure on the other guy, who knows this might be his one chance to make history."

That Wimbledon season, Borg once again hit hundreds of balls at the Cumberland Club, a valuable locale to any player given how hard it was at the time to find grasscourt practice facilities in

London. There, Borg was the guest of Tommy and Dot Nutley, who managed the club's restaurant. Dot was said to prepare all his favorite food and wash his clothes. Tommy Nutley, a retired jockey and a tennis fanatic, was extremely loyal to Borg, who felt the horseback rider was his good-luck mascot and would bring him to all his matches. "When Björn stops winning Wimbledon, I'll sell the bar in Cumberland and move to Greece," the jolly Nutley told Simionescu. "I'll open up a taverna there with a small garden inside."

That would be the last year that Borg would practice at Cumberland, because IMG was said to be no longer willing to incur the high costs of his stay there. Nonetheless, in 1980 he reveled in his routine. He called SW19 "My Wimbledon," and went on to have a garden party the likes of which Nutley couldn't have imagined.

He knew the world's eyes were upon him, but he didn't go and hide. "I know I can't win forever, and the other guys are usually playing well against me because they have nothing to lose. I'm the one who has all the pressure on me. No one will say anything if they lose in three straight sets, but if they win it is a big thing. It was the same for me when I was coming up. When I was playing the top players, I felt I had nothing to lose, everything to gain."

Fortunately, he wouldn't face a truly elite player until the final, but there was much work to do. His first contest would be against the big server Ismail El Shafei of Egypt. Simionescu thought it should be a cakewalk, but Borg knew that every match had its curves, and while reading a newspaper that morning he shouted out, "I just want to remind you, Mariana, that there's no such thing as an easy match. A player who thinks that way might as well give up. And I have no intention of doing that."

Borg was a bit concerned because the Egyptian was capable of hitting a hot streak on his serve, but the Swede returned competently and got through 6–3, 6–4, 6–4. In the car on the way back to Cumberland, Nutley was joyful and happy and called Wimbledon an old whore who as years go by puts on more and more makeup and doesn't understand why youngsters like Borg continue to woo her.

Rain poured down at Wimbledon that year, but Borg was very patient and knew that long delays sitting around the locker room or back at their hotel suite were merely part of the process. When the tarps were pulled off the court, he faced Shlomo Glickstein, the first Israeli to make it to the second round. He had little trouble with his nerves or his strokes in a 6–3, 6–1, 7–5 victory.

What's particularly fascinating about tennis is its different styles of play: how a player strokes the ball, how deeply he bends his knees, firms or loosens up his wrist, how he moves his feet to set up and strike. But Borg didn't focus on technique during tournaments, saying that it would be too distracting, instead concentrating on being efficient with his shot selection.

In the third round, Borg would face a milestone as he got the opportunity to tie Laver's mark of 31 straight wins at the Big W. He would confront another Australian named Rod, Rod Frawley, a middle-of-the-road player, but one who had experience on grass. "I'm against playing Sir Rod," he said to Simionescu, who wasn't quite sure of his meaning. "That's right, Sir Rod, Sir Rod Laver. I must win my 31st straight to hit his mark."

Borg had put the weight of the record on his own shoulders, relishing the torturous effort it would take to succeed. He did not play brilliantly, but competently enough, and pushed through 6–4, 6–7, 6–1, 7–5.

Borg was bubbling with happiness, and the next day he brought Gerulaitis over to practice leading into his match against the tricky Hungarian Balázs Taróczy in the fourth round. The workout served him very well as he wasted his foe 6–1, 7–5, 6–2. He knelt down in relief and joy, as Laver's record was now history. Borg and Bergelin returned to their flat and spent countless minutes retuning the strings on his racket, which Simionescu compared to a harpsichord routine.

Next up would be the American Gene Mayer, who hit his peak that year, winning five titles. This was the season when the Long Island native finally came into his own, when he learned that having tremendous variety in his game didn't necessarily translate into victories. It was his brother and doubles partner, Sandy, who showed him the light of day.

"I finally understood what it took to win day in and day out," Mayer said. "Sandy said to me one day in practice, 'If you learn to confuse your opponents as much as you do yourself, you'll win a lot more matches.' He was right. I was making too many mistakes and didn't understand how to properly construct points. Once I learned how to use my strengths and string things together, I found my game."

Mayer finished the year ranked No. 4, and at the concluding Masters played in January 1981, he took down McEnroe, Borg, and José Luis Clerc before falling to Ivan Lendl. Mayer was putting his tools to use.

"Against McEnroe, I made sure to stand in as close as I could on my returns and make sure that he didn't have an easy first volley," he said. "Once he started to control the net, you were out of the point. I had to go for my returns more. Against Borg, I really had to push myself, because for me, I liked to play four to five balls to establish myself before trying to close points out. Against Borg, I had to make sure not to give him easy mistakes, which he lived on, but keep my balls deep or to angles. I really had to focus on not giving him anything easy, or he would dominate me. He rarely missed."

Armed with a keen intellect, the former standout at Stanford found a way to keep himself competitive in a rough peer group. Mayer reached the quarterfinals of the U.S. Open and Wimbledon, and won two doubles crowns at the French Open with his brother, Sandy, but never led the pack by its nose. Mayer was in the thick of things that year, but could never crack the top echelon of what he called a superclass: Borg, McEnroe, and Connors, followed by himself, Gerulaitis, Vilas, and Brian Gottfried.

"It was as tough as it ever was and as it ever will be. I may not have had the outright talent of those guys, but I studied the sport and analyzed my own game," said Mayer, who collected 14 singles and 15 doubles crowns. "I improved my court positioning and shot selection. The only regret I have is that when I was younger I didn't realize the benefits of off-court training, and if I had been smarter about taking care of my body early on, I may have been able to avoid injuries."

When Mayer went out to face Borg, he didn't yet sense that Borg and Mac would become an all-time great rivalry. He knew fellow New Yorker McEnroe well and believed in his potential, but thought he might be still a little too raw to stare down the Swede. He thought that by employing a relentlessly attacking, whizzing all-around game, he himself had a shot at upsetting Borg.

"At Wimbledon, there was never a sense he wasn't beatable, he was constantly struggling and down," Mayer said. "Björn beat you by letting you beat yourself. He didn't do it by pressuring you or that you had too much discomfort with his balls; he hit too many good passing shots and good returns and you were worn down by relatively unimpressive stuff. That's what truly amazes me about Borg and Wimbledon—let alone winning five in a row—is that everyone thought they could beat him and they couldn't, where on clay they could have brought out a cardboard figure of Borg and they would have shaken hands with it and said, 'I can't beat you.'"

Borg consistently said the return of serve was the most important shot on grass, and it's hard to quibble with his reasoning. At the time, the competitors were still playing with wooden rackets with smaller head sizes, and it was much more difficult to meet a searing serve in the center of the racket and rip it back. Today's souped-up graphite rackets with space-age strings are much more responsive all over the frame and allow players to return bullets from way deep in the court and even outside of it. With wood, hand-eye coordination was a bit more important because the frames and strings weren't as forgiving.

"His return was sneaky and ridiculous in how accurate it was, but I wouldn't put in it Connors's class, which was more powerful," Mayer said. "I think I was a better returner than he was, but he was a better passer. He served extraordinarily well and got a huge amount of unreturnables on his serve and a lot of free points. He even came in some behind his first serve because he served well enough and the grass was different then and gave you more volleying opportunities. When he came into net, he was really well set up. And he got enough quality returns to set up his passing shots. Even after you played him a few times on grass, you thought you could beat him. The impressive thing was that he just didn't lose and figured out a way to win. It seemed like he was down two sets to one with a break every year to someone but managed to win. As a competitor he was so consistent. Not glamorous, but efficient. It's amazing how the game was supposed to be played on grass and how he actually played on it, where logic dictated differently."

Against Borg, Mayer served for two sets, and had he managed to scrape one out, he might have garnered enough confidence to get under the Swede's skin a little. But once again, Borg took full ownership of the big points and won going away 7–5, 6–3, 7–5.

"He made all the returns and I didn't serve well enough," Mayer explained. "I felt very comfortable with him. When I played Connors one Wimbledon, he returned so well that I didn't want to come in as much. I loved playing Jimmy because after a few balls we'd get loose, running side to side. His balls were always hard and deep, and I never felt I could stay with him in the backcourt. Björn was not as punishing, but he was so quick, got the few extra balls, that he squeaked it out. Against the best players, he was unflappable. You knew what you would get—there weren't errors, and for all the things he was known for, his consistency impressed me the most. Even if he doesn't play well, you have to play *too* well. So quick and so many balls."

Borg knew what he would get out of American Brian Gottfried, whom he had played before and with great success. Gottfried was a very good but not a great player, a right-handed workaholic who tried to master every shot in the book but at times found that he was limited against more naturally talented players.

The curly-haired Baltimore native was good enough to have reached No. 3 in the world in 1977, the year in which he reached fifteen singles finals, winning five titles. Gottfried was an excellent junior player, winning fourteen national titles. He won the 1962 National twelve-and-under doubles title with Connors, and in 1970, as a freshman at Trinity in Texas, won the prestigious USTA Boys eighteens singles championship, as well as the doubles championship with Sandy Mayer. He was the runner-up in NCAA singles and doubles in 1972.

Gottfried turned pro before Borg and well before Mac came on the scene. In April 1977, he was playing so well that *Newsweek* wrote he was "simply the best male tennis player in the world at the moment." He came down to earth a bit in the French Open final, where Vilas wasted him 6–0, 6–3, 6–0. However, he did win the doubles title with Raul Ramirez, his longtime partner from Mexico, with whom he also won Wimbledon in 1976.

Gottfried's game was described as technically flawless, and he owned a penetrating forehand volley that was admired by one and all. He was a purist and perfectionist and a true gym rat. He once missed a scheduled practice in Miami in order to get married to his wife, Windy, but made up for it by putting in a double session the next day.

At the historic Queen's Club—the traditional Wimbledon warm-up—Gottfried faced McEnroe in the third round and lost a 7–6, 7–6 decision. He wasn't thrilled with his Davis Cup teammate's behavior on that afternoon.

"His tantrums didn't distract me," he said, "because with my style, I could block out what was going on, so I didn't mind playing him or Nastase. But having said that, I felt he was a guy who took advantage of certain situations. Some players will question calls when they are bad, but I really felt there were times he did it to change the direction of the match. At Queen's, we had words after the match, but we weren't ready to put the gloves on. But I questioned why with all the talent that he had to do things like that. At 5–5, you could tell when a guy was going to try and change the flow of the match."

Gottfried got over the incident, won a grasscourt tournament at Surbiton, and quickly found his groove at Wimbledon, not dropping a set in his first four matches and scoring impressive wins over Stan Smith, Phil Dent, and Wojtek Fibak. He was owning the net, and going into his match with Borg, he felt that he might be able to suffocate him.

"It was strange to play for three weeks on grass and not hit many groundies and then all of a sudden to play a guy who seemingly not ever got a bad bounce," he recalled. "To me one of the miracles of sport was Borg winning Wimbledon five times with the way he played. The courts weren't the same quality as they are now. There were real divots in them. He just moved so well and seemed to get the balls back faster. Grass was more suited for serve and volley, and that's what you did during the grass season: I practiced my serve, volley, and return of serve, and all of a sudden you are playing someone whose second serve you can attack, but he's playing from the baseline and you are struggling to know as to how to play."

On that day against Borg, Gottfried tried to force the action, but kept getting pushed back, mentally and physically, in a 6–2, 4–6, 6–2, 6–0 defeat. Borg was playing with a pulled stomach muscle, so he actually tried to shorten points and volleyed reasonably well for a man who largely made his living well behind the baseline.

"He moved so well and passed so well that you had to do something special with your first volley," Gottfried said. "He was so good under pressure, and was incredibly fit. I think grass helped him in two respects: he could still crack a first serve when he was down, and he came into net with a little slice backhand that was effective. He didn't hit a firm volley, but the ball would just die. I served and volleyed on most first serves, and on my second serves I tried to come in sometimes, but against him it didn't seem to matter at all as I was just getting worn out. The night before, we had beat the Amritraj brothers 19–17 in the fifth set in doubles and I was a little tired. If I had done any better in that semi, maybe it wouldn't have been the great Borg-Mac final. People should probably thank me."

Due to the rain, Borg would have to wait to find out whom he would play in the final: Connors, whom he had thumped the last two times at the All England Club, or McEnroe, who was closing in on him, but was far less experienced. Simionescu and Nutley wanted it to be Connors, as he was more of a known quantity for their beloved Swede, while McEnroe was more unpredictable, like Nastase.

On the BBC, Arthur Ashe, now serving as a television commentator, picked Connors to best Mac. Nutley, watching TV at the Cumberland Club with Borg and Simionescu, commented, "The old man must have gone gaga." Borg was wordless for a moment, then laughed and asked Nutley for a beer.

He watched Mac's victory, but didn't offer a comment. Simionescu recalled what Borg's grandfather had explained to her about his Swedish heritage. "For him, Björn is Odin, the Scandinavian god with his eight-legged horse, Sleipnir, that runs like the wind. He says Borg can run faster than the horse. When he enters the fray, like Odin, his mere appearance makes all blind, deaf, and powerless."

But his foe in the final would be McEnroe, who was more than ready to cowboy up and ring a lasso around his ankles.

18

True Nature

Leaving his conflict with Stacy Margolin behind him, McEnroe went to the 1980 Queen's Club, got revenge on Paul McNamee, and won the historic Wimbledon warm-up without dropping a set, crushing Kim Warwick 6–3, 6–1 in the final.

He was prepared for Wimbledon, but England wasn't exactly prepared for him. The British papers were out for blood. McEnroe and his screams and antics were perfect tabloid fodder, with the headlines calling him, among other things, "the Brat," "the Incredible Sulk," "the Merchant of Menace," "the Prince of Petulance," "the Rude Dude," "the Super Brat," and "King Sneer."

"He is the most vain, ill-tempered, petulant loudmouth that the game of tennis has ever known," one of the tabloids proclaimed.

Even though he waltzed through the Queen's draw, Mac still found reasons to blow his top. As his Davis Cup coach Tony Trabert said, once Mac lost it, he was pretty much gone, regardless of how many times he vowed to maintain his cool prior to a contest. Once he began to see red, he frothed at the mouth like a rabid dog.

"I grew up in New York," McEnroe explained. "You go from the airport to your house and you're lucky if ten people don't call you an asshole. Look at hockey players—put a mike on them or put a mike on the football field. I'm just like those guys, but they made it look like it was all different. The game was so stiff. It felt like everybody's collar was starched, like the next thing they were going to do was ask me to wear long pants. So if there was one thing I wanted to change that was it. It became like this cause for me. But there are demons. There have always been questions on my mind on the tennis court. Off the court I'm way better able to keep things under control than on the court. When I get on the court it is unpredictable; I don't even know myself what's going to happen. You ask, 'What percentage of you is actually pissed off?' I'm not sure. And when people ask I always say, 'Look, did you want me to be pissed off? Or do you want me to say I'm pretending?' I just go along with whatever one they say just for lack of having to discuss it at any serious level, because ultimately it's all superficial anyway."

McEnroe was fighting an uphill battle in Britain, where Margaret Thatcher had brought an edgy new conservatism to a traditionally conservative people. Under her policies, known as Thatcherism, the rich grew richer and the poor grew poorer in her attempt to build a larger middle class and encourage entrepreneurship. The left and trade unions resented her for obvious reasons, but so did a portion of Britain's ruling class, who had set up the welfare state in their favor, keeping the poor and the small middle class in their place and the nation's riches very much to themselves. The bluebloods disdained the nouveau riche and loudmouthed celebrities like McEnroe who didn't have the proper breeding. The more stoic Borg, who largely kept to himself and knew how to bow to royalty, was more to their taste.

Like Thatcher and Ronald Reagan, who was looking toward the Republican nomination that summer, McEnroe, a maverick who forged his own path, was not well liked in establishment circles. Yet despite being an antihero to the punk rockers and street toughs who revolted against Thatcher, Johnny Mac was no man of the masses and rarely concerned himself with the mind-set of the general populace. It was one thing to butt heads with officialdom; it was another to embarrass a middle-class steward or linesperson who was merely there to watch him ply his craft. McEnroe did plenty of that, which is why it took him years to gain a substantial fan base in Britain.

While watching the curly-haired avenger curse and sneer was always great theater, many folks were simply embarrassed when he went overboard. At Queen's in 1981, he called the chair umpire an "idiot" and yelled out, "Over a thousand officials to choose from and I get a moron like you!" When Mac saw his opponent, the relatively unknown Leif Shiras, who would later become his friend and broadcast partner, looking amused during his outburst, he pointed his finger at him during the changeover and warned, "I've been around a long time and I don't want to take that crap from you."

But he was as irresistible to watch as a street performer trying to tear his hair out after dropping two of his balls while juggling in front of a mocking crowd. Mac tortured himself with contorted body gestures after a bad shot or call, and tormented officials with his outbursts and opponents with all-too-frequent stoppages of play. Fans wanted to see the crazed artist jump off the bridge, canvases in tow.

"I'm sick and tired of [McEnroe's] bullshit," said South African–born player Johan Kriek. "If I'm the only one that has the guts to say he needs to be kicked off the tour, fine. I work too hard to be treated like this. That guy McEnroe has got a screw loose."

His career was one long psychodrama, which combined brilliant shotmaking with immature tantrums. He would twist his serve, caress an impossible volley from his shoetips that landed just over the net and close to the line. Just a few seconds after mouths fell agape at the heavenly show, a linesman would signal "out" and he would grind to a halt, put his hands on his hips, clench his teeth, and erupt.

"I could have controlled it better," he said. "My parents always thought so. On some level I didn't control it because I didn't want to. But I took economics at Stanford and it's the law of diminishing returns. I did feel out of control, and I didn't like it."

There were so many things that upset him: bad calls, not getting what he wanted, a camera snapping at an inconvenient time, and of course, being a perfectionist and wanting everything right. Plus, he wanted to be recognized for his true persona, but he wasn't sure exactly what that was.

"People had no idea what they were clapping for," he said. "I wanted to change the system. Umpiring in tennis is so much worse than other sports, it's ridiculous. You go to the [U.S.] Open, you get the same people who were working the Easter Bowl for me when I was twelve. Or who work for my brother in the juniors. I'm serious. It'd be like refs in the NBA doing a CYO game in Great Neck. How can you respect them? Now, I know I'm wrong sometimes, because I can't take no for an answer and I keep rubbing it in and nail them to the wall. I know I'm wrong there. But I know I can see the ball so much better than they can. As many balls as I hit, I can feel it when I hit a serve out. But they don't understand that. I have zero percent doubt that I see balls better than they do."

The establishment was appalled and most of the British press despised him. One newspaper opined, "It is to McEnroe's eternal discredit that he has repeatedly let loose the howling dogs of war— interrupting play by stalling, ostensibly to regain his composure, by whining about a line decision or some trivial distraction; by shouting sometimes disgusting abuse at court officials; and by whipping his racket about as if intent on dismantling adjacent furniture. Had some of his language been uttered in the street, he would have been knocked down by the addressee or cautioned by police."

There were those who defended McEnroe to some degree, including his official biographer, Richard Evans, who argued that as a perfectionist, McEnroe demanded perfection from everyone else, and that he was essentially arguing against perceived injustices. But that's not all Mac exploded over; it was also his own poor play, his inability to execute even though he knew which shot to hit.

"Nobody seeking justice can arrogate the roles of judge and jury," Rex Bellamy wrote.

Even Wimbledon champion Pat Cash, no easygoing chap himself who is now a friend of McEnroe's, would say, "The rule book was like a hundred pages long. By the time McEnroe retired it was like 250. It's phenomenal how many rules they had to bring in for him. I see it but I don't understand it. It's a fine line between genius and insanity in anybody who's the best at anything. John is the best player that's ever walked on a tennis court in my opinion. He also always walked that line. Sometimes he goes over it."

Boris Becker, another combustible Wimbledon champion who would also become a friend of McEnroe's and like John is very much a free spirit, added, "He was the most difficult player to play against because it was always personal with him. It was never just about tennis."

In some ways, his old Davis Cup captain Ashe agreed with psychologists Jim Loehr and Allen Fox, that McEnroe would become more explosive when he faced lesser talents. "He had very few peers," Ashe said. "So he gets bored and condescending with others and has to manufacture controversy to stay interested."

But that summer in England, McEnroe was by no means bored. Even though he was butting heads with the establishment, the very sight of Wimbledon gave him the chills. "I always viewed Wimbledon as a faraway incredible place you always wanted to get to, even though I ball-boyed at Forest Hills and I loved the Open. It was magical. It's our Augusta, our Masters," he confided.

But McEnroe did not treat the tournament the same way that he might have cared for the long and luscious fairways of Augusta National. Some said he treated it no better than a dingy diner on Queens Boulevard. "The boy wonder is upstairs, eating the traditional strawberries and cream without benefit of the traditional spoon," one locker room attendant scoffed.

That may not have been a habit John learned at home, but it was one he displayed in Douglaston. Mary Carillo recalls McEnroe coming to dinner at her parents' house and digging in with his hands, and also remembers an occasion when she invited twelve-time Grand Slam champion Billie Jean King over to dine with John and her. They were eating pizza and ice cream and McEnroe decided not to use the available silverware.

"Billie was mesmerized by his eating habits," Carillo said. "She just couldn't imagine him playing some big tournament with ice cream dripping all over his shirt. She just sat there with her arms crossed and giggling out loud. My parents still talk about him. My mom would serve rice, and after he got up there was rice every-where. It seems in some ways he tried breaking every rule, every social custom there was."

McEnroe's father is also a temperamental Irishman but says that nationality had nothing to do with it when it came to his family's problems in England, which had ruled Ireland with an iron fist for centuries. Even though he admits that his son went over the line, he blamed the officials for patronizing him, which further aggravated the situation.

"It was all very spontaneous. He couldn't tell himself not to do it; he had to do it. But if you look and see the people sitting in chairs and the way they would look at some players and sneer at them and John would yell, 'Answer my question! Answer my question!' And they would say, 'Play right on, play right on' without listening. They were just supercilious and ridiculous. It was stiff-upper-lip horse-shit. It was just outrageous."

McEnroe wasn't acting, but he gave Academy Award–worthy performances. Actor Tom Hulce studied him for his role as the loony yet brilliant eighteenth-century composer Mozart in the 1984 film *Amadeus*. The band members of the Rolling Stones and Pink Floyd, as well as the singular David Bowie and Eric Clapton, wanted to meet him. Andy Warhol followed him around with a camera. Mac was too cool to change for anyone.

"I think back in the early eighties he must have been one of the five most recognizable people in the world," recalled Fleming. "There was Ali, Pelé, Reagan, but John was right up there and people acted very, very strangely around him. It was a trip just to experience it."

It was also a trip to see him lose his marbles. "Look, even my friends know I have no control," Mac would later say. "I just go into the ozone. There've been times, I swear to you, five minutes before the match, five minutes, I've said to myself, 'Now John, don't do anything today. Just go out and play,' and two games into the match—two bloody games—I've lost complete control. People think I plan all this stuff? I've gone nuts in exhibitions. I've lost it completely."

Given that tennis is a game, McEnroe was frequently asked why he never smiled, and he gave a simple answer—because he was a workingman simply doing a workingman's job, no frills included. He was asked why he was rude to officials and said it was never his intention. He claimed he had better vision. "I just think my eyesight at twenty is better than some old man's at seventy, however much he might love tennis. When you lose, you really do feel like a loser. I view it as more like I was more of an average person than I was portrayed. Tennis is a very frustrating sport and people get upset playing it. Go to any public court and you see that. I showed emotion on court, and I think initially some people couldn't see through that and just thought of me as a guy who yells at umpires."

The problem with defining McEnroe's behavior and attempting to discover a consistent, discernible pattern as to how he would react in a given situation is that his behavior has been unpredictable. To some, he's a humble, angelic, silent contributor to numerous charities. To others, he's a rude, brazen, selfish person who doesn't really care about anyone except for himself and his family and friends.

Said Carillo, "There's a theory out there that John has this canny legal mind that he got from his dad and he could quickly see an injustice, and there's part of that that's true. Look, I've known this guy for a long time, and anything that you say about him, I believe, anything that you say about John is true. Someone will tell some glorious story about him giving money anonymously or stepping out of his way to, you know, do something great, I've heard a lot of those stories. But somebody will tell me a story about what a dickhead he was on a plane ride, and you know, they're all true! Nobody has ever told me something where I had to say, 'There's no way that's true.' My general instinct is, there's no way that's false."

McEnroe would later say that he didn't play Wimbledon in 1986 or 1987 because, despite his success (he had won three titles by then), the entire experience had taken too much of an emotional toll on him. That process began in 1978, and by 1980 he was a marked man. "It wasn't even like I was playing opponents at a certain point; it was like I was battling everyone over there. I felt like I had to be okay as a person and they make it seem like tennis is the most important thing, but it isn't the most important thing."

The All England Club cared about its tennis and how its players behaved. Given that Borg uttered nary a peep of objection and personified what the British considered to be perfect manners, Mac's back was up when it came to behavior.

Bellamy described Borg as a solid yet dull man, who was accused of being greedy and selfish, but "where it mattered most, on court, he was an exemplary sportsman and champion." But not McEnroe, who Bellamy said needed to polish a tarnished image and thus enforce a "reappraisal of a great tennis player." Results be damned.

Some American journalists were not much kinder to the young McEnroe. "McEnroe does most of his pouting on the courts," wrote *Newsweek*'s Pete Axthelm. "In private, this devastating athlete can be a nice enough kid . . . but when he steps to the service line, with his perpetually put-upon expression and his insistence that every line call and crowd reaction go his way, his public posture is all too easy to understand. Call it spoiled."

The *Washington Post*'s Barry Lorge said, "He came across as a precocious brat—immensely talented, spoiled and rather obnoxious. On the court, he pouted, cursed, threw his racket. . . . He was a crybaby. Off court, he demonstrated little savoir faire."

But McEnroe couldn't care less that his behavior was affecting the press's opinion of him. As the renowned tennis historian Bud Collins recalled, he once went to talk to McEnroe about his awful behavior in a match in Boston against Jimmy Connors and told him that he was destined to be a great champion, and that the greats, like

Jack Kramer, Rod Laver, and Ken Rosewall, "didn't sully their reputations with bad acting. For one thing they thought too much of themselves and the game."

"He said, 'Thank you. You're right. I'm working on it, and it will never happen again.' I left him feeling good. That was 1977."

His brother Patrick observed, "Part of John enjoys chaos. He likes things to be a bit unsettled. Wreaking havoc, what unsettles others, he can handle."

But at 1980 Wimbledon, there would be no early major outbursts. He vowed before the outset of the tournament that he would try to be calmer and hoped to have no explosions. He wanted England to give him a second chance, because he didn't feel like he was getting one.

"I think the public wants a villain, needs one, and I have been given that role. I don't like it. Who would? Borg is the epitome of a tennis player, but if everybody were like him then the game wouldn't be so exciting. You'd have a bunch of robots out there who are afraid to say something. . . . I'd like to tell you, 'I promise you there won't be any more outbursts.' I would. But I can't say that because I don't know. I'm sorry, I don't."

In the first round, McEnroe crushed Butch Walts 6–3, 6–3, 6–0, but then seriously struggled in a 4–6, 7–5 6–7, 7–6, 6–3 win over Aussie journeyman Terry Rocavert. "I was not meant to be a champion and McEnroe was," Rocavert said. "You have to be a certain kind of person to fit into all of this."

He then wasted Tom Okker 6–0, 7–6, 6–1. "He killed me," said the Dutchman, who by then was past his prime. "On grass the ball stays low and McEnroe could move it around very nicely with his wrist." The New Yorker then outserved the huge-serving Kevin Curren of South Africa, 7–5, 7–6, 7–6, who at the time still considered himself an up-and-comer even though he had played McEnroe in college when he competed for the University of Texas.

"He had this presence and could control the crowd, the court, the match," said Curren, who in 1985 upset Wimbledon champions Stefan Edberg, Mac, and Connors en route to the final, where he lost to Becker. "I didn't play that badly. I served pretty well, but I didn't have enough confidence yet to play with him. But he's the kind of guy in a big situation that you would ask to play for your life. I felt the same way about Borg. They were able to raise their games when it counted most."

In the quarters, McEnroe would face Fleming, who wasn't in the physical or mental shape to keep up with him. He was bothered by a foot problem and felt a little out of shape, and Mac thrashed him 6–3, 6–2, 6–2. "From the day the draw was made and I realized I'd have to beat him if I was to reach the semifinal, my ambition was simply to make the quarters," Fleming recalled. "And that is not the attitude of a champion. I just wasn't ready to compete and he just killed me. He played incredible and I couldn't come close to matching him. I was pretty confident before that he could go all the way, and after that even more so, but he had some tough matches ahead."

The first match that would test his will was against Connors, who was becoming a more and more hated rival. Mac knew it would be an emotional contest and said that the bad blood between the two had begun to boil and they were nothing if not testy around each other. They trash-talked each other during changeovers. Connors called McEnroe a baby in what was an ugly match, with Connors's lack of shotmaking and both of their lack of sportsmanship plainly evident. It was more like a spitball contest between two middle school bullies than a Wimbledon semifinal.

"He got under my skin and I got under his skin too and I don't blame him," Mac said. "He had a young guy taking away his thing, and he'd do everything he possibly could to make me suffer."

Mac would say what a great guy Borg was, but he didn't take to his in-country rival Connors. However, he held his abilities in high esteem. "Despite the fact he was a complete asshole, I had complete respect for him because no matter how hard I'm trying, he's trying harder. Borg was just a physical freak of nature. When you look at Connors you see intense will and desire—I've never, ever played against a guy who tried as hard as him. I kept digging in and saying, 'I'm going to try even harder and show this guy,' but no matter how hard I dug, it seemed he dug deeper, which I found absolutely amazing."

Allen Fox saw a lot of similarities between the two type-Triple-A personalities, even though they were dissimilar in that Connors rarely lost his cool when he was ahead and McEnroe was capable of going ballistic against everyone except for Borg. But they both exposed their human side publicly and it wasn't always pretty.

"McEnroe had his failings, but he's a genius," Fox said. "His brainpower is very high. He's very honest and will tell you how it is. He has the bullshit detection system, and if he smells the bullshit you are gone. He's a person who is powerfully driven. Tennis is a game that requires honesty. It's not like the real world where you are dealing with manipulating people, or you have to be PC and have to deal with being PC. The tennis court is all about production. You either have the cards or you don't. You have to play your best hands and the other guy does too, and if you make excuses, lie to yourself, and play games it all comes out on court. You are naked, you are what you are, and the other guy is going to find out. You don't get anywhere dealing in subterfuge. If you lose, you have to find out what went wrong, and how to fix it."

In the semis, McEnroe told Connors he could kiss his ass. Connors, upset with Mac's outbursts, told him that the next time he would let his son play for him, as he and the New Yorker acted the same age. Both men were irascible and stalled frequently, but McEnroe served too cleanly and volleyed too effectively for Connors to step in and take control of the match. It was a gray day, punctuated by McEnroe's sour attitude, where he asked fourteen times to see the tournament referee, which drew the first public warning ever issued on Centre Court.

Nonetheless, McEnroe anticipated where his foe was aiming with his passing shots and punched his way to his first Wimbledon final in a 6–3, 3–6, 6–3, 6–4 victory. He was agile and quick at the net and served with amazing variety. Connors simply couldn't get a good enough read of Mac's intentions and was spun off the court.

McEnroe would meet Borg for the first time at a Grand Slam.

Peter Fleming, who felt bad that he had to drag Mac to the doubles court the next day (they fell in straight sets to McNamee and McNamara), knew that, in great form, his buddy had a terrific opportunity against Borg. He wouldn't guarantee victory, but he saw the road very well.

"I thought that John had a great chance," he said. "It was clear. They had already had a number of matches. If you can play with somebody like that and you're a naturally gifted grass player, then there is a possibility. But Borg was an animal and I knew it would be tough."

His friend knew it would be difficult too, physically and mentally. McEnroe believed that he had the goods to triumph but also felt that the conditions weren't quite as ripe as they could be.

"I had put a lot of pressure on myself and I felt my game was better suited for grass, but I had choked some matches," McEnroe said. "I was so caught up and wrapped up, and the press was all over me, I was exacerbating the situation and inflaming it. But I was thinking and felt like I should win the match, that this is the time I should win it. But the fact I had to play Jimmy on Saturday because of the rain and also play doubles—Björn had some time off and even without that was fitter than I was. That was on my mind."

19

"Something in Me Wilted"

John McEnroe has the momentum and a great chance to step on the Swede in the opening game of the fifth set. Borg looks impatient to start, bouncing the ball off the grass again and again before serving while McEnroe crouches and sways. Borg comes in off a deep approach and McEnroe hooks a backhand pass off his back foot that careens off the Swede's racket. Then a bending Borg pops up a volley and McEnroe full-throats a running backhand swing volley past him. He's hyperaggressive and superconfident, up 30–0. But Borg is by no means done. He cuts in an excellent first serve. He hammers a groundstroke combination. He efficiently puts away an overhead and places a drop volley just where it needs to be. The Swede has held to 1–0 and Mac can't make him work hard enough.

"I kept saying to myself, 'Oh my God, I've got to break him now,'" Mac remembered. "You'd think maybe just once he'd let up and just say forget it. No. What he does out there, the way he is, the way he thinks . . ."

Borg is simply not willing to relinquish his crown without throwing everything he has against the cagey kid. He rubs his arms with a green towel and telegraphs to his younger foe that there are more balls to play, that there will be no rapid secession from the king. Borg will attempt to grind Mac down.

"If you lose a match like this, the Wimbledon final, after all those chances, you will not forget it for a long, long time," Borg said. "That could be very, very hard. It was my serve to start the last set. I lost the first two points. But then, I say to myself, I have to forget. I have to keep trying, try to win."

After those first two lost points on his service game, Borg serves twenty-nine more times in the match and wins twenty-eight, the only mishap coming while he is ahead 40–0 in the ninth game. He never develops a fluid technique on his serve, which is odd, considering that his groundstrokes run as true as a great river diving over the widest and highest waterfalls. He doesn't bend his knees enough and isn't explosive through his motion, but his ball toss is appropriately high, he cocks his cobra of a wrist and has such a strong, whippy right arm that he generates sizable power on his first serve, and he is calm and savvy enough to spot it well.

Borg is just too strong physically. He is involved in a Superstars cross-training competition again, this time not a made-for-TV sports circus but a Wimbledon final, where Mac can't keep up with him on the final legs of the high hurdles. Borg appears fresh, and Mac is drained.

"Something in me wilted," he said.

Sitting forward on a couch in the clubhouse, Fleming thinks, "John looks fried."

The American keeps clawing, but Borg's lungs and champion's reserve are fathomless. Mac has lost a step and Borg has gained one, just as the mythical horse Sleipnir could when called upon to perform heroic acts.

The American is too slow up to the net and can't bend his knees deeply enough to hit an effective half volley. His second serves land short and Borg punishes them.

He's holding, but it is getting more and more difficult. Somehow he fights off four break points in the second game, but his back is pasted to the wall. At 3–4 with Mac serving, Borg races ahead to 0–40. This could be it. But McEnroe goes to his service slider, which Borg pokes into the net; he adeptly covers the net with a forehand volley; and then when the Swede runs around his backhand and sizzles a forehand return down the line, Mac reads it and punches a backhand volley into the open court. Three break points saved. Although he's slower to net, McEnroe finally holds to 4–4 with a swinging forehand and looks relieved. He's not spry, but he's maintaining some hope.

But Borg is holding with such ease that all Mac can do is put his hands on his hips and shake his head. The BBC's Dan Maskell says he's living on pure nervous energy. The Swede holds to 5–4 with a booming ace.

McEnroe still has his wondrous serve and volley, so unless Borg comes up with top-drawer returns and passes, the American will be able to take care of business on his own serve, but not forever. He's huffing and puffing after flailing at a backhand volley and it's 30–30. He's two points from defeat again. He nets a first serve and barks out, "Oh yeah" in disgust. But he hooks a fine, deep second serve into Borg's body and then grunts loudly while he cuts a backhand volley crosscourt, and he has held to 5–5.

Borg seems to be gaining speed. At 30–0, he dances over to pick up a hard low pass and the crowd is wowed. McEnroe then pushes a pass wide and Borg has held at love again to 6–5. The American's chin sinks into his chest and he licks his dry lips. He has a few breaths left and holds to 6–6. But Borg is locked in and holds easily to 7–6. With Mac now serving, the Swede blowtorches a forehand return down the line and then rifles a backhand at the American's shoetips to gain his eighth and ninth match points at 7–6, 40–15.

As it should be, Borg's signature shot gives him his fifth trophy, a wrists-cocked, hatchet follow-through, seeing-eye crosscourt backhand pass in a 1–6, 7–5, 6–3, 6–7 (16), 8–6 victory. They shake hands quickly at the net and Mac thinks, "I knew I could beat Borg, but Wimbledon still belonged to him."

Of the 482 points played, Borg won 242 to McEnroe's 240. Simionescu and Bergelin are beside themselves with joy. Borg then quietly breaks into tears and flashes a small knowing smile.

"I was so driven," he said. "It was an unbelievable feeling. If he had broken me in the first game of the fifth set I would have lost, but I won from love–30 and then I played just unbelievably well, hardly lost a point on serve and won the match. That was the strongest set, mentally, in my tennis career."

After sitting with his hands in his head on his chair, fingers full of wilting black curls, McEnroe bows to the duchess to accept his runner-up trophy, clearly saddened and looking downward, but he shows tremendous humility during the trophy presentation. He has yet to be knighted, but everyone in England is now aware of just how lethal his sword can be.

"Part of why I lost to Borg was if I knew that I could get to a fifth-set breaker, I think I could pull it out," Mac said. "But there's no fifth-set tiebreaker at Wimbledon. I wasn't getting the job done on his serve. He was serving so big and holding easily. Whatever he had inside himself was beyond anything I could imagine."

20

Living the Moments

John McEnroe and Björn Borg were not fully aware of the impact of their rivalry on the world in 1980, but what they did know was that tennis was huge then and celebrities wanted to inhale its spirit. That year, a famous photo was taken of the award-winning director Woody Allen and actress Diane Keaton appearing to have a long conversation. Allen is holding a Dunlop racket bag—Mac's weapon of choice. There's another picture of a sexy Bianca Jagger walking down Fifth Avenue with a racket-carrying Ilie Nastase.

All of Mac's and Borg's peers described how the two were treated like rock stars, how the spotlights turned on them everywhere they went. They both had long and stylish, if not funky, hair. When Borg went clubbing, his colorful outfits shifted into overdrive. Denim was in, and Mac felt just right in dark blue, light blue, gray, acid—any kind of jeans jackets. Leather shoes with no laces or buckles tromped across New York City and Paris, and loafers became as common for men as high heels were for women.

"I came in at a good time with a lot of personalities; Nastase was full of life and Björn had the most incredible aura ever," Mac recalled. "I've never seen anyone still to this day with 250 to 300 girls screaming outside of the locker room like they were for Björn. There were Connors, Vitas, Vilas, even guys ranked 100 in the world had fans, there was something about tennis then and with money starting to come in—it was an incredible combination for me. I was saying, 'This is exciting and they will pay us more than we deserve.' There was an incredible allure. There was a sense of tremendous excitement. If you would have told me then that golf would now get double or triple the ratings than tennis does I would have said you were crazy. And they had some attractive guys—Lee Trevino, Arnold Palmer, Jack Nicklaus, Tom Watson, and people knew them, but we were in a different league, There's that famous cover shot of Borg and I on *World Tennis* magazine, standing back to back as gunfighters, and I had a lot of national covers too."

After the Wimbledon final, Borg and Mac's popularity took off like the Stones' Keith Richards blazing a guitar riff in "Sympathy for the Devil." They were celebrities on both sides of the Atlantic.

"From a British perspective, [McEnroe] was the icon of all the antiestablishment guys," said Peter Fleming. "Walking down the street with Junior was a trip. He always walked fast, just to sort of be behind him and see people's reactions, people freaked out. It was a big deal. This guy was something special. That matchup in England was history."

McEnroe later recalled his first trip to Ireland when he went to look up a relative, who was then in her eighties. "The first thing she said to me was, 'I like Björn Borg better than you.'"

Sports psychologist Jim Loehr believes that the fascination with the 1970s and 1980s is not accidental. "That's where the public's fondest memories are," he said. "You had great rivalries, with players who kept showing up every Sunday, and the personalities became bigger than life. There was a consistency among the players, and we could identify with them. The players were in the game much longer and they didn't get rich as quickly. There's a correlation between passion for the game and the players' longevity. Today, people can't play the game they're watching on TV. It's like it's become a sport outside their reach, so they go back to a time when life was slower, the ball was slower, and the rackets were primitive. The players were human and you really felt you knew them. People today get lost in the pace of life. They might find the tennis exciting, but they don't identify with it. The players were around for a very long time, you got to know them. . . . They were always there on TV when you turned it on. They never went away. There weren't as many choices on television then as there are now."

Loehr describes the connection to those players as "clearly a nostalgia phenomenon. . . . People like Connors, Chrissie, McEnroe became family members. You grew up with them, in an extended family. You got to know Mac's quirks, and you either loved him or hated him, but he was in front of you all the time."

Loehr believes that in today's game the fans don't have as much time to get to know the stars because they get injured more frequently, or leave the game early because they have already made their fortunes. "They disappear because they got rich real quick and lost their motivation. Big money has changed the game. If players had to continue to work to make a living for a long time, it would be different for how long they chose to stay active. The average life span of a player now is maybe seven years, and back then, although Borg was a slight exception [even though Borg retired at twenty-six, he began playing on tour at sixteen], many of them played well into their thirties and, with Connors and Rosewall, until forty."

Borg was not a complicated man—he was a very simple one—but his aura alone was enough to knock 'em dead. Pam Shriver, who reached the 1978 U.S. Open final, was never overtaken by his spoken words, but by his very being.

"I looked at Borg like a superstar in our sport," Shriver said. "I was even afraid to say, 'Hi.' This guy was too big. He had the hair, the headbands, tight shirts, the incredible heartbeat; he had all these legendary things about him. He had a physical aura, but when you sat down and talked to him it was like . . . okay."

Borg's personality was the perfect contrast to that of Mac and Connors, and fans liked seeing the regal Old World gods fending off the upstart demigods who appeared too big for their britches.

"The contrast was incredible," Loehr said. "Borg not only had the long hair, but he was a free spirit, a man unto himself who was unfettered by what was going on around him. He wouldn't change for anything, he had no ego, wasn't boastful, wasn't very in-your-face, but he'd show up and beat you like a drum if you weren't one hundred percent. He almost never had bad days. He was the man of steel, nothing changed him and he played like a bloody robot. He created his own style and people just liked to look at him. It was intriguing to watch him hit shots that no one can teach . . . he was more of a mystery man. No one really knew him except that he wore his hair different, had nerves of steel, and no one else hit the ball the way he did way behind the baseline. He'd get inside people's skins with a quiet and steady elegance."

That was not McEnroe, who got under people's skin with a loud, brash riot of sounds and a vast cornucopia of wondrous shots. "The contrast with someone who was screaming and yelling and cussing was right there," Loehr said. "With Mac, fans liked his drama; it was like going to a hockey game to watch the fights."

When folks discuss how effusive and attractive the personalities of that era were, part of their reasoning is that angrier men make for better theater. Moreover, men like McEnroe and Connors, who showed disdain for societal rules, more or less embodied antiestablishment and working-class values. They weren't exactly saying "Fuck the rich" as the era's socialists did, but "Fuck the officials who shower us with antiquated rules" did them just fine. The Old World fought back with a vengeance and tried to rein in their explosions, but to little overall effect.

"That's what the sport didn't realize, or maybe they did, when they changed all of the rules and tightened it up on me and Jimmy," McEnroe said. "It was, 'Let's drain as much personality out of the sport as possible.' We came at a time when the money was just coming into the sport but there was still a sense of enjoying yourself and you went out and had fun. You weren't sitting around counting the chocolates on your pillow at the hotel."

Shriver called the period "the boom time," saying after she reached the U.S. Open final in 1978 against Chris Evert as a sixteen-year-old—where she was defeated by her more experienced opponent—the feeling of popularity was palpable. "Tennis was transcending the sport. People knew who played it, which important people followed it—it spanned pop culture more."

Shriver, a distant relative of former vice presidential candidate Sargent Shriver (who ran with George McGovern in 1972 against Richard Nixon and Spiro Agnew), has played tennis on the White House courts and hobnobbed with plenty of VIPs, including her distant cousin Maria Shriver, who is married to "the Terminator," the actor and governor of California from late 2003 through 2010, Arnold Schwarzenegger. But nothing in the following years came close to what happened to Shriver in 1978, when simply being a successful pro tennis player meant that you got on the A-list at parties.

"That was my huge sensational splash," she said. "I had *People* magazine knocking at my parents' back door. I had *National Enquirer* at my high school. That's never happened since. Do I think in 2008, thirty years later, if I got to the finals of the U.S. Open that would happen again? No. I think maybe people would have called and asked for an interview, but that's it. Tennis these days has been pretty good about trying to place its players outside of the sports pages and into the mainstream, but the world today is a different place and they aren't always front and center. With real celebrity, it's whether you can stand the test of time, and I had multiple exposures playing doubles with Martina Navratilova and your face is out there and it kind of builds up. But it has never been like it was that summer."

Tracy Austin was a minor celebrity by the age of thirteen, having already played against Bobby Riggs in exhibitions and winning multiple junior championships. *Sports Illustrated* put her and her pigtails on its cover, and she was touted as the next big thing, but it wasn't until 1979 when she upset Navratilova and Evert to become the

youngest player to win the U.S. Open title at sixteen years and nine
months that her life really changed.

"Winning the nation's most important crown on the country's
grandest stage over America's sweetheart, 'Chrissie,' who had won
four straight titles, really put me on the map, and after that, sponsors, media, and fans began to demand a large piece of my life," she
said. "It didn't hurt that I was seen as an 'attractive Californian girl'
sporting pigtails and freckles, but I was also a person that showed
no fear on court and displayed a mental toughness not often seen
with someone so young."

Austin was named the Associated Press's Female Athlete of the
Year and quickly became one of the most popular athletes around.
"Sponsors swamped my agent with business opportunities and journalists kept ringing up my mother, Jeanne, trying to get exclusives.
I was a squeaky clean All-American kid whose image fans and sponsors bought into," she recalled. "I very much tried to stay in my
tennis bubble and continue to lead a normal life off the circuit, but
it wasn't that easy. There were constant, extreme demands on my
time. There were many times when I felt there were too many things
on my platter and others didn't understand the meaning of the word
'No.' At times, there were too many balls for me to juggle."

Austin put tennis first on her plate, but accepted a number of big
sponsorships, including her own signature lines with Avon, Spald-
ing, Pony, and the Japanese clothing company Gunze. She appeared
in heavily promoted TV commercials for 7-Up with basketball phe-
noms Magic Johnson and Larry Bird, but her eyes were more
focused on the top ranking and winning more Grand Slam titles.

"At sixteen years old, you don't quite realize how big the world is
yet and what your role is in it," she said. "As I reached adulthood,
the pressure began to increase, because I realized how big the occasions were. In 1980, when I became number one for the first time,
I was clearly a hunted player and my competitors' perceptions of me
had changed."

Austin loved to watch McEnroe face off with Borg or with
Connors, and enjoyed the Jimbo vs. Borg contests, too. Like Shriver,

who played juniors around the same time as McEnroe, Austin found McEnroe more approachable than Borg, which was partly because they were both American. She could feel, too, the intense mental competition between McEnroe and Connors, both type-A personalities who didn't want to be viewed as the second best American, each resenting the other man for pushing him off the top of the heap, privately and publicly.

"Really competitive types get along with noncompetitive types," said psychologist Allen Fox, who played against Connors and knew him well. "But really competitive types don't get along that well." As McEnroe later admitted after his failed marriage to the feisty actress Tatum O'Neal, they were too competitive with each other.

Although Jimmy Connors was right in the mix, it was the Borg-McEnroe rivalry that dominated the summer of 1980 and helped to fill a gap for an America that saw its Moscow Olympic dreams disappear in the boycott over the Soviet invasion of Afghanistan. The nation had been extremely excited about what was to come that summer, especially in competition against its archrival and host, the chest-pounding USSR. The fervor had begun at the Lake Placid Winter Olympics in February of that year, when the phenomenal twenty-one-year-old American speed skater Eric Heiden won five individual gold medals, and the U.S. hockey team—a collection of wide-eyed college kids and lunch-bucket journeymen—stunned the seemingly unbeatable Russians in what became known as the "Miracle on Ice."

During those same games, one of Borg's heroic peers, the Swedish Alpine skier Ingemar Stenmark, won the slalom and giant slalom in an ethereal and balletic display that made him just as popular as Borg or even more so in a country that reveled in sliding through the snow.

A few months later in America, however, where sweltering temperatures, a sluggish economy, and a faltering White House held sway, the summer boycott of the Moscow games licked the icing off the sweet winter Olympic cake.

"The country was in one of its worst conditions under Carter," Loehr said. "When people's lives get to the point when a recession or depression is weighing on them, they want to go out and are looking for some kind of excitement, looking for a release. They need a little joy in their lives. When you had the kind of drama you had with Borg and Mac and there is staleness in the air, it was a great release where people could leave the depressed state they are in, go into this magical game and watch them duke it out. Sport had always been a rescue for people when their lives are really challenged. The challenge of sport gives them a little relief and I'm sure it happened then as well."

What McEnroe recalls about that summer is how hard he burned inside after his loss to Borg at Wimbledon. "I didn't have worldly matters on my mind at that point," he said. "The one thing about tennis is you live in cocoon. People's attention was on us and I can't say whether the Olympic boycott was a factor. Maybe it was, but I wasn't thinking about it then."

What was apparent, though, after the smoke had cleared in London, was that McEnroe and Borg would take over the sporting scene for the rest of the summer. Few could wait for the U.S. Open, which would begin in seven weeks' time.

"Wimbledon 1980 put them into a different sphere," Loehr said. "Sports then were more of staple to get a break from what was going on, the hostage crisis and the Olympic boycott. It seems today that while the sports landscape has grown, everybody is so into their PDA and cell phones they don't sit down and pay attention. Back then, people would sit in their living rooms and really live the moments."

PART TWO

THE U.S. OPEN

21

Rock of Gibraltar

It is bright and sunny on September 7, 1980, for the U.S. Open final. There is almost no wind, literally a godsend, as Flushing Meadows typically has at least a light breeze pushing down its long stems of grass—what's still left of them in the fading marshes near the old World's Fair grounds.

Former Davis Cup captain Tony Trabert, commentating for CBS, believes that McEnroe is in good enough shape to shake off the effects of the marathon clash he had with Jimmy Connors the previous evening, but Mac had gotten to bed late. As almost always, Borg looks fairly well rested. Both men look like they have just showered when they come on court.

Borg tries standing a little closer in to receive Mac's second serves, but he is still wary of the New Yorker's searing first serves and bends low a good eight feet behind the baseline. As Trabert says, both men are feeling the tension of the occasion. It is an apocalyptic type of rematch.

Borg rips a backhand crosscourt winner, and Trabert opines that we'll see that plenty. That will certainly be the case, as the Swede is nowhere without his money shot, and if he's wristing balls in rapid-fire succession as he did at Wimbledon, McEnroe could be in for a very long day. In the same vein, if Mac is nearly errorless with his too-hot-to-handle volleys, Borg will surely strain.

CBS's play-by-play man, Pat Summerall, says this is one of the toughest tickets ever for a U.S. Open final. It's absolutely packed.

In the second game, Borg revolutions a spinning backhand lob at Mach 3 speed that dips so quickly everyone in the building knows that if Mac is going to be successful coming in on Borg's backhand he has to disguise his approaches, hit deep and to sharp angles. On the other hand, this is not grass, where Borg's short volleys will die on a brown spot. This is concrete, where the bounces are higher, and the Swede must keep his volleys deeper, as the short sliders that work on Wimbledon lawns will only become slow, crushable curveballs on cement.

The eager tennis writers who sit above the back of the court watch the shadows coming off the stadium to the west, only covering about a quarter of the court from the brilliant sunlight. Mac's hair is still long and curly, but his headband—black today instead of his trademark red—rides so high up on his head that his poofed-up hair reminds one of actress Adrienne Barbeau after a one-hour blow-drying session in the hit 1970s TV show *Maude*. Borg's headband is dark blue, moodier than the one he wore at Wimbledon.

If Mac gets any floating topspin ball to his backhand, he will lean in, slice hard, and charge. Much of the outcome will be determined by whether Borg is baiting him and waiting for him to come in Russian roulette fashion, at which point he can gain an excellent shot at the pass, or whether Mac has limited Borg's options so much that the percentages weigh in his favor.

At times, though, it doesn't make a difference, as even the so-called low-percentage volley or pass leaves tongues wagging, both men nailing impossibly difficult shots that most mortals cannot conceive of pulling off. The term "low-percentage shot" does not apply in this titanic contest.

Borg has a break point at 2–2, and after a cat-and-mouse rally, he barely misses a backhand pass down the line that he believes is in. He then scalds another one of his legendary backhands cross-court, but Mac grunts and nails a hard ace down the T. A third break point and Borg nets a return. McEnroe begins to fiddle with the second hand on his service watch, and Borg breaks the glass with a searing backhand cross. Mac denies him by jamming his serve into Borg's forehand. The American hits a terrific forehand volley in the corner and Borg ricochets a forehand down the line for a winner. Will the match last until Monday?

Mac pummels a lefty forehand again and finally holds with a brilliant, forceful volley into the corner. "Technically, McEnroe's backswing is so short, his strokes so correct, biochemically he's so perfect it looks magic," noted the legendary coach Vic Braden, who is known as tennis's mad but happy scientist. "His instincts have always been exquisite. He can't drop-shot any better, disguise lobs any better, intimidate any better, scheme any better. This is it. This is the time you want to pay good money to see him play."

It's 3–2 and the mental marathon is on. Borg is cracking his serve and Mac isn't driving the ball enough from the backcourt. It's 4–4 and Borg mis-hits a forehand crosscourt that lazily sails over McEnroe's head and stays in the court. It's triple break point. Standing way off the court and anticipating a slice serve into his backhand, Borg rockets a backhand return down the line and breaks Mac at love. For the New Yorker, there is trouble afoot.

It's 5–4 Borg, and the Swede is looking to serve out the set. If he can get a leg up in this contest, he can play more freely. He knows that and tightens just a smidgen. McEnroe senses it. Former U.S. Open champion John Newcombe notes that both of defending champion John McEnroe's ankles are taped. Trabert talks admiringly about Mac's willingness to slap and charge off Borg's second serves, and moments later McEnroe calls himself a lazy bum after he's slow to attack the cords and nets a forehand volley from his navel.

Johnny Mac drills a quick forehand down-the-line pass. Borg misses an easy backhand pass down the line. On break point, Mac muscles a forehand crosscourt return and follows it up with a leaping overhead winner. Now they are deadlocked at 5–5.

Just two months prior, Britain's Mark Cox, commentating for the BBC, said this of Borg during the Wimbledon final: "His temperament is as solid as the Rock of Gibraltar." But not so, early on this day in New York, as doubts keep creeping into his head. Maybe a plane overhead belched out an annoying burp; maybe he caught the whiff of a burnt hot dog or heard a strained siren wailing miserably in the distance. His look is downtrodden, not one of an invincible deity.

McEnroe isn't floating in the heavens either. At 5–5, he double-faults, errs on a simple forehand half volley, and then with a forehand volley on his racket that he should have contained down the line, he nudges it wide yet close. Mac almost never gets upset against Borg, but he objects to the call, skipping across the court, circling a mark, and telling chair umpire Ken Slye that the ball was right on the line. But Slye, who is sitting right on top of the white stripe, denies him. Mac yells, "It's only break point at 5–5!"

The New Yorker is down 6–5 and he's churning inside, but he begins to raise his level, hitting two terrific volleys, and then watches Borg double-fault. Why can't the Swede serve this set out? Because this is not his venue. He is a little unfortunate as he is late to a simple forehand and then flies a routine backhand long. He is broken at love to 6–6, maybe by all five boroughs of spooky New York. McEnroe had little to do with that implosion in particular.

They go into a tiebreaker. Remember that? The better server always has the advantage, since he doesn't have to defend as much. Borg sneaks ahead 2–0 after blasting an overhead. McEnroe slaps his hip, but the Swede again begins to err and allows his opponent a chance to breathe.

McEnroe inhales deeply and fools Borg with a topspin second serve out wide to his forehand in the deuce court that is called an ace. Borg is disgusted, rearing his head back, putting his fingertips on his eyes, then staring down Slye. But he doesn't say a word down 2–3. "That's about as much emotion as you'll see from Borg," Trabert notes.

Borg smokes a service winner and it's 3–3. They quietly change ends. A stumbling Borg falters on a half volley and the shadows are now halfway across the court at 4–3. Mac is superambitious and is willing to charge off the most marginal of approach shots. His instinct takes over as he knocks off one winning volley, barely misses another on an excellent dipping return by Borg, authoritatively punches another into the open court, and then wins the set that should have been Borg's with a bump and run, punctuated by another quick-fisted volley winner. The New Yorker has seized the first set 7–6 (4).

The Swede must feel jinxed by NYC, or maybe, for the first time in his career, he's feeling that his best might not be good enough.

22

The Cowboy Bucks Up

After his epic loss at Wimbledon, John McEnroe and company got on the first available flight out of London to New York. His childhood friend Mary Carillo, still not rolling in the big bucks that she would later earn from broadcasting, was sitting in coach and caught wind of the fact that the McEnroes were up in first class.

"I'm back in cattle class, but I sneak up into the first-class cabin and pull back the curtain, and John is out cold, asleep," Carillo recalled. "Mr. McEnroe had picked up all the Fleet Street papers and every other paper he could get his hands on and had them spread across his lap. He's opened to a double-page spread and the stewardess is telling me to go back to coach and I point over and say, 'I know them, I know them!' Mr. McEnroe heard my voice and looks up and there's a great big tear rolling down his face. He's reading about his boy, the crabby guy who a lot of Wimbledon had rooted against, and now in defeat after that magnificent match, the country had come to embrace him."

John McEnroe Sr. remembers carrying his son's runner-up trophy onto the plane and reliving the match. It was an exhilarating two-week trial for the headstrong family from Douglaston, Queens, especially the final, where every ounce of emotion had been wrung out of them.

"I was a little teary because it was so unexpected," he said. "John beat Jimmy and then fended off all those match points in the fourth set against Björn; he was just getting confidence in knowing what he can do. And then in the fifth set, Borg plays incredibly well and I'm thinking, 'How can he feel this good about himself after what happened in the tiebreaker?' But he keeps getting better and better. I'm thinking, 'My God, this is unbelievable!' I wasn't happy with the result, but proud of how John played. Donald Dell [an agent and broadcaster] came up to me and said, 'He may have just lost a match but he just won a country.'"

While McEnroe was proud of his effort too, he was by no means pleased to be on the losing end of the historic match. He was steaming.

"All the memories I have of what happened after 1980 Wimbledon and before the U.S. Open was being in that match and I was steaming for a couple of weeks. I should have won the second set and won in straights and I blew it. Tennis is so mental. I was physically tired, and I tried to hang in there because I thought for sure I was going to win. But Björn rose to the occasion in the fifth. My biggest mistake was thinking that he'd be discouraged because he had almost won in four, and it was an amazing effort that he found something within his soul when he had almost blown it. It's hard to get that out of your mind."

But clearly, something magical occurred that sunny day at the All England Lawn Tennis Club on July 5. For all intents and purposes, McEnroe tattooed the tiebreaker score 18–16 to his forehand and will carry it to his grave. He also carried the memory of how he had fallen in London to New York, where the two ultimate rivals would meet again in the U.S. Open final.

"It's the match I'm most proud of and the match people have talked to me about hundreds of times—they whisper, 'The tiebreaker, the tiebreaker!' That match is the one where I can really look my kids in the eye and say that the cliché that says there are no losers in a match can be true. And people damn well know that someone lost, but I thought I came out ahead getting more respect from players, fans, and a more positive view of me from folks in general. I felt something electric going on, which is very rare in a match, especially in the tiebreaker, which is incredible because Centre Court has a pretty quiet crowd. To be part of tennis history is a fantastic feeling."

Another part of history was taking place in July 1980 at the White House, where for all of his humanitarian virtues, for all of his deep intellect and his softhearted people skills, President Jimmy Carter was stuck in the mud. Iran had gone off the board, the economy was sinking, and he inspired confidence in almost no one.

America needed a big-thinking cowboy carrying a big stick of knotted oak, and Ronald Reagan was just the ticket, although his cowboy image was carved in his television and movie days rather than from actually rustling cattle or getting his hands dirty shoveling horse manure inside rickety stables. Still, he talked tough and told Americans what they wanted to hear.

"All of us have been dishonored, our credibility as a great nation has been compromised, to say the least," Reagan said in one of his stump speeches on his way to crushing George Bush in the Republican primary. "Our shield has been tarnished. Pride in our nation is out of fashion. Let's not consign the American dream to the dustbin of history."

Although it may seem a stretch to compare a twenty-one-year-old tennis player with a man who would become president of the United States, there were some genuine similarities between Johnny Mac and Ronald Reagan in the appeal they had for the American people that summer. Like McEnroe, Reagan was no fan of compromise or being proverbially held hostage by another person's rules or regulations. To Reagan, the world had to be refashioned in an American way, his way, with his nation leading the charge, guns blazing, across the international plains and shooting down all who opposed him. When confronting his enemies, there was little emphasis on sportsmanship. When devising his game plans, there was no need for an Old World style of diplomacy.

Like McEnroe, Reagan felt he was constantly in the right, and those who opposed him were essentially viewed as enemies of the state. There was a defined American way for Reagan: stand up straight, chin high, shoulders back, fists clenched, and arms ready to deliver a knockout punch. "I've never seen anyone insult Jack Dempsey," he once said in reference to a foreign policy question.

It was the end result that mattered to Reagan, and, just as McEnroe often thought minor players didn't deserve to be on the court with him, Reagan's journey would not include being tossed around by minor world players like Khomeini or Cuba's Fidel Castro. It would be traveling up the highest mountain roads to battle Russia for world supremacy. He foreshadowed a shootout at the OK Corral, where after a potentially dark night, it would be morning again in America. "We cannot play innocents abroad in a world that is not innocent," Reagan would say.

Reagan was, like so many world leaders before him, a charismatic authoritarian who made heartfelt emotional appeals during troubled times. McEnroe, although the only world he was trying to change was tennis, had similar qualities. When he returned stateside after Wimbledon and moved toward the U.S. Open, it was his ambitious, charismatic personality that captured the nation and his tough-talking, authoritative game that shook the earth.

To put it simply: in the summer of 1980, Reagan and McEnroe were a couple of American cowboys bucking up for the blazing gunfight.

McEnroe's politics are now on the liberal side (he donated to left-wing comedian Al Franken's Minnesota senatorial campaign in 2008), and he doesn't recall being swept up in the Carter-Reagan debates in 1980, but has strong memories of both presidents overall. He remembers writing a song about Carter in 1976, the first year he voted.

"I remember thinking, 'This guy is incredible, man, there is something about him,'" he said. "It was like, God, anything is possible. You had this feeling like anything was possible. But I was too young—then all of a sudden it felt like a letdown because here was this guy that was so smart and so great, like supposedly cared so much about people; was like a brilliant guy—here he is like bombing out as president. That was sort of deflating. Then you have this actor and I remember I went to the White House, I think because the Davis Cup team and the Olympic team were being honored or whatever, and Bush was in the room. No one was even talking to him, and he was the vice president. It was pretty funny. Then Reagan came in. He was this tremendous storyteller. He obviously knew nothing about tennis but . . . you really liked the guy." So did most of the nation that had voted for him.

Less than pleased with his loss to Borg, Mac arrived at his Douglaston home, slept, and hung out with friends. He was much more of a celebrity now and letters flooded his parents' home, some addressed to "John McEnroe, U.S.A." Rocker Eddie Money asked him to come onstage to play the tambourine at a Central Park concert.

John McEnroe Sr. called the Wimbledon match "absolutely glorious," but of course, he would have preferred a victory. "John helped change people's perception of what he is all about. They saw that part of his intensity is pressing himself to the limit."

Junior's doubles partner, Peter Fleming, saw a more depressed side of him. "He was bummed. No other way of putting it. It was tough. But there even was a part of him that was exhilarated; everybody knew there was something special."

McEnroe's reception was grand as everyone praised his performance in the historic loss. A lot of folks told him it was the best match they ever saw and that there were no losers who left the court. "I've had a lot of problems with the fans. I know that. The match at Wimbledon was kind of a new start. I still showed my emotions, but I wasn't bad. It was natural, the emotion I showed, and people liked it. I still showed my personality out there, but it was mostly just two people going at each other. I know I gave my best, and I was satisfied with that, but you wouldn't want to celebrate it. You wouldn't want to settle for second best."

There was work to do, and McEnroe went back to his coach Tony Palafox for a tune-up. "The panic button had set in," Mac said.

Palafox tweaked a few things prior to the summer hardcourt season. They didn't immediately fall into place, but in seven weeks' time, he was clicking.

"He almost never verbalizes about his game," said Peter Rennert, his rival in the juniors. "Everything is instinctive. The one guy he listens to is Tony. When Palafox says something, John pays attention. Otherwise, he'll just pick and choose and maybe say something months later. Mainly, he just does what feels right, and with him it ends up being good."

Palafox was more convinced than McEnroe that he was about to hit his peak. "He has gained two things: some new fans who found out that he's not as bad as they thought he was, and a lot of confidence. He knows how to beat Borg, and he's ready to do it."

But until he arrived at the gates of the USTA National Tennis Center, Mac went into a seven-week funk. He was close to drinking from the golden chalice, and he had a hard time getting up for the in-between events. Had he come off a Wimbledon title, he might have stormed through his matches, but he couldn't find the fire within or the rhythm in his strokes.

He played the South Orange, New Jersey, Canada, and Atlanta tournaments, but took losses in all. He lost in the final at South Orange to José Luis Clerc, defaulted in the Canadian Open because of a sprained right ankle, and lost a first-round match in Atlanta to John Austin, Tracy's brother. "Part of it is I don't want to reach my peak too soon," McEnroe said at the time. "Maybe I'm not working as hard as I can to make my career last. I've never really felt in my life that I was in great shape. I've just relied on talent. It's easy to say to yourself, 'I'm number two in the world, so why should I train hard?' But my body has gotten to the point where I have to work on it."

Harry Hopman, who was then running his own academy in Florida and was still on the forefront of conditioning work, noted the difference between the American and the Swede in the Wimbledon final. "The way Borg finished with such stamina, so fast and so well, might influence John to do a little more off-court training," he said hopefully. "And when I say a little, I mean some. John is not very keen about that form of life. But he needs his agility. He is so intense that he's using himself up all the while, and he has to be fit. I also would like to see the inner fitness that comes out because you've worked very hard, because of daily habits."

McEnroe's father conceded that his son was no great fan of practice, saying, "Twenty guys on the tour can beat him in practice," but noted, as his son did, that he got his workouts by playing doubles.

McEnroe never got serious about off-court work until after his hiatus in 1986, but he was determined not to tire the rest of the summer. Mentally, he was still on edge. There were still some fans who, even if they respected him now after Wimbledon, got on him, and that didn't please him.

"After Wimbledon, you expect a positive thing when you go out on the court," McEnroe said. "But some people are still egging me on. I don't think that Wimbledon totally changed everything. It's not a one-match-type thing. It's going to take a while, but the Borg match showed me that it doesn't have to be that way. Sure, I want to be appreciated. When I quit tennis I want to be remembered as a tennis player, not some jerk."

Hopman was rightfully concerned about what could happen at Flushing Meadows. "There will still be times when John, in his intensity, will not hold himself in. Particularly in New York, where the gallery is very vociferous and sometimes vulgar, that sort of thing could trigger him off."

Hopman was correct, but Mac wasn't quite a rebel without a cause like his folk hero, James Dean. He knew what he was after. He was more than just an antiestablishment guy who wanted to be wild and cool for the sake of it.

"I thought Dean was great," McEnroe said. "I think the unfortunate thing—like he killed himself at twenty-four, running a car a
hundred miles an hour into a tree—that is not the part I liked about
him. The intensity he had—it is like his pain—I like pain with
intensity. I like people with intensity. It is clear from the way I am
that I prefer that, sitting there and looking at someone who is like
a Borg—if everyone acted like Borg, we would all be sleeping. If
everyone acted like me, we would have an explosion."

23

"I Didn't Know What Was Happening"

The man who was largely responsible for waving good-bye to old money and welcoming the new into USTA coffers, Slew Hester, is sitting beside Marv Richmond, who is to be the next president of the USTA. Wearing light gray blazers, they watch intently with long gazes. Richmond is wearing a short-brimmed straw hat, a signature cap in the stadium's President's Box that is still worn to this day.

Borg's fiancée, Mariana Simionescu, dressed in a pink short-sleeved shirt, has her lips pressed tightly together. Frequently she pulls a gold lighter out of her handbag and lights another Marlboro.

It's the second set of the 1980 U.S. Open final, and Borg is missing everything. A simple half volley is yanked way wide. A routine two-hander crosscourt flies lazily away. McEnroe is so confident that he's nimbly moving around no-man's-land and short-hopping impossible winners. Tony Trabert calls it a "symphony in motion," and Mac breaks Borg in the opening game by powering an approach shot deep down the middle and then taking Borg's pass attempt and gently dropping it over the net. The 20,000-plus who came to applaud do so in resounding fashion.

The U.S. Open has set a new attendance record of more than 364,000 fans going through the gates, a mark that will be smashed time and time again as the grounds are expanded and a new, cavernous stadium is added in 1997, but those folks who helped set the mark in 1980 on that sunny Sunday will always remember the final as one of their most cherished spectator moments.

Borg doesn't seem to believe that he can break McEnroe's serve, and when the American holds at love to 2–0, the despondent Swede doesn't even run to chase down a volley. Trabert is wondering whether the thought of the New York jinx is running through Borg's head. Pat Summerall says it must be.

Borg misses a sitter overhead when he doesn't properly set up for it and double-faults to be broken at love to go down 0–3. He is in a huge funk. His head is too far down and he has no rhythm.

Trabert says that if Borg goes down two sets to love, he's toast, but he doesn't think he's going into the tank this quickly. He mentions Borg's comeback over Kriek, and while this is New York, where he has never been able to find his closer's instincts in finals, his champion's mettle can never be entirely dismissed.

Borg briefly comes alive. He curls a forehand down-the-line passing shot and then Mac floats a backhand long. Borg grabs one break back to 3–1, but the Swede still isn't completely confident. He hesitates on a backhand overhead that lands long. Mac tosses up another lob over Borg's backhand side and his overhead bounces down before the net. The Swede hesitates on an inside-out forehand that lands wide, and then a despondent Borg double-faults and he's broken to 4–1. He seems cursed.

The crowd is silent as they feel Borg's pain. Simionescu scratches her head. McEnroe's serves are so varied that it would take a three-hundred-year-old psychic to know where he is aiming. He is torturing Borg's forehand with varied serves and the Swede is late and unsure of himself. One return goes down the alley, and Borg's final one, a blocked backhand, flies way long. Mac's sunnier and ultrase-rious side is shining through and he easily holds at love to 5–1.

Even when the Swede is running the right plays, he's erring near the goal line, pushing two simple forehand volleys into the net. At 30–30, Borg misses a routine forehand and then a backhand and loses the second set 6–1. An hour and forty-five minutes into the contest, Mac is deep into the proverbial zone while Borg has yet to reenter the hemisphere.

"I didn't know what was happening," Borg said when discussing his total lack of feel.

McEnroe said his foe looked "distant."

24

The North Star of Vitas

While John McEnroe fiddled with his strokes, Björn Borg had reason to celebrate in Romania: a new wife and another Wimbledon title. He and Mariana Simionescu were married just after Wimbledon at a Greek Orthodox church in Bucharest before two hundred family and friends, with tennis friends Ilie Nastase, Vitas Gerulaitis, and Vitas's sister, Ruta, in attendance.

The wedding and ceremonies were organized by Regine, the proprietress of jet-set nightclubs, and the photo and film rights to the wedding were sold by International Management Group. Simionescu was ready to put a marriage crown on Borg's head and felt like whispering, "My husband, the King."

Ruta Gerulaitis, who was still a pro then and once reached the French Open quarterfinals, recalls it as a royal type of affair, but because of shortages in Romania at the time, it had its glitches.

"It was fabulous," she recalled. "But it was so different there in Romania, and it was really hot and we got all dressed up and they had these public buses taking us around. When we got to the reception, it was outdoors; there were two little bowls of ice cubes we were all fighting over. Ice cubes weren't plentiful then."

There was also a reception for friends in Monte Carlo, and then they were off to Marbella, Spain, for their honeymoon, followed by a trip to Borg's island in Sweden, where they fished, picked raspberries, and sailed.

Ruta Gerulaitis, who was close to Simionescu, wasn't convinced it was a marriage made in heaven. It was far from that, and Borg is now on his third wife and also fathered a child with a Swedish teenager, Jannike Björling, whom he didn't marry.

"I didn't think it would last," Ruta said. "Just being around my brother and his friends and knowing how they talked and how they laughed and what they talked about, I couldn't see it. He had an exciting romantic life. I think he really loved Mariana and she filled a need, too. She was supportive and his best friend at the time, and you need someone like that. He didn't trust a whole bunch of people. He wasn't like Vitas, who let a lot of people in. She became part of his circle and it was a small circle. He had Lennart, Mariana, his parents, and maybe a friend or two in Sweden, and I'm not even sure about that. But as they grew and went through life changes and then after he retired, it's a second life and it's difficult."

After their languid days on the island, Borg and Simionescu went back on tour. Simionescu said that Borg never mentioned anything, but she felt he was out of rhythm, and she could see cracks in his legendary mental armor. He was facing intense psychological pressure and it was wearing him out. She believed that as a player, he might no longer be eternal and invincible. "This unusual summer couldn't pass without leaving marks on his formidable psychophysical complex," she said, "which had topped everything in world tennis during the last five years."

Simionescu was prescient. Borg went to Canada for the big hardcourt warm-up and beat Gullikson, Rennert, Sadri, and Sandy Mayer before retiring in the final against Ivan Lendl with acute pain in his leg.

His celebrity had begun to wear on him, and he had risen to such heights even in the United States that there were demands on every minute of his day. "He no longer belongs to himself. He can no longer say yes or no when he pleases," Simionescu complained. He had grown testier with reporters too, saying after a defeat, "I lost because I am not God."

That summer, he and Simionescu would buy a five-bedroom home in Sands Point, Long Island, complete with a pool, where his grandparents and parents eventually hung out. But before the Open, they all set up camp at Gerulaitis's dream home in Kings Point, which Vitas bought from the winnings from his only Grand Slam title, the 1977 Australian Open. It featured a backyard hard court and had enough bedrooms to fit their parents, Borg, Simionescu, and Bergelin. Gerulaitis's parents, Lithuanian immigrants who had lived in Queens, were in heaven, and Borg and his friends shared a little slice of it.

"They camped there," Ruta recalled. "Björn found that little haven where he was comfortable at our house. It was a quiet place to practice. He loved my mother and dad. Our interest was with making my brother comfortable, but Björn too. My mom used to cook and it seemed so normal then, but now looking back I guess it was really exciting. They had those legendary practice sessions where they would go for seven or eight hours. It was neat. The neighbors always knew Björn was coming and would come over and watch."

Mary Carillo, who would stop by to hit with Ruta, recalled, "Vitas loved to drill but John didn't. John always wanted something on the side. He played a lot better if he had a little skin on it. Vitas had to practice and always felt confident if he was in tremendous condition, and man, did he and Björn ever practice!"

Gerulaitis reveled in his own celebrity, especially in New York, where he was a tabloid favorite. He once drove a mustard-colored Rolls-Royce that matched his hair, and although he ground it out on the practice court daily, he loved the nightlife and the dance floor. He got along with every other player of note and was Borg's best non-Swedish friend.

"Vitas was the center of everything and people wanted to hang out with him," Ruta recalled. "He was the life of the party. He was so charismatic and just a magnet. If he had a few issues with people he'd never admit to that. Björn was so wonderful when he came to stay—so kind and soft-spoken, a real genuine person. He was authentic. But when he and my brother went out, it was a different story. It was a good time in our lives and the best memories ever, and when it ended, it was kind of depressing. It was like a fairy tale how we went from Queens to Kings Point. Vitas was a star anywhere he went. I remember being in Paris together and he was like a rock star. He always wanted to be Mick Jagger, and at that point, he seemed like one. He loved that role. Not everyone can do it well and like it."

Whether their relationship was good for Borg is debatable, but clearly the Swede loved and admired him. "Björn was a great guy—quiet and honorable and had a good sense of humor," Sandy Mayer said. "But he was so one-dimensional and focused that he started hanging around with Vitas and decided that fun was a good thing to have. But he didn't have the moral compass to decide what's good and bad."

Gerulaitis loved being in the center of the universe, and there's no doubt that eventually the nightlife won the battle over his day job. He ended up fighting a cocaine addiction for nearly a decade, but that summer he was still in good form on court, and although he and Borg were rivals in their matches, no bitterness came of the Swede's constant victories over the American.

"It never crossed Vitas's mind," Ruta said. "Once his matches were over, he'd let it go. There was no tension at all between them. Jimmy [Connors] stayed with us years later and that was a little different, but Björn and Vitas were like brothers; there was no jealousy factor whatsoever and it really worked for them because they both got a lot out of their practice sessions."

Ruta said that by that point, the always smiling Bergelin was no longer giving Borg much technical instruction, just handling the day-to-day routines and making sure that his pupil was comfortable and motivated. Vitas was motivated too, but because he had reached the U.S. Open final the year prior, fans expected more out of their local boy.

"Vitas felt that it was his hometown tournament and there was more pressure for him to do better there than anywhere else," Ruta said. "I remember that summer, he had opened a foundation for children and there were a lot of things going on and it was all leading up to how he would do at the Open."

Whether Gerulaitis was thinking about the four times he had lost to Borg in 1980 when they whacked balls at each other in Kings Point is debatable, but he ended up having a disappointing U.S. Open, as he was upset by the big-serving Californian Hank Pfister in the second round. He did put in heavy on-court hours prior to the tournament, but perhaps he had already begun his downward spiral around that time.

"My brother spent a lot of time working on his game, and that was a little overlooked, but he was equally excited about going out and treating everyone," Ruta said. "He was too generous and had a need to have a lot people around him. He was not a loner and was always surrounded by a lot of people. Who wouldn't want to be a part of the excitement, even Björn? They both had their evenings. They got along so well and respected each other too. They really were like brothers. That was the beauty of their relationship."

Gerulaitis and McEnroe got on too (Ruta said it was Vitas who really introduced John to rock 'n' roll), but Ruta didn't see much of her fellow New Yorker at Kings Point. McEnroe would have more than his fair share of late nights out, but he didn't stretch himself to the limits that summer, as defending his U.S. Open title was paramount. He may have admired Gerulaitis as a people magnet as a teenager, and how folks naturally gravitated toward Borg's supercool Nordic persona, but he needed to prove himself on court before he was willing to totally let his guard down.

"I wasn't an innocent bystander," McEnroe said of the period, when cocaine was the sexiest drug around. "I could see early on that it wasn't something I could do if I wanted to keep playing. It's a whole process, you're up late, and then you want to sleep all day. It wasn't conducive to being a professional athlete."

Gerulaitis died prematurely in 1994, at the age of forty, of carbon monoxide poisoning while asleep at a friend's Long Island cottage. Some say he was well on the road to recovery, and whether that's the case or not (others disagree), the sport lost its social cornerstone of the 1970s and early 1980s.

"The nightlife took a toll, but he lived more than most people lived," Ruta said. "His life was unfortunately cut short but he lived strongly. Three or four days before he passed away, someone handed me an article where Vitas said, 'I made a lot mistakes, but I've had a great life and I have no regrets.' And he really meant it."

McEnroe made his mistakes too, but in August 1980, he was determined to make none that would cost him the U.S. Open title.

25

Willing and Able

Down two sets to zero and looking like a lost puppy, Borg is going to have to come up with something extra special to pull off his first U.S. Open title. McEnroe is not about to allow him room to breathe and knows that he must suffocate him.

But Borg will not relinquish easily. He fights off two break points at 1–2 with a brilliant pass and a volley and has new life, even squeezing his right hand in a subtle fist pump.

The camera pans to the new U.S. Davis Cup captain Arthur Ashe, who is sitting with his new wife, Jeanne, a strikingly beautiful photographer. Ashe is watching the guy who will bring him utter joy and total angst in Davis Cup competition, the man who will force him to look deep inside himself to discover whether sportsmanship or victory is more important.

Tony Trabert, whom McEnroe for all intents and purposes has just had fired as Davis Cup captain (years later, Mac would apologize to him publicly), says during the telecast that Ashe will make a magnificent captain and adds that he will let go of his post reluctantly, but thinks it was the right thing to do.

Mac attacks early in the fourth game with a vintage chip and charge. But McEnroe overplays a drop shot and Borg easily passes him. The American waves his hand in disgust. Maybe he can't do everything. Borg misses a wide-open pass into the net and Mac has two break points for a chance to go up 3–1. If he gets an early break here, this might go down as the Swede's worst defeat in a Slam by a long stretch. Sitting courtside, three-time U.S. Open champion Fred Perry has his mouth agape watching Borg struggle. But the Swede responds with a quick backhand pass. McEnroe is going to chip and charge again, but gets jammed by Borg's serve and is forced to retreat. Borg seizes the opportunity to come in and hits the crispest volley he's struck all contest. It's deuce. McEnroe makes two unforced errors, the last a lazy backhand, and he takes a practice swing in hopes of quickly retooling. It's 2–2.

Trabert discusses McEnroe's "happy feet" and how lightly he's moving toward the ball. He doesn't feel the New Yorker's level will drop and thinks Borg will have to make something happen. He does a moment later with a vicious inside-out backhand return into the corner. But McEnroe booms an ace down the T and appears to be sitting pretty at 3–2. But he's not. In the sixth game at 30–30, Borg smokes a backhand that clips the line, and the New Yorker grows agitated, thinking it fell wide. Then Borg finds another corner with an ace and they are even at 3–3.

In a marathon seventh game at deuce, Borg nails a backhand down the line that Mac can't handle at the net, and in frustration the American nearly crushes a ball lying on the ground with his wooden frame. It's break point, and Mac takes a superslow windup and hits a topspin second serve off the let cord that falls out and is broken to 4–3.

The Swede is playing more consistently, pressing Mac, inviting him to physical battle. Borg is running with abandon now and the crowd is trying to pull him back into the match. The masses succeed; Borg is now literally skipping into winners.

All niceties have been put aside and the tension inside Louis Armstrong Stadium is as thick as one of the trumpeter's low notes.

At 5–4, Borg once again serves for a set. But he's not anticipating as well as he did without the pressure on him. Mac wins a cat-and-mouse point at the net with a lob over the Swede's craning head. Mac pushes Borg way off the baseline, sprints in, and knocks off a forehand volley winner. He pumps his fist, and Borg mutters a few unkind words at the stands.

It's 5–5 and Mac is just two games from the match. Trabert says he's steamrolling Borg. Lennart Bergelin's tongue is clenched between his teeth. Mac holds easily at love, but with new balls in his hands, Borg steams an ace out wide and they go into another tiebreaker.

Fans think back to their Wimbledon encounter and the first set of their New York clash and wonder: can the legendary Swede actually win one against the hot-serving McEnroe?

Maybe. Borg begins the breaker with a dipping backhand pass down the line and the fans are living and dying with every point. They want a classic. At 6:35 p.m. with the sun dipping, they must have a classic.

Mac's simple backhand volley into the open court dies in the net and he's cracked the door open for a Borg charge. He swipes at the net with his frame. It's 3–2 for McEnroe, and a successful Borg backhand crosscourt pass off a bump and charge by Mac incites the American to throw his towel on the court. The boos rain down, and all of a sudden he's yelling at chair umpire Ken Slye: "You've just made the worst call I've ever seen in the biggest match of all time!"

Borg is swinging hard and his topspin is jumping off the cement. After a successful Borg volley and a McEnroe ace down the T, it's 4–4. Mac serves back down the center to Borg's backhand, but the Swede reads it and scalds a winner down the line. Then another Borg two-handed pass whizzes down the line to 6–4.

It's double set point for Borg, but he misses a simple backhand to 6–5. Maybe he'll never be able to shoot Mac through the heart during sudden death. Then, almost inexplicably, McEnroe misses a leaping high backhand volley in ugly fashion. Borg wins the third set 7–5 (5). He's down two sets to one, but he's back in the match.

Now he can make this a titanic test of physical conditioning, just how he likes it.

Vitas Gerulaitis's dad, a teaching pro, is in the house, sitting next to Bergelin. They perk up. The gold chain that hangs off Borg's neck appears to have loosened and he looks more determined. He survived Roscoe Tanner down two sets to one. He survived Johan Kriek down two sets to love. His body is willing and able. Now it's just a matter of his mind accepting that he can triumph on hard courts, go full circle in his career, and snare the one big title that has eluded him . . . and do what so many say he cannot.

26

Among the Bad Actors

In the steamy week of August 26, 1980, the U.S. Open began, and defending champion John McEnroe had a reasonable first-week draw. He wasted France's Christophe Roger-Vasselin 6–3, 6–4, 6–1 and then plastered American Steve Krulevitz 7–6, 6–0, 6–2. In the third round he'd face a familiar face from Port Washington Academy, Ricky Meyer, who caused him a bit of trouble in Mac's 6–1, 6–1, 4–6, 6–2 victory in muggy 95-degree heat. A red-faced McEnroe didn't take too kindly to some overbaked fans who were loudly cheering his double faults and errors. He exchanged some choice words with a few of them. Streetwise residents of Gotham like Johnny Mac can't resist responding to even half-empty taunts.

"There are more people rooting for me, but New York's always going to be the same, no matter what happens," he said. "You're never going to get rid of all the bad actors. I mean, during our doubles yesterday, there were people fighting in the stands. It looked pretty interesting for a while. I figure I'm about ten Wimbledon finals exactly like the last one away from getting those people on my side."

Razzed by the crowd and barking back at them, Mac lost his cool against Meyer in a contest that he knew was entirely on his racket. "Most people can't get away with that, even the aggressive types," sports psychologist Allen Fox observed. "It's very unusual. Connors and Gonzalez could do it, too. It's very hard to lose control and gain control the next point. You have twenty seconds to do it and if you really get emotional it's hard to get the fine motor control. You have to be flexible and relaxed from being super angry in just twenty seconds. You have to have a lot of confidence. If you mix anger with fear it's a problem. If you don't have a lot of fear it's easier to do it. Somewhere in the recesses of John's brain, he thinks he can do it. He may not do it, or be certain that he can, but he *thinks* that he can."

In the fourth round McEnroe defeated Frenchman Pascal Portes 6–2, 6–4, 6–2, but that would be his last predictable win. Going into week two, he was somewhat pleased. "When you lose a set, I guess it's good in a way, if you win the tournament and look back. Like when I lost a set to Nasty last year," he said. "I think I really picked up after that. Hopefully, it'll be the same thing again. I think each match I've gotten a little better, which is important. I can't say that I'm playing at the top of my game, but the guys I've played haven't been at the top of their games either, so it's hard to really judge. I just feel that I'm a lot sharper than I was at the start of the tournament."

His 4–6, 6–3, 6–2, 7–5 win over Ivan Lendl in the quarters would portend another incredible rivalry to come. The stone-faced Czech would become not only one of McEnroe's greatest rivals but one of the best players of all time, winning eight majors and reaching the U.S. Open final on eight consecutive occasions. He was incredibly fit and brought the game to a new level, powering balls off both wings and rarely mixing in soft stuff. In 1980, however, Lendl was still very much a young work in progress and hadn't figured out the proper strategy against Mac in the New Yorker's victory.

"I had trouble beating John at that time," said Lendl, who would end his career with a 21–15 record against McEnroe. "I was also way down in the matches with Jimmy. So what I did is I sat down and looked at it and said, 'What do I need to do to get better so I can overtake them?' It was mainly quickness. I had to get around the ball a little bit quicker so I wasn't always on [the] defensive and catching the ball on [the] last stride, that I had [a] little more time. Once I was able to get [a] little bit quicker, then it has helped me a lot."

Ruta Gerulaitis saw Borg and her brother leave the Gerulaitis family compound to go off to Flushing Meadows during the early days of the Open. She knew that the Swede was on a mission, but it might be an impossible journey. "Maybe he was a little psyched out," she said. "I'm sure that was really upsetting to him, not winning the U.S. Open, because he was really serious about his tennis."

Borg's practice partner Billy Martin hated Flushing Meadows, saying it was too noisy, smelled, was disruptive, and didn't fit his character. After he lost in the first round of the Open in 1979, he never went back again as a player and said he was better off for it.

Borg entered the Open being called the wealthiest athlete in the world, earning an estimated $5 million per annum. He was ready to go where he had never gone before, even entertaining questions about the possibility of winning the calendar-year Grand Slam and signaling a willingness to head down under to Australia for the first time to complete the Slam if he won the U.S. Open. Instead of denying the possibility, the Swede took the challenge head-on.

"If he's looking for pressure, he's certainly found it by talking about it," observed Rod Laver, the last man to go around the block, in 1969.

In New York in 1980, there were few matches where Borg played great, but he displayed a tremendous amount of guts time and time again. He took a quick win over Argentine Guillermo Aubone in the first round, was able to stave off John Sadri's bombs 7–5, 6–2, 2–6, 6–0, overcame the trickery of Peter McNamara 7–6, 1–6, 6–2, 6–0, and then walloped the still raw Yannick Noah 6–3, 6–3, 6–0.

Three years later Noah would become the toast of Paris by being the first Frenchman in thirty-seven years to win his home-country title.

"Björn wins and will keep winning because he doesn't push his luck," Mariana Simionescu said. "He never wages a psychological war against his opponent, because out of decency, he would never defeat his rival by talking him out of it. He never assumes poses for TV close-ups, never mimics detachment from what's going on around him, never gloats over his best shots, and never wrestles with God when the ball won't go over the net. He's just a man who goes to his work with the confidence of one well prepared, who knows he cannot do less or more than he is able. Björn does not believe in miracles."

But perhaps in New York, a few days of walking on water would have helped. From the quarterfinals on, life would get tricky, oh so tricky. He would once again face Tanner, the man who had bullied him under the lights the year prior. But this time, Tanner couldn't hold on, and when the big moments came with the American ahead 2–1 in sets, 4–2 in games, Borg responded by moving in closer to return serve and dipped one return after another at the Tennessee native's feet. He survived 6–4, 3–6, 4–6, 7–5, 6–3. "Always the guy who is ahead gets tight at the end," Borg said. "I know I'm more relaxed playing from 2–4 behind."

In the first match of the semifinals on Super Saturday, he would find himself in a worse position against the muscular, zoning, and quick South African Johan Kriek, down two sets to love. "Borg knows how fast I am," Kriek said prior to the match. "He can't hurt me with his topspin. He'll have to kill me to beat me."

That's exactly what happened. Borg dared Kriek to play steady with him, and by the third set he had taken his legs out from under him. The South African could no longer plant properly and the errors rained down. "I was just so tired," Kriek recalled. "He was in incredible shape—better than me. I just couldn't stay with him." Borg was through to the final in a 4–6, 4–6, 6–1, 6–1, 6–1 victory. The Grand Slam was in sight.

27

Frozen in Time

After he loses a torturous third set to Borg, John McEnroe's legs are dead. He cannot seem to get to anything. "I felt my body falling apart," he said.

He is mis-hitting groundstrokes that he handled with ease in the previous two sets. Borg is serving bigger, snapping his topspin with increased verve. McEnroe's face is puffy and red as the sun drops behind Manhattan. This might be his twilight as well, but somewhere deep down maybe he can convince himself that he has a little more left in the tank.

Mac means it, too, when he says to himself during the fourth set that he has to find a deeper reserve. He's up two sets to one, but Borg is prepared to play all night if he has to in a match of his otherworldly lungs against his opponent's.

"I learned my lesson from my last mistake," McEnroe said. "I came in more prepared, dug deeper, and got better from losing. I beat Lendl on Thursday night in a close match, then I had five sets of doubles, then I beat Connors. The next day I'm on the verge of going five with Björn again. I thought that at Wimbledon I had lost an opportunity and dug a little deeper. The problem when you get older is sometimes you don't learn from mistakes and your fear of failure becomes more prevalent. When you are younger you are not afraid, and I said, 'I'll suck it up and not let it happen again.'"

At 3–3 in the fourth, Mac briefly objects to a call, hands on hips, and he shakes his head. American Don Budge, who won the Grand Slam in 1938, chuckles a little in the background, as if to say, "I've been there too, and it sucks."

Mac nudges an awful approach shot and Borg easily passes him. Mac's serve is the only thing that is holding him in the set, but Borg has heated up his first forays too. Mac has to be thinking about the fifth set at Wimbledon, when he couldn't make even a minor impression on the Swede's serve when all the chips were on the table.

But a couple of nervous shots from Borg at 5–5 and it's 30–30. Mac is just two winning points from serving for the match. Then he flies toward the net and knifes a crisp backhand volley winner. Feeling confident on a Borg second serve, he hammers a forehand approach shot, but it's an inch long. He had chosen the right tactic, but the execution is slightly flawed. Borg then pokes away at Mac's weaker backhand and the American is slicing high as the Swede successfully closes. Borg closes out the game when Mac backs off a dipping approach that he could have put away and flies a forehand long.

It's 6–5 Borg and the pressure is squarely on Mac's aching shoulders. He muffs a half volley. The McEnroe family is fidgety in the Friends' Box, and they watch Borg whip a two-handed pass down the line that goes just long. Borg's frown dips past his strong chin, but every shot he strikes seems to be a winner now, and if Mac doesn't come up with something special himself, he will lose the set.

The American fights off one set point with a forehand volley out wide that the Swede nearly chases down. McEnroe double-faults on a game point, then Borg muscles a forehand return past him at deuce. On set point number two, Mac swerves a left-handed curveball to the Borg backhand and the Swede is all over it, flipping a cute angled backhand to a spot in the service box that McEnroe cannot locate.

Borg's clan leaps out of their chairs and the noise is deafening as all 20,000-plus fans are standing on their feet, with the exception of the McEnroe family, who are frozen in time. John's dad is chewing on something furiously.

28

"You Are Not Going to See a Tougher One"

In the middle of Super Saturday at the 1980 U.S. Open, Chris Evert, Jimmy Connors's former fiancée, stops the wondrous variety of Czech Hana Mandlikova in a three-set final. Six years prior, Connors's coach, Pancho Segura, forbade Evert to enter Connors's hotel room the night before he waxed Ken Rosewall for the title, reducing her to tears when he said that his boy needed proper rest.

Now in 1980 it's showtime, the match everyone has waited around for six hours for: Mac vs. Connors, a true late afternoon brawl. "We got the real sports fans into the game," Connors says of himself and his brash young rival. "I wanted the fan sitting there who worked his tail off to make his money and paid for his ticket because he wanted to be there."

Connors walks on court with a thin beard and a goatee, not the stuff of a grizzled offensive lineman, but for the soft-skinned, pale man an obvious statement that he wants to appear tough.

Mac starts strong and is largely in control. He approaches the net in more straight-ahead fashion, skipping in the backcourt, mixing in soft stuff that Connors hates and taking whatever opportunity he can to move forward. He knows what he has to do: get to the net at all costs and impose himself and not get too crazy trying to conjure up magic from the backcourt, where Connors reigns supreme. His job from the baseline is to blunt Connors's pace, find an approachable ball, or put more steam on shots when Connors occasionally attacks the net.

Connors owns the baseline rallies, where he can bend down superlow and rifle flat shots into the corners. McEnroe mixes up his serve well and dictates the ball beautifully with his volleys. Connors knows that he has to push the younger American more this time than he has in the past, that he must lean in returning second serves and take some chances. He has to push the rabid Mac off the net.

Early on, though, Jimbo cannot do enough with McEnroe's second serve and is unable to string him around from the backcourt, as Mac easily takes the first set 6–4.

Connors has more jump in his step in the second set, but still, McEnroe is determining the pace of the match, and with Connors serving at 4–5 deuce, the contest hangs in the balance. McEnroe bumps and charges and gains himself a set point. But then the tide turns with the arrival of a Belleville tsunami, and the wave that McEnroe has been comfortably riding envelops him in its pipeline.

Connors hits a lefty serve wide to the other lefty's forehand and Mac parks one long. The crowd screams in delight. They know they have a match on their hands now. Connors holds serve and then breaks McEnroe with an almost unthinkable shot for a man with a two-handed backhand—a one-handed backhand pass on the dead run. Connors then holds at love to take the set 7–5, and they are dead even at one set apiece.

Mac is peeved and things begin to spiral out of control. Upset with a call on what he thought was a perfect touch backhand volley on the line early in the third set, he barks at umpire Don Wiley, "When are you going to get one right, Mr. Incompetent?"

He is already down a break at 0–2 and faces two more break points. Suddenly his chances of defending his title look slim. The day before, he and Fleming lost the doubles final to familiar Davis Cup faces Smith and Lutz, and he might have peaked.

One break point is gone with a hard serve into Connors's body. Then Mac whips a twisting serve down the middle, which barely nicks off his opponent's racket. Jimbo keeps coming, launching into returns, and gains his third break point with a laser shot. Mac is broken again, this time with a bullet Connors return at his feet. On the changeover, Mac asks that Wiley be replaced. He is denied.

McEnroe appears mentally out of sorts and confused. He's frustrated and angry and Connors's often combustible forehand is deep and true. He's serving well and moving more lightly. Mac is nudging back his returns. Connors wins the third set 6–0, and a rematch of the Mac-Borg Wimbledon final seems like a pipe dream. Connors is launching passing shots from all over the place and now owns the crowd. He's finding acute angles from the sidelines while leaning backward on his returns.

There is a palpable feeling in Armstrong stadium that the New Yorker has become part of the gas shortage. But to Mac, this isn't any old foe. It's the patronizing Connors at the U.S. Open. This is the enemy and he must stand and fight. The actors Jack Nicholson and David Keith are sitting in the player guest box as McEnroe's guests. Keith knows little about tennis and on occasion applauds after a Connors unforced error (a move that is considered unsportsmanlike for fans). As Patrick McEnroe tells it, after one such applause after a critical point, Connors walked over toward the McEnroe box, "hawked up a real nasty lougie [and] spit it right at us, just short of the box. He snarled at David, 'Why don't you pick that up?' There was brief moment of silence, whereupon Nicholson, totally unruffled, drawled in that unmistakable voice of his: 'Sure . . . tomorrah.'"

At the start of the fourth set, J.P. McEnroe changes seats. Patrick, just fourteen years old, stares straight ahead. At the beginning of the fourth set, Connors hits a beautiful offensive lob and Mac is stuck at the net. He faces a break point and Connors rips a return right past him and is up a break at 1–0. Connors has won 10 straight games, and Mac is very slow to the ball from the backcourt. He is sloppy, and the planes taking off from LaGuardia Airport are simply deafening.

"I was losing my mind," McEnroe later said.

Those tennis luminaries in the house—Connors's former coach Pancho Segura, former U.S. Open winners Jack Kramer, Don Budge, Bobby Riggs, and Fred Perry—sense that McEnroe is too sluggish and is pouting too much to win. Segura has taught Connors to play a thinking man's game, while Connors's single mother, Gloria, had emphasized that they would always be outsiders from East St. Louis and needed to maintain a little hate at the hostile world that was trying to take something from them.

Just where the hell is the fathomless reserve that Mac was discussing during the lead-up to the Open? McEnroe goes down 0–30. If he gets down two breaks, dozens of fans are sure to start ringing their favorite restaurants to make their reservations for a late dinner in Manhattan. But Mac crunches an overhead, and Connors misses a sitter swing forehand volley. Mac finally holds and stops the losing streak. He's nowhere near the driver's seat, down 1–2 and a break, but he hasn't been thrown under the bus yet.

Connors holds to 3–1. Just three more holds and he gets a crack at Borg again in the locale where he most likes to face him. He gets up to serve again at 15–0, softballs a skyhook overhead instead of cracking it, and Mac lofts a lob past him. The crowd is growing restless. At 15–30, Connors decides to serve and volley and dumps an easy backhand volley into the net to go down 15–40. He denies one break point with a crisp forehand volley behind his foe. Mac misses an easy forehand return long but grabs another break point. Then, in an incredibly athletic point that sees Connors come to the net, get pushed back, and come in again, he just misses a backhand volley wide and is broken.

Game back on at 3–3, and from there, McEnroe begins to fly again. His touch has returned and every spin and speed he is attempting is well within his capabilities. He is pumped up and light on his feet. Before Connors can shake the missed volley completely out of his head, McEnroe has grabbed the fourth set 6–3.

The crowd is lusting for more. Connors is broken to open the fifth set on a steamrolling McEnroe backhand volley and has now lost six straight games. The match has lasted over three hours. It's getting darker by the second. Connors is in substantial trouble, but he scratches his beard, maybe catches an odd piece of stubble under his fingernail, and positively digs in.

He fools McEnroe with a wonderfully disguised backhand lob winner and then breaks back with a fine volley into the open court to 1–1. Johnny Mac explodes, throwing his racket as hard as he can onto the concrete and then watching it bounce away over Connors's head onto his opponent's side of the court. As McEnroe goes to the sidelines to get a drink of water and a new stick, Connors tosses Mac's busted Dunlop to him.

The crowd roars with bloodlust as Mac explains to Wiley that he lost control of his wet grip and didn't mean for his weapon to whiz the net. Amazingly, the judge he wanted removed from the bench excuses him.

Trabert says, "Whoever wins this is going to have to go home, have a shower and dinner, and say, 'Whoops, I have to wake up and go up against Björn Borg.'"

They are fully chained inside the Queens thunderdome now, and both guys realize that it will be guts and willpower that will bring them through. McEnroe breaks Connors again, this time to 3–2, when Connors nets an easy backhand. The crowd grows quieter, waiting for the next huge moment. Connors holds two break points and can't convert, and all of a sudden Johnny Mac is serving for the match at 5–4.

Then Connors decides to let it all hang loose. On the first point he hustles down a drop volley and McEnroe muffs a reflex volley. The crowd goes wild and urges Connors to bring it to a tiebreak. At 30–15, a nervous Mac overswings on a forehand volley and the ball falls wide as he raps the net cord in disgust. At 30–30, Connors rips a forehand crosscourt that clips the top of the net and bounces past McEnroe for a break point. Connors quadruple fist-pumps. Mac then twists in a deep second serve and Connors nets the return and angrily bites at his fingers.

"All of a sudden I don't even feel tired," says the dry CBS play-by-play man Pat Summerall, a former New York Giants football player more suited to deep-throating fullback rushes into the middle of the line than to describing deft volleys, yet a man with a keen sense of the big occasion.

Connors wakes himself up further by gunning a two-handed backhand return winner past a stunned McEnroe. Holding another break point, the Belleville Basher lands a jaw-crunching blow to break with an inside-out backhand return winner that Mac can't even touch.

Finally, Connors seems to have the momentum back, but does he really? A full-stretch backhand volley winner—a pure adrenaline shot—earns him another point. He holds at love to 6–5, and now Mac will have to serve with his back plastered firmly to the Louis Armstrong Stadium wall.

Mac skies up for an overhead on the first point, takes a deep breath, and shows Connors he's not going to give the contest away now. He dares Connors to pull off brilliant returns, and the older man is just catching the top of the net tape. Mac holds at love.

The bolder man will win this fifth-set tiebreaker, the one who is clearheaded, the one who will execute. Is this really Johnny Mac's New York, or is Connors really the adopted mayor? "I felt I was going to tear my heart out if I didn't win," Mac said.

The first point is brilliant. A great lob by McEnroe, followed by an over-the-shoulder bullet by Connors, who is running backward, and then a solid volley by Mac. The real New Yorker has won the critical first point.

With Mac up 2–1, Connors takes a high forehand volley sitter and slaps it into the net. It's a huge mistake. He then flies a backhand deep off an unimpressive McEnroe angled return. "Abortionated points. The two worst points of my life," Connors growled after the match.

Two more mistakes by Connors and a service winner by McEnroe and the kid holds five match points. One crisp volley by Connors takes one away. A crosscourt forehand volley steals another.

Now it's step-up time for Mac. Two points on his serve and he only needs one. He muscles up and nails a screaming serve down the T that Connors can't handle. That's it! It's 6–4, 5–7, 0–6, 6–3, 7–6. McEnroe throws his arms up in the air in triumph and looks over at his joyous family, who give him a hearty round of applause.

"You are not going to see a tougher one," says Trabert.

If only he really knew.

Going into the final, Mariana Simionescu thought Borg was at a disadvantage, being "blinded by John's lights and deafened by John's planes."

Fleming sensed that his doubles partner was ready to expose Borg's softening underbelly. "The hard courts were fast. On a slow hard court, he was brutal. But on a fast hard court he didn't return serve as well. It wasn't his major strength."

McEnroe spoke of a golden opportunity, a chance at redemption. "He's going for the Slam; I won the tournament last year. There are a lot of factors, and after Wimbledon, people want to see the matchup again."

29

"Poetry Written on Water"

Mac has taken the first two sets of the final, Borg has muscled through the next two, and the ultimate rivals will play five sets again in the summer of 1980, just as they are destined to do—the world will have it no other way. The match time is approaching four hours. Pat Summerall says the jury is still out as to whether the 1980 Wimbledon final is the best match of all time, that it could be this one right here.

Borg has not lost a five-setter since 1976 and has won 13 in a row. How could he possibly lose one when he is in full pursuit of the golden chalice that is the calendar-year Grand Slam? "When it comes to the fifth set, I always believe in myself," he said.

McEnroe walks over to his chair and takes a long drink of water. He knows that he has to get his head together. "There were times out there I started to think I was never going to beat the guy. At the end of the fourth, I thought I was really in trouble because I was tired and he just keeps getting stronger. Right then I thought my body was going to fall off. I had to start pushing again. I knew that."

Peter Fleming said, "I knew he could do it if he just hung tough."

In the fifth, Mac tries something the observers had hardly seen that day—a backhand drop shot—and it works, as even the fastest man in tennis can't run it down. McEnroe is prepared to cowboy up as he spins his racket in his hands like a Wild West gunslinger twirling his six-shooter.

McEnroe is volleying with a heavenly touch. Borg is salivating when whacking his groundstrokes. Both men's energy level has picked up. Mac steams a wicked forehand crosscourt past Borg after an exhausting end-to-end point to hold to 2–2 and he's huffing and puffing, but his well is running deeper than he ever thought it could.

Now it's Mac who is serving massively. Borg stares into Mac's brown eyes and sees nothing but red fire. At 3–3 on the opening point, Mac pushes a forehand return down the line that Borg decides not to play and it's called good. Borg is none too pleased and stares at Mariana and Bergelin as if to ask, "What the hell just happened?"

The Swede usually regroups, but not quickly enough this time. A double fault off the top of the net has him behind 15–30. "I've never served that bad in a final," he would say later.

Tony Trabert mentions that whenever he's behind, Borg attacks. He successfully does so on one point but then remarkably double-faults in the deuce court again. Mac has a break point and comes in off about as bad an approach shot as a man can hit—down the middle, right in the center of the court, and Borg easily passes him.

Then at deuce the Swede tries to get too cute with a topspin lob, and on Mac's second break point, Borg approaches to his backhand side. McEnroe leaps into a backhand crosscourt and Borg cannot lift the steaming ball above the net. The New Yorker has the break and screams out, "Yes!"

Now all McEnroe has to do is hold two more times and he will defend his crown and yank Borg back to the same earth where he and the rest of the human race reside. He's taking forever to serve, as he wants to make sure that every one matters. And they do— twisters, sidewinders, flat ones, high-hopping topspin, body blows.

His hands at the net are remarkable, slicing biting volleys, stabbing mean-spirited ones, firming up on solid approaches.

The New Yorker easily holds to 5–3. Mac conserves energy on Borg's service game while Borg holds at love to 5–4.

This will be the most important game that Mac has ever contested in New York. Throughout his life, he has competed in hundreds of memorable contests, from knuckle-bruising stickball games that ended under fading streetlights in Queens to his seizing of the king of New York tennis tag from Gerulaitis in 1979 and his punch-out of the monarch of U.S. tennis, Connors, the day before. Mac's parents are sipping out of the same beer. His mother, Kay, and his girlfriend, Stacy Margolin, cannot sit still.

Borg is still thought of as the world's best and Mac has to beat him right here, right now. It's the only way the crowd can exit Louis Armstrong Stadium saying that their homeboy is better than the planet's most regal tennis player. The Nordic god must be vanquished in order for folks to get back on the No. 7 train and pound their chests, saying, "Did you see our boy steal Zeus's thunder?"

Mac steps up to serve, rocks back and forth five times in his inimitable fashion, and charges in off a fine entry, picks off a tough return, and drops a volley down the line, and Borg just misses a crosscourt drop shot himself. But Mac is clearly tense and takes a crazy swing at a forehand volley, missing it wide. It's 15–15.

He calms himself down waiting to serve and flames a scorcher down the T that careens off the top of Borg's racket and skyrockets above the bleacher seats. Then he gets a little lucky, as he decides not to go nuts on his next forehand volley and pushes it toward the Swede, who, flat-footed, stands still and lets it bounce too close to his body. Borg nets a sloppy reply.

Double match point for McEnroe. The New Yorker plays it smart, deciding not to give Borg room to breathe, and he hooks a body serve right at Borg's exposed jugular. The Swede can only push a half overhead in front of his angular face toward the center of the court, and Mac closes like a starving tiger, nailing a ferocious forehand volley crosscourt winner.

The Wimbledon king has died in New York, and without question the guard has changed. Johnny Mac is the new ruler of tennis. He bends his back, pumps two fists in the air, and smiles as widely as he ever has. He lightly jogs up to shake hands with the man he so admires, whom he has caught and will soon pass.

He no longer wants to be Borg; he is convinced he is his own man now, with his own way to win, with his own ship to steer, with the world at his feet. It's time to take down the worn-out poster hanging in his Douglaston bedroom. "When we shook hands, I could see he was devastated," Mac recalled.

The McEnroe family joins him. Bergelin and Mariana exit, stunned.

McEnroe is being interviewed by former U.S. Open champ John Newcombe, and the crowd interrupts them with screams of empathic triumph. Mac turns to them and with a grin that reaches from ear to ear yells, "Aaaahhhhh!"

"The U.S. Open was my greatest actual effort, it was mind over matter," McEnroe said after his 7–6, 6–1, 6–7, 5–7, 6–4 victory in four hours, eleven minutes. "I figured if I was ever going to beat him this was the place to do it. This is my best surface and probably his worst. If I didn't beat him here I didn't know when I would have beaten him."

It was at that point that most people close to Borg knew that his cloak of invincibility was gone. So did he. Borg knew his uninterrupted reign was over, and Mac had put more than serious doubts in his head.

"I hate to lose, but I accept it more easy now than maybe five or six years ago," Borg said. "There's no way you can keep going winning all the time. I hate to lose more than I love to win, so when I lose I get very depressed right after the match."

After press interviews, Borg and Mariana leave quickly, not responding to the fans and autograph seekers who shout encouragement while they dive into their car. Borg says he has many more years to come, but there will only be one more that really means anything and he will navigate his career from the backseat. He says that the level of play and intensity was higher at Wimbledon, but that was more from his side.

Johnny Mac contested the match of his life, and this time he came up the victor. "We both can play better," Borg says in a hollow tone. "You will see the best matches, the best tennis, from us in the future."

In the locker room, McEnroe says that what the victory means to him is that he "likes to win," and he adds that anytime you beat No. 1 in the world it's special, "but beating him to stop the Slam makes it even better."

Night has fallen on Flushing Meadows.

The next year, Borg and Mac reprise their rivalry in Wimbledon and the U.S. Open finals, and then it's clear who the more motivated player is, the one with unshakable confidence, the one with the higher-level game. That man is John P. McEnroe Jr., who convincingly wins both contests and becomes a dominant No. 1.

As thrilling as both those later matches were, they didn't come close to the sheer magic of the pair's clashes in the summer of 1980, which became woven into popular culture as tightly as Bergelin's strong masseur's hands pulled Borg's gut strings through the holes of his black Donnay racket. The Swede and the American had the entire tennis world—and lots of the rest of it—on the edge of their seats.

"That's the funny thing about tennis and games," McEnroe recalled. "They may be awe-inspiring at the moment, but then the moment is gone. They are a little like poetry written on water."

The End of a Great Rivalry

By the time you read this, at least thirty years will have passed since the 1980 Wimbledon and U.S. Open finals, and both McEnroe and Borg have lived very full lives since then.

In 1981, McEnroe took over as the king of the tennis court, putting his foot on Borg's throat and never letting up. While race riots shook London (its worst rioting in a century), McEnroe would finally top Borg's streak and win his first Wimbledon. However, on his worst behavior, he became the only player in history not to be granted an honorary membership to the All England Club when he won Wimbledon for the first time. (He was later given one.)

It was that year that he unleashed his most infamous tirade in the first round against Tom Gullikson. After having one of his serves called long at 4–3 in the first set, McEnroe smashed his racket and lit into chair umpire Ed James. "Man, you cannot be serious!" A disputed Gullikson serve in the third set saw McEnroe demand to see the tournament referee, Fred Hoyles, before tossing in another bon mot: "You guys are the absolute pits of the world, do you know that?" Both phrases would become as connected with McEnroe as the handle of his tennis racket, and *You Cannot Be Serious* became the title of his autobiography.

Later in the same tournament McEnroe called another umpire "an incompetent fool, an offense against the world," which would elicit a $10,000 fine.

"I've never seen Wimbledon so mad, so burning," said Arthur Ashe. "Not even when Connors insulted the queen by not showing up for the centenary celebration in 1977."

Mac's father, who was at his side most of the time, defended him then and still does to this day. "John was right most of the time," J.P. said. "When they brought aggravated behavior against him in 1981, when John said 'pits of the world,' the umpire wrote down 'piss of the world.'" McEnroe asked to see the referee, who agreed with the umpire and walked away. Mac called him back and said, "You are just as big a shit as the rest of them."

As J.P. explained, "They then gave him a warning for abuse of the referee, but the guy still wrote down 'piss of the world' . . . then later John is accused of calling the umpire, George Grime, a 'disgrace to mankind' even when John was quite clearly talking to himself. [Grime] wrote it down as if he called [him] a disgrace to mankind. If you took those two things away, there would have never been a charge leveled again him."

Despite the fact that McEnroe was ahead during most of the match and won in straight sets, when he hit a volley long in the second set, he screamed out, "I'm so disgusting you shouldn't watch. Everybody leave."

He was concerned that he might lose to Gullikson, whose twin brother, Tim, had upset him two years prior. Just the sight of a Gullikson brother (although this one was a left-hander) was enough to set his stomach churning. "I was as tight as a piano wire," he said.

Despite his histrionics, McEnroe stopped Borg in the Wimbledon final in a tight yet authoritative 4–6, 7–6, 7–6, 6–4 victory, and two months later trounced the Swede in the U.S. Open final 4–6, 6–2, 6–4, 6–3. He became the first man since the great American Bill

Tilden in the 1920s to win three straight U.S. Opens. Those were two of the best matches of McEnroe's life, and by then he clearly had Borg's number. "I felt I could do anything," he said.

By no means did Borg have a terrible year in 1981. Prior to Wimbledon, he won his final Grand Slam title at the French Open, besting a real up-and-comer and future Hall of Famer, Ivan Lendl, in five sets, for a record sixth crown. In reaching the final at Wimbledon in 1981, he stretched his winning streak to a then record 41 matches (Roger Federer eventually passed him), a more than admirable tally, even if he couldn't push McEnroe past his limits in the contest.

"It was the first time in my life I wasn't really disappointed," Borg said. "Here I am in the biggest tournament in the world, and I wasn't hurting deep in my heart. I realized something was wrong. When I left the dressing room I knew something in my mind wasn't there and my focus wasn't just on tennis anymore."

Given how mentally tired he had become, reaching the U.S. Open final again was an achievement in itself for Borg, and had he won that match and captured the one major title that eluded him, his inner engine might have kick-started again, but he was body-slammed on hard courts and his pistons stopped accelerating.

"He didn't feel young when he quit. He had dried up that well," Mary Carillo said.

After the 1981 U.S. Open final, Borg walked off the court before the trophy ceremony began, and those who knew him sensed that he might never return. He played a little more, twice in the fall and then once the next April in Monte Carlo, but he was done as a big-time competitor. His entire life had been wrapped up in whacking balls between the white lines and he understandably needed a new form of motivation in different life pursuits.

"He was clearly burned out," said Sandy Mayer. "He needed something else in his life, even if he didn't know what that was yet."

In January 1983, Borg officially announced that he was retiring from tennis at the age of twenty-six, and even though those who knew him sensed that he had grown bored of the game, they thought that with an extended break he would begin to rekindle his fire. McEnroe and others tried unsuccessfully to persuade him to continue, but they would have no effect. His mind had gone elsewhere.

"When I stepped away from the game . . . I didn't enjoy it," Borg said. "I didn't have motivation."

McEnroe was stunned and less than pleased that the man who got his juices going the most wouldn't return. Borg's exit robbed tennis of its greatest rivalry. Their career head-to-head stands at 7–7 (they would play five more times after the 1980 U.S. Open, three wins for McEnroe and two for Borg), which is where it should be, as no two elite players during the Open Era have been so closely matched.

Even today, McEnroe somewhat resents Borg's retirement, but they have become close friends, even attending each other's weddings.

McEnroe did continue his teeth clenching mano a mano with Connors, developed a terrific rivalry with Lendl, and had some glorious matches with Swedes Mats Wilander and Stefan Edberg as well as the bellowing German Boris Becker. But it was Borg who first fueled his fanatical drive toward perfection.

The New Yorker would win four more Grand Slam titles, including 1983 and 1984 Wimbledons, and in 1984 had one of the best seasons ever, winning Wimbledon for the third time and the U.S. Open for the fourth time, but in what he calls the greatest choke of his career, he was unable to hold off Lendl at the French Open, letting go a two-sets-to-love lead. He finished the season with an 82–3 record and won a career-high thirteen singles titles.

Yet in the back of his mind, he wanted to battle with Borg again and again on the world's greatest stages, to relive that glorious summer of 1980. What he didn't realize in 1981 was that in some ways, his incredible play drove the Swede from the sport.

"I loved playing Borg," McEnroe said. "I wish I had played him more. That was the ultimate rivalry that I had. He was the guy I thought could bring me to the top of my game."

After retiring, Borg hit the party circuit with a vengeance. He divorced Mariana Simionescu, married the colorful Italian singer

Loredana Bertè, then left her for a seventeen-year-old Swedish girl, Jannike Björling, whom he met at a wet T-shirt contest, and with whom he had a son, Robin, and fought an ugly custody battle. He didn't marry Björling, but Robin ended up playing collegiate tennis in the United States.

Borg was alleged to have had a drug overdose, and was said by some to have attempted suicide, a charge he disputes. A business partner, Lars Skarke, whose credibility was in question, wrote a scandalous book about going into the fashion business with Borg, citing repeated decadent incidents of drugs and sex and alleging that the tennis legend became "engulfed by the darkness in his soul." That business, the Björn Borg Design Group, fell apart, and Borg was forced to sell off homes, boats, and life insurance policies to pay off millions of dollars in debts.

"The only plan was that I know I'm going to step away from tennis," Borg said. "I just wanted to learn about this other life from tennis. I learned about all kinds of different things—good things, bad things."

In 1991, at the age of thirty-four and needing income, Borg returned to the tour in Monte Carlo wielding one of his favored wooden rackets, an outdated and poor choice of weaponry given that everyone was playing with the more powerful graphite stick by then. He would play eleven more tournaments in 1992 and 1993 and, sadly, didn't win a single match, only stretching three opponents to three sets.

He returned to Sweden and became a bit of a recluse, although he did mix in some play on the senior circuit, but because he was no longer as fast or as powerful, he lost time and time again to Connors and McEnroe, who had made significant necessary adjustments to their games as they got older.

In 2002, Borg married Swede Patricia Ostfeldt and became a father again as well as a stepfather to her two other children. The following year, clearly stressed financially, Borg shocked the world and said he was planning to auction off the five Wimbledon trophies he won between 1976 and 1980 as well as two signed rackets at Bonhams salerooms in London. They were collectively expected to bring in around $525,400. In a statement, the then forty-seven-year-old Borg said he decided to put the items up for auction because he and his family needed long-term financial security and mentioned that they were merely getting dusty in the attic.

The tennis world reeled and circled its wagons. The immensely popular Andre Agassi began to put together a consortium to buy Borg's five replica trophies so as to keep them in the tennis family. "It's not right," he said. "The only way you should have a Wimbledon trophy is if you win it, not buy one. I can't make any judgments on Björn, but I can say that the thought of a Wimbledon trophy being in the hands of somebody who has a lot of money is upsetting. Wimbledon is the greatest tournament in the world."

McEnroe went quickly into action and convinced his friend to stop the auction. "I called him up and said, 'Are you out of your mind?' I know Björn pretty well, and sometimes he decides things without thinking."

Borg was moved. "I could never imagine that it would be such an unbelievable response from the whole world. I was touched that so many people around the world [were] very concerned."

A more stable Borg now occasionally coaches and competes in European-based senior tournaments and has started a new fashion business, Björn Borg underwear, and an online dating site. He lives in a large mansion on the water about twenty-five minutes outside of Stockholm.

McEnroe never calmed down on court and has had some choice moments off the court too. Not only did he conduct his infamous "pits of the world" tirade at 1981 Wimbledon, but he was thrown out of the 1990 Australian Open for swearing at officials. In 1985, he reached his last Grand Slam singles final at the U.S. Open, where Lendl crushed him.

Playing badly and head over heels in love with the volatile actress Tatum O'Neal, Mac took a six-month break from the tour in 1986; during the break he and O'Neal were married. While personally the break it may have been a wise decision, professionally it did him little good. The first half of his career, 1979 to 1986, was full of prosperity, but from 1987 to his retirement in 1992 he only managed to win seven of his 77 singles titles.

He and O'Neal had three children (Kevin, Sean, and Emily), but because neither of the two type-A personalities knew how to give enough or compromise, and possibly because they spent too much time partying, they divorced in 1994. A bitter custody battle ensued and McEnroe was awarded full custody of their children, as O'Neal continued to have drug problems. Arrested for drug possession in 2008, she now has limited visitation rights.

McEnroe's personal life improved when he met the gentle-spirited rock and roller Patty Smyth (she and her band Scandal had the hit song "The Warrior") and married her in 1997. They had two children, Anna and Ava, and Smyth brought along her daughter, Ruby, from Smyth's previous marriage to rocker Richard Hell, bringing the couple's grand total to six.

McEnroe's last great performance came in 1992, when he and a U.S. Dream Team (McEnroe, eight-time Grand Slam champion Agassi, fourteen-time Slam champion Pete Sampras, and four-time Slam champion Jim Courier) teamed up to defeat Switzerland 3–1 in the Davis Cup final in Texas, where McEnroe won a doubles match with Sampras.

After a very public campaign, McEnroe was named the U.S. Davis Cup captain in September 1999, but his reign was short-lived, as he didn't have the patience to deal with star players. In 2000, his squad beat Zimbabwe and the Czech Republic, but just after Wimbledon, when an exhausted Sampras and Agassi declined to compete against Spain, McEnroe's makeshift team was buried 5–0 by Spain in the semis, and the captain blew a gasket, publicly calling out Sampras and Agassi, who took none too kindly to the criticism and went right back at him. McEnroe resigned in November 2000 after just fourteen months on the job and was replaced by his less temperamental brother Patrick, who led the team to the title in 2007.

McEnroe today is something of a Renaissance man with little fear of failure. In 2004, he began a CNBC talk show titled *McEnroe* that was canceled after five months and had the dubious distinction on two occasions of earning a 0.0 Nielsen rating. He also hosted the quiz show *The Chair* in both the U.K. and the United States, but that show also bombed. He became an art collector and owns a New York City art gallery, which has had marginal success.

The chatty New Yorker has had tremendous success as a TV tennis analyst, working for NBC, CBS, and the BBC, among other networks. He also plays on two senior tours, one in the United States and the other in Europe, and after two years of frustration he won two singles titles in 2008 at the not-so-tender age of forty-nine and another one in 2009 at the age of fifty, beating men some fourteen years his junior.

Borg and McEnroe share many memories, and even today their rivalry is still a benchmark for greatness. It took twenty-eight hearty years for the so-called greatest match of the twentieth century, Borg's 18–16 in the fifth set spectacular over McEnroe in the 1980 Wimbledon final, to be challenged in quality and drama by one in the twenty-first century. In 2008, they were both at Wimbledon to watch the Roger Federer–Rafael Nadal final as the Swiss Federer attempted to break Borg's record of five straight crowns, but the Spaniard stopped him 6–4, 6–4, 6–7 (5), 6–7 (8), 9–7 in what some now call the greatest men's final ever.

McEnroe himself said it was the best match he had ever seen, but his father, J.P., would later caution, "He said it was the best match he ever *saw*, not one that he played in, a very crucial distinction."

As always, J.P. defended and clarified the play, thoughts, and emotions of his fiery namesake, who defeated the most dominant player of his time and changed the way tennis would be played for decades to come.

BIBLIOGRAPHY

Books

Adams, Tim. *On Being John McEnroe*. New York: Crown, 2003.

Aitchison, Alex. *A Tennis Experience and All of That . . .* New York: Vantage Press, 2006.

Austin, Tracy, with Christine Brennan. *Beyond Center Court: My Story*. New York: William Morrow, 1992.

Baltzell, E. Digby. *Sporting Gentlemen: Men's Tennis from the Age of Honor to the Cult of the Superstar*. New York: Free Press, 1995.

Barrett, John. *Wimbledon: The Official History of the Championships*. London: CollinsWillow, 2001.

Bellamy, Rex. *Love Thirty: Three Decades of Champions*. Bath, U.K.: Simon and Schuster, 1990.

Bodo, Peter. *The Courts of Babylon: Tales of Greed and Glory in the Harsh New World of Professional Tennis*. New York: Scribner, 1995.

———. *Inside Tennis: A Season on the Pro Tour*. New York: Dell, 1979.

Borg, Björn, with Eugene Scott. *Björn Borg: My Life and Game*. New York: Simon and Schuster, 1980.

Borg, Mariana. *Love Match: My Life with Björn Borg*. New York: Dial Press, 1981.

Cantor, Norman, with Mindy Cantor. *The American Century: Varieties of Culture in Modern Times*. New York: HarperCollins, 1997.

Caraccioli, Tom, and Jerry Caraccioli. *Boycott: Stolen Dreams of the 1980 Moscow Olympic Games*. New York: New Chapter Press, 2008.

Collins, Bud. *My Life with the Pros*. New York: Dutton, 1989.

———. *The Bud Collins History of Tennis: An Authoritative Encyclopedia and Record Book*. New York: New Chapter Press, 2008.

Drucker, Joel. *Jimmy Connors Saved My Life: A Personal Biography*. Toronto: Classic Sports Books, 2004.

Evans, Richard. *John McEnroe: Taming the Talent*. New York: Stephen Green Press, 1990.

———. *Open Tennis: 1968–1988: The Players, the Politics, the Pressures, the Passions, and the Great Matches*. London: Bloomsbury, 1988.

Flink, Steve. *The Greatest Tennis Matches of the Twentieth Century*. Danbury, CT: Rutledge Books, 1999.

Folley, Malcolm. *Borg versus McEnroe*. London: Headline Books, 2005.

Kramer, Jack, with Frank Deford. *The Game, My 40 Years in Tennis*. London: Andre Deutsch, 1981.

Little, Alan. *Wimbledon Compendium Annual*. London: All England Lawn Tennis Club, 2008.

McEnroe, John, with James Kaplan. *You Cannot Be Serious*. New York: Berkeley Books, 2002.

McEnroe, Patrick, with Peter Bodo. *Hardcourt Confidential: Tales from Twenty Years in the Pro Tennis Trenches*. New York: Hyperion, 2010.

Nastase, Ilie, with Debbie Beckerman. *Mr. Nastase: The Autobiography*. London: CollinsWillow, 2004.

Nathan, Fernand. *Borg by Borg*. Paris: Octopus Books, 1979.

Scanlon, Bill, with Sonny Long and Cathy Long. *Bad News for McEnroe: Blood, Sweat, and Backhands with John, Jimmy, Ilie, Ivan, Björn, and Vitas*. New York: St Martin's Press, 2004.

Scheer, Robert. *Playing President: My Close Ecounters with Nixon, Carter, Bush I, Reagan, and Clinton—and How They Did Not Prepare Me for George W. Bush*. New York: Akashic Books, 2006.

Skarke, Lars. *Björn Borg: Winner Loses All*. London: Blake, 1993.

Tanner, Roscoe, with Mike Yorkey. *Double Fault: My Rise and Fall and the Road Back*. Chicago: Triumph Books, 2005.

Magazine Archives
Inside Tennis
Sports Illustrated
Tennis
World Tennis

Newspaper Archives
Associated Press
Daily Mail
Daily Telegraph
Guardian
Independent
London Times
Los Angeles Times
New York Times
Reuters
Washington Post

INDEX